Praise for *Inspired Philanthropy, Third Edition*

"Gary offers extensive strategies, tools, and wisdom in an easy-to-read format so that funders with all levels of experience will be prepared to take action."

— Alison Goldberg, author, *Creating Change Through Family Philanthropy*

"*Inspired Philanthropy* is a comprehensive and valuable resource that helps individuals and families give away money in effective ways."

— Charles W. Collier, senior philanthropic advisor, Harvard University, and author, *Wealth in Families*

"I enthusiastically encourage all generations to read *Inspired Philanthropy* and discover ways to transform your giving and legacy planning."

— Taij Kumarie Moteelall, executive director, Resource Generation

"From basic giving plans to transformative philanthropy, the new version of *Inspired Philanthropy* gives solid tools to donors and community leaders."

— Paul Shoemaker, executive director, Social Venture Partners

"This book helps donors realize they can give more than they ever thought possible, and that strategic planned giving is the best way to improve our world."

— Kim Klein, author, *Fundraising for Social Change, Fifth Edition*

Praise for *Inspired Philanthropy, Second Edition*

"*Inspired Philanthropy* is a good book—don't miss it. It is a most ingenious mixture of philanthropic philosophy, personal accounts of how some individuals have handled their giving and, most interesting, a rich section of exercises that leads you through the gift-making process. This book makes you want to do philanthropy the way it should be done. It is suitable for all people touched by philanthropy—givers and takers, big and little. The field will owe these authors."

— David R. Hunter, philanthropic advisor

To help you develop and update your charitable or legacy giving plan, all worksheets and exercises in this book are available free online.

To download electronic versions of the worksheets and exercises, go to **www.inspiredlegacies.org**

JB JOSSEY-BASS

Inspired Philanthropy

YOUR STEP-BY-STEP GUIDE

TO CREATING A GIVING PLAN

AND LEAVING A LEGACY

THIRD EDITION

Tracy Gary
with Nancy Adess

Foreword by Suze Orman

BICENTENNIAL
1807
WILEY
2007
BICENTENNIAL

John Wiley & Sons, Inc.

Published by Jossey-Bass
A Wiley Imprint
989 Market Street, San Francisco, CA 94103-1741—www.josseybass.com

Wiley Bicentennial logo: Richard J. Pacifico

Jossey-Bass books and products are available through most bookstores. To contact Jossey-Bass directly call our Customer Care Department within the U.S. at 800-956-7739, outside the U.S. at 317-572-3986, or fax 317-572-4002.

Jossey-Bass also publishes its books in a variety of electronic formats. Some content that appears in print may not be available in electronic books.

Cataloging-in-Publication data on file with the Library of Congress.

ISBN 978-0-7879-9652-9

Printed in the United States of America
THIRD EDITION
PB Printing   10 9 8 7 6 5 4 3 2

CONTENTS

CD-ROM CONTENTS

EXERCISES

6.1 Your Funding Areas

7.1 Your Giving Plan

8.1. Giving Methods

10.1 Level of Engagement

11.1 Checklist for Assessing an Advisor

11.2 Becoming a Legacy Partner

11.3 Who Are You Planning For?

11.4 Current Wills, Legal Documents, and Titling of Assets

11.5 How Advisors Can Help

12.1 Mentoring

13.1 Giving from Assets

WORKSHEETS

6.1 Evaluating a Group for Possible Funding

7.1 Your Giving Plan

7.2 Multiyear Giving Record

7.3 Giving Intention

7.4 Results and Impact

7.5 How You Did as a Donor

10.1 Inspired Philanthropist's Checklist

10.2 Preparing for Site Visits

APPENDICES

Appendix A: Tools for Partnering Effectively with Advisors for Your Inspired Legacy

Appendix B: Partnering with Clients for Inspired Outcomes: Notes to Advisors and Nonprofits, by Phil Cubeta

Appendix C: Creative Ideas for Giving

To donors and people worldwide eager to make a world that works and survives for everyone. May the extraordinary inspiration of Rita Thapa and the transformative community of the women, men, and children of TEWA, Nepal, give peace and hope to the survivors of New Orleans, the Gulf Coast, and all displaced people who have lost their familiar community. May giving and love and others' generosity of spirit support you to find your way again.

The Power of Doing Good: Giving to a Worthy Cause Is Worth More Than You Know

When charitable requests come in the mail, making a pitch for your support to stop global warming, prevent cancer, fund a local food bank, or protect a nature preserve, do you read the letters? Do you throw them away with the supermarket circulars? Or do you give as much as you can?

There are scores of good causes, and many of us feel we can't afford to give to all—or to any. The larger view suggests that we can't afford not to give to some causes. There's a moral component to the issue, of course, and everyone has to decide privately how much he or she owes the world. But there's another factor to consider, one that's not often mentioned. When you donate money to a cause you believe in, you're giving yourself the gift of power.

Here is a familiar scene: you're sitting in front of a stack of monthly bills, writing checks and watching your balance shrink. You come upon an envelope from an organization that supports a charity you care about, or maybe a cause you've given to before, when you felt flusher, or a group whose work you've always admired. Hard-pressed this month, you toss the envelope away, gather up your paid bills, head for the mailbox, and set out to run some errands. You feel depleted.

Let's play it another way. While writing checks, you discover an envelope you know contains a worthy plea and, instead of throwing it away, you open it, read the letter, and write another check—for $25 or $100; the amount doesn't matter as long as it won't break the bank. As soon as you've signed your name, the light dawns: hey, come to think of it, you can spare a little money this month. Later, when you head out to pick up the kids from their soccer game, you're lighter on your feet—having discovered new resources of both good fellowship and funds, you're a little less pressured. You're buoyant, proud. Confident, curious. Ready to give and receive. And that's when wealth of all kinds comes your way.

It's really this simple: by giving, you become the receiver of gifts—not the smallest of which is an acquaintance with your own power of choice and your freedom to exercise it for the good.

Suze Orman

PREFACE

Come, my friends,
'Tis not too late to seek a newer world.
Push off, and sitting well in order smite
The sounding furrows; for my purpose holds
To sail beyond the sunset, and the baths
Of all the western stars, until I die.

—Lord Alfred Tennyson, *Ulysses*

Giving has become hip and cool. The greatest transfer of wealth from one generation to the next is taking place while sports figures, media moguls, and entrepreneurs across the globe amass new riches. Using some of those fortunes in the service of humanity has become headline news:

- Lance Armstrong's simple yellow LiveFree bracelets start a fashion craze while raising millions of dollars for cancer research. Hollywood and other superstar givers grab headlines and draw attention to those in need at home and abroad.

- Oprah Winfrey builds a $40 million school in South Africa for girls.

- "Giving kiosks"—donation ATMs—make giving at some churches as familiar as withdrawing money at the bank, while faith-based initiatives attract the support of those at the highest levels of government.

- Ted Turner gives $1 billion to the United Nations, encouraging more global giving; Warren Buffet gives $31 billion to the Gates Foundation, creating a cascade of other mega-philanthropists "giving while living."

- Technology millionaires such as eBay's Pierre Omidyar, Paul Brainard, and Jeff Skoll champion venture philanthropy.

- Philanthropy across the globe expands at the speed of an Internet connection.

Philanthropy itself is changing, as donors discover and create new ways to give:

- Donors place nearly $1 trillion in donor-advised funds at community foundations and family foundations.[1]

- The Internet democratizes the philanthropic landscape through expanded online donations, and supports a new emphasis on youth service to their communities and the world through sites enabling adults to fund—and youths to direct—youth giving accounts through Youthgive.org.

- Women become the leaders of innovation in the nonprofit and foundation industry with programs such as Women Moving Millions of the Women's Funding Network, the United Way's Women's Initiatives, The Women's Philanthropy Initiative, and hundreds of giving circles and women's foundations worldwide.

- Family foundations wake up to the use of activists in their decision making and their community-based philanthropic foundations, and giving federations encourage partnerships of giving between activists and donors, including major donors of colors.

- Wealth advisors and giving coaches emerge to improve our giving focus and follow-through.

- Neighborhood funding led by Bread for the Journey enables anyone to be in on the simple acts of giving in our own backyards.

- Donors, advisors, and nonprofits find shared joy and values expressed in the integration of giving, social investing, and legacy planning.

More and more people are discovering that philanthropy and acts of generosity and kindness can become lifelines. Money wisely placed and invested in people, research, or projects becomes the way to substantive change. Even small amounts can change a life, village, or system when the potential of the gift is matched or properly leveraged by a caring community and thoughtful leadership.

You may be naturally asking, "Can I give more, or are there better ways to give?" "Could I be more engaged with the nonprofits or leaders I respect? And will I find tools here that will advance my effectiveness?" Here, too, we ask you to think about a lifetime of giving and consciously passing on your legacy so that your full intentions and giving potential are achieved.

Since *Inspired Philanthropy* first appeared in the fall of 1998, the world has changed dramatically. The September 11, 2001, attacks on the United States, the tsunamis worldwide, the shocking realities of the hurricane damage to the Gulf Coast and other areas—all have humbled us and shown us what real security and our government's true capacities are. Globally, wars and insurgencies still rage on, with devastating results on people, communities, and the planet.

But a larger and even more powerful awareness has also set in: the awareness that in times of chaos, war, disaster, and with the acceleration and unraveling of daily life, what can sometimes settle and calm us are simple interactions of love and support. What we see consistently is that recovery from trauma, violence, and disaster comes from the deep and immediate empathy and caring that are expressed by so many through giving. Giving of ourselves and giving meaningfully transforms us all. Adults and kids fundraised for the New Orleans and Gulf Coast victims of the 2005 hurricanes, and restaurant owners in Florida sent the dollar bills pasted on the ceiling of their café to the widowed wife of the restaurant owner on the top of the World Trade Center. Neighbors living on less than $2 a day gave to the Nepal Women's Fund-TEWA, even during war and displacement. Through such actions, we send love, hope, and encouragement to people we have never met. These good deeds and donations from strangers lighten the despair of the recipients and restore people for yet another hour or day. With more people giving, these days can turn into weeks and months of actual survival.

We are now in the middle of not only the intergenerational transfer of wealth but also the intergenerational transfer of leadership. How we carefully and consciously transfer our money and the leadership of our organizations must be sacred work by us all. Passing on core values and shaping a better world is not to be done in isolation or silence. Done in community, with great advice, we truly can have inspiring outcomes for our families and our communities. But we must first agree that the process will take time and that expert advice and partnership are essential.

I believe that generosity as a global shared value and practice has a powerful role to play as the yeast to get many solutions to social problems, now stagnating, to rise. Giving, properly timed and directed, can change communities and change ourselves and our sense of what's possible. In lives that have become obsessed with work, giving is also fun, creative, and enormously meaningful for both the giver and receiver. Let giving and supporting change and culture become the standard for our busyness—not only work that depletes us and our planet. For philanthropy to partner with the government and for-profits to make for a great society for all, we must change the giving process and the practices of most of us who give. If philanthropy is to facilitate substantial changes needed and to serve or even preserve humanity and the planet, then all of us—donors, novices and experts, new and old—must put more planning and engagement into our giving. Adding new thoughtfulness and advisors and others to our giving process is the way to better giving and better living. Alone, it is just too confusing to figure out what to do, with whom, how, how much, and when.

This book presents tools and stories you can use to improve your lifetime giving. To respond to the times we find ourselves in, we must evolve to considering how "my" or "our" giving plans can be infused with consideration of what now must be our collective giving plans for the greater good. We must ask ourselves deeply, "What is needed and how may I serve for even greater results?" And we must find more engaged giving with the people and projects that will only not crack open our hearts, minds, and purses but whose effectiveness is clear. For it is in these relationships that the true transfer of wealth will occur.

There are now more than 1.5 million nonprofits in the United States alone.[2] It can be overwhelming to know where your donations will do the most good or have the most impact, especially if you want to be strategic or involved in substantive change to address the root causes of social inequity and global distress. It takes a great deal of experience, consciousness, research, and time to become a good donor. We cannot afford to waste a dime. So much is at stake. After nearly fifty years of giving, I am still learning, still inspired to improve and be a better leader, and loving every lesson.

Melissa Kohner and I wrote the first two editions of *Inspired Philanthropy* as a tool to help make more order out of our own and others' intentional generosity. We had heard from so many donors that they loved to give but felt less effective than they wanted to be. Many said they knew that for the sake of humanity and improving the state of the world or their communities they "really should get more organized or focused" in their giving. We knew the feeling.

Melissa and I were both donor activists, having been raised by socially active parents, giving grandparents, and religious traditions that showed us how to extend grace and goodwill to others. We were told to "leave the world a better place" or to "do something" for the city, country, and community in which we lived. Our parents and those who came before them, along with our mentors, showed by their examples the amazing gifts received from being a giving person—that true abundance within comes from giving and being connected to community.

In the preface to the first edition Melissa noted that religious congregations and circles everywhere are successful in raising money because the collection plate keeps coming around. There it is: you give. As Melissa wrote:

> It was from that collection plate that I understood that this was how the church kept itself in this building. But for other nonprofits, we must be much more decisive. The appeals come in the mail—what do you want to support? Thinking ahead of time about what you're committed to and what you want to give to commits you to accomplishing a goal. Putting your values and mission and commitment on paper challenges you to be as serious about your giving as nonprofits are in needing your support. Most important, it holds you accountable to giving of yourself and your money.

Here from the preface to the first edition was part of my motivation:

> At the height of my giving in my early 30s, I was receiving requests from more than 700 groups a year. Unlike my parents, who are very organized about their philanthropy, as a younger donor I was not so organized, and I found myself bouncing around from project to project, reacting to whatever came along. I came to realize that not only was there a personal consequence to my disorganization, but that it also affected others when I couldn't find proposals sent me or wasn't sure if there was any logic to supporting one project over another. I needed to refine my methods.
>
> I had noticed that foundations had guidelines and statements of purpose or missions for their work. As a result, they knew what they

wanted to fund year by year; groups seeking funding saved countless hours by knowing a foundation's priorities. Following their example, I began to put my own vision for my work into words, stating what my dreams were and what communities had taught me was needed and refining them in a manner that could be shared. This process gave me added energy and the focus to find partners for my work.

I had started as a child of privilege, with a powerful yet "limousine liberal" education and a family history of philanthropy in the established white Anglo-Saxon tradition. When I came of age, I responded to what is deepest in that tradition by giving away the fortune bestowed on me and devoting my life to helping others do the same. A child of the 1960s and affected by all the tragedies and social changes of the Civil Rights Movement as well as the deaths of so many fine leaders, I emerged as an activist in the women's rights movement and discovered many great leaders in the expanded civil rights arena who were working for society's change. I made my home in the San Francisco area, where I learned from mentors, both older and younger, who enhanced my sense of possibilities and practices as a nonprofit partner and donor. I moved as a leader in the refined circles of heirs and entrepreneurs, as well as among activists with bold ideas and the passion to fulfill them.

I found so many nonprofits and donors that I respected that I was propelled to travel the country and abroad to seek more donors and best practices and to start foundations that could help fund and build more change. At the turn of the millennium I moved for love to Houston, where my beloved selflessly serves community through helping people with AIDS and tending to distressed or unwanted animals. Together we engage our neighborhood association and diverse community, and discuss with the people of Houston over dinners the amazing faith traditions of the people of Texas and how to transform giving and the planet. People care everywhere.

I found myself speaking in places such as Dallas, Austin, and Birmingham, preaching giving in the language of progressives—the language that had become second nature to me, the language that deep conservatives love to hate. It was new to me to be received from time to time with fury, dismay, and consternation. We are still a divided nation. Since then I have sought how to build with others at Reuniting America a new concept, transpartisan philanthropy.[3]

I have come to care deeply about poverty and how our country, among the greatest and wealthiest of all nations, could eliminate it, and how to make the promise of this democracy truly work in the United States and globally. Even so, I know I come from a particular progressive stance.

I do not mean to offend, nor to shut the mind of the more traditionalist reader. Old linguistic habits do die hard. Words such as *ageism, sexism,* and *anti-militarism* may inadvertently offend as being too politically correct. But I have made the decision to write this book as a transparent reflection of who and what I am, and I invite you to use the tools presented here to articulate and advance your own views, to clarify your own personal vision, to use your own voice, and to come to action. Through giving we create a life and a stronger family—we strengthen our respective communities and, if we work at truly caring together, even the world. Out of the collision of warring communities, out of culture wars, can come not civil war again but the tumult of a vibrant democracy. So whatever your traditions or values, whatever your side of the culture wars, whatever ideal you hold holy—welcome. Let us pursue our differences passionately with faith, hope, and love. Let the spirit of those we serve guide our greatest generosity.

Creating a giving and legacy plan and being proactive with it may not only change your life, it might change the world. We have seen the remarkable gap that exists between people's stated desires for societal change and their irregular practices at contributing to making that change. Consciously accepting responsibility for our individual and collective roles in shaping the direction of our society is one solution to the distance between nonprofits' needs and donors' giving. Awareness of our participation as donors and thoughtful decision making—at every financial level—will help create a more compassionate world for ourselves and the planet.

In a moment of prayer after the exposure of the Abu Ghraib prison abuses, I asked how I might better serve humanity. A voice came to me—whether from within, without, above, or in harmony, I do not know, but the sacred message was clear: *"The only way to counterbalance exponential violence, greed, and injustice is with exponential love, generosity, and care."*

Let us imagine anew our collective abilities to align our dreams, deeds, and dollars for the good of the planet.

With gratitude and love to all who inspire us to greater impact and engagement.

Tracy Gary
Houston, Texas
and Ross, California
July 2007

ACKNOWLEDGMENTS

This third edition of what was originally called *Inspired Philanthropy: Creating a Giving Plan* has been substantially revised and updated to reflect new ways of giving and new resources to do so. I am hugely appreciative of the talents and commitments of several mentors and giving partners whose voices and influence echo through every word here. To collaborate in this third edition with writer and editor Nancy Adess, with Allison Brunner and Jesse Wiley, and the whole team at publisher Jossey-Bass is to return to a well of substance, faith, and excellence. There are simply no words to properly describe the humble and remarkable partner that Nancy Adess has been as an accompanist wordsmith and patient craftswoman in shaping this volume of tools. I pray for one ounce of her talent and her grace under fire. I deeply miss my original coauthor, Melissa Kohner, who is now pursuing a doctorate degree. Her audacity and that of her generation inspire my own hope and fifty-year engagement with giving and its transformative contributions. Melissa's brilliance still fills these pages.

I make a deep bow to my creative partner, advisor, and self-proclaimed "charitable cheerleader" Phil Cubeta. His questions, "Why haven't your previous versions said more about legacy planning?" and "How may I help?" were the impetus for both this book and Inspired Legacies, the nonprofit through which we develop tools and build connections for donors, advisors, and nonprofits, and which is referred to frequently throughout this book. Phil's diligent feedback helped make many parts of this book stronger; his wisdom and years of experience with donors and advisors can be found especially in Chapter Eleven. I shall be ever grateful to him and to the donors and nonprofits worldwide who have taught me that the missing piece is often the deep translation of values through our families and advisors to our nonprofits and the leaders that make them magnificent.

Credit for the many new ideas for this edition goes to the participants at several conferences on philanthropy (including the Tipping Point Network and the Philanthropy Salon on the Evolution of Philanthropy: Love, Social Justice, and Evolution), the Transformative Philanthropy Strategic Leadership Circle, as well as exchanges among women donors, community foundation donors and advisors, and young donor groups and our communities and partners at Inspired Legacies and Changemakers. I also extend thanks to readers of the first two editions of *Inspired Philanthropy* for sparking my own sense of possibility by your communications, feedback, stories, and examples. Thanks especially to Lorrie Lampson, Jean Russell, Karen Payne, Elizabeth Share, Anne and Christopher Ellinger, and Duane Elgin, who along with Phil Cubeta researched or added their original thinking or added their direct research. Many others, including Luis Gilberto Rivas, Sondra Shaw-Hardy, Melissa Milos, Pilar Gonzales, Melissa Kohner, Jean Beard, Laura Loescher, Michael Feder, Tammi Wallace, Terry Larimore, Paul Shoemaker, and Bonnie Kell gave feedback, support, writings, interviewing, and suggestions. The resource section was updated due to the generosity of Colin MacKay and expanded by the work of Alison Goldberg and Karen Pittleman and Resource Generations's *Creating Change Through Family Philanthropy.* It's the inspired stories told here that belong to donors and advisors and nonprofits.

Finally, to the boards, staffs, and donors of Inspired Legacies and to Changemakers—the two nonprofits that over the past ten years have supported me as a staff person or consultant in my work with donors, advisors, and nonprofits that has resulted in so much of this learning—my personal and profound thank you. I would never have had these opportunities to traverse the country and the world without your investment in my leadership. This book is indeed the work of that village, which has built not only my knowledge but my heart. I have been the vehicle for making visible the good works of many people and organizations. Of course, any omissions, improper crediting, or errors are entirely my own.

To Tori Williams, who is at the center of that heart, I say thank you for your faith and patience in the six months taken between our rich and full lives to write this book.

THE AUTHORS

Tracy Gary has spent her life transforming communities as a donor activist, philanthropic and legacy advisor, and nonprofit entrepreneur. She has given away more than $1 million that she inherited at age twenty-one and another $1 million that she has earned since. She has served on more than thirty boards of directors and has helped to start eighteen nonprofit organizations and foundations, including Resourceful Women, the Women Donors Network, and Changemakers. Tracy's latest adventure is Inspired Legacies, which helps to catalyze millions of dollars of the public good through linking powerful donors, activists, and advisors. Inspired Legacies provides exceptional donor and legacy education materials and workshops for nonprofits, advisors, and donors wishing to "unleash the generosity generation."

Tracy works to promote and inspire greater and more strategic lifetime and legacy giving. Her work includes supporting donors, family foundations, financial service organizations, and nonprofits, and educating them about the stewardship of money and about leadership and philanthropy.

Tracy works as a philanthropic coach and legacy advisor for a wide array of groups. Corporate clients have included American Express Financial Services, New York Life Insurance Company, PNC Wealth Management, and US Trust Company. Other clients have included the Women's Funding Network; the Institute of Noetic Sciences; regional grantmaking associations; and many private, family, and community foundations; donor networks; and grassroots community groups. Traveling all fifty states and numerous international locations, Tracy promotes service, impactful lifetime and legacy giving, and leadership.

Tracy can be reached at www.inspiredlegacies.org or tracy@inspiredlegacies.org or at donordiva@inspiredlegacies.org or by phone at 713/527-7671.

Nancy Adess is a freelance editor with specialties in social change, nonprofit functioning, and health care. In the field of philanthropy and fundraising, she has edited numerous books, among them the first two editions of *Inspired Philanthropy; Fundraising for Social Change, Fundraising for the Long Haul,* and *Fundraising in Times of Crisis,* all by Kim Klein; *The Accidental Fundraiser,* by Stephanie Roth and Mimi Ho; *The Nonprofit Membership Toolkit,* by Ellis Robinson; and *Grassroots Grants,* by Andy Robinson. In the health care field, Nancy has edited chapters of *OurBodies OurSelves: A New Edition for a New Era,* and numerous reports and policy briefs.

Nancy has been active in the nonprofit community for thirty-five years as volunteer, board member, executive director, and fundraiser. She can be reached at naedit@horizoncable.com or 415/663-8562.

Inspired Philanthropy

INTRODUCTION

We have to share with our people. Suffering today is because people are hoarding, not giving, not sharing.

—Mother Teresa

When you give money or time to a cause, does it speak directly to something you really care about? Do you feel confident that your money, time, or influence will make a difference, will help improve or even save the world? Do you feel sure your resources will be used wisely? Are you concerned that those you love may not know your charitable or legacy wishes? Do you know you care but have yet to prioritize how you will give back or pay forward the generosity you have received?

If you want to become a better giver, or to consider how to reflect on the alignment of your values and the practice of giving, or to work with your advisors or family on how to shape your legacy, this book is for you. It will tell you how to become more organized and engaged in your giving and how to work to achieve your highest aspirations. If you want to connect with others, the extensive resource section will point you to a variety of groups working on many issues as well as to advisors and foundations with whom you may want to work. Welcome to philanthropy!

Here you will find you are not alone, that you are in fact on a path with many others who are also dedicated to a stronger and more caring world. You might try a few new ideas gathered from thousands of donors, nonprofit leaders, and financial and wealth advisors on how to engage your highest self, invest your resources in inspired plans, and catalyze others for the public good.

Helping you move from "obligatory giving" to "inspired giving," as shown in Figure I.1, is what this book is about. Most people's charitable gifts fall into the "obligatory" category at the top of the inverted pyramid. By working through *Inspired Philanthropy,* you can reverse that assignment so that most of your gifts come from your passionate belief and elegant planning and fulfill your vision of how to transform the world. By the time you have completed the exercises in this book, you will be more confident of the impact you can have by directing your giving to organizations that truly speak to your values. You will be closer to being a passionate giver—both effective and inspired.

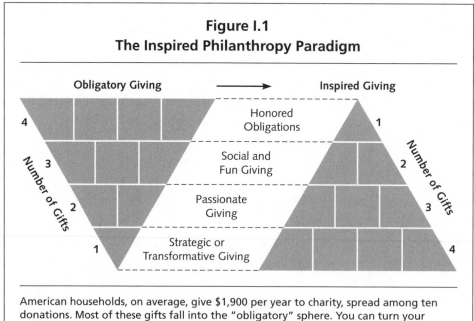

Figure I.1
The Inspired Philanthropy Paradigm

Obligatory Giving → Inspired Giving

Number of Gifts

Honored Obligations
Social and Fun Giving
Passionate Giving
Strategic or Transformative Giving

American households, on average, give $1,900 per year to charity, spread among ten donations. Most of these gifts fall into the "obligatory" sphere. You can turn your current giving upside down with inspired philanthropy.

An inspired giving plan has a time horizon of more than one lifetime. Such a plan includes within it a prudent estate and financial plan for the giver and the giver's family. An inspired plan is passionate, prudent, heartfelt, and also effective. The goals set for self, family, and society are systematically advanced. With an inspired plan, a person or family comes into their own as a force for the good, establishing traditions that will last many lifetimes.

Financial advisors and community, family, and public foundations will find this book helpful as a resource for clients and donors. Readers have told us that previous versions have been used to give an overview to the emerging industry and infrastructure of giving. In fact, the previous edition was found to be the most frequently used donor education source among more than eighteen hundred donor education providers across the United States. This book would make not only a good gift for clients or donor advisors, but a great tool for your own social investing or legacy planning. *Inspired Philanthropy* aims to turn your limited time into more effective uses of your money and influence.

HOW TO USE THIS BOOK

Inspired Philanthropy will lead you through the steps to align your giving with your dreams of a better world. Creating and using a giving plan will give you a sense of control, purpose, and direction and will inspire you to become more proactive in organizing, managing, and taking charge of your financial life in general. A thoughtfully developed and conscientiously implemented giving plan will tell you where your philanthropic hours and dollars are going. Because it reflects your personal priorities and dreams for creating a better world, it will be an active ally in supporting the issues that are most important to you.

The early chapters of the book cover the basics of organizing your thinking and your process of giving. They begin with an overview of the many ways the nonprofit world benefits our lives, our communities, and the world. In Chapters Two, Three, and Four, workbook exercises give you a chance to explore your values and passions and begin to shape a mission and a method for your giving. In Chapter Five, there are exercises to help you decide how much to give. Chapter Six looks at how to find out more about where to put your philanthropic dollars, including how to evaluate groups. By the time you get to Chapter Seven, "Creating a Personal Giving Plan," you have all the pieces you need to create a plan that will reflect what you most care about and the generosity you wish to express.

Chapters Eight and Nine provide more detail about ways to move your financial gifts to the nonprofits you've chosen, including individual and group giving methods as well as giving through family foundations and donor-advised funds. Chapter Ten explores deepening your development as a donor through your relationships with groups you fund and by growing into an inspired philanthropic leader. Chapter Eleven discusses the crucial piece of creating your legacy through estate and better lifetime philanthropic planning and working with advisors for greater effectiveness.

Chapter Twelve looks at how to engage the next generation in giving, with examples from people who got useful early lessons in being philanthropists. Chapter Thirteen addresses donors who have much more to give. The book concludes with a chapter on "transformative giving"—how careful strategies and courageous actions might enable our communities and our world to thrive. Although all of the stories in the book are true, most names have been changed to preserve privacy.

Along the way, "Donor Diva" comments offer insights from the field. These reflect an inspired perspective on giving that comes from years of experience working with donors and seeing change happen. They are my own pearls of wisdom, added to simplify your journey.

You may find from the table of contents and index exactly what you feel you need right now and leave the rest for future perusal. Or you may focus on a few exercises that will get you reworking what may feel like a currently chaotic approach. If you are new to giving, or want to overhaul the way you give, starting from the beginning and working through the exercises will give you a more comprehensive approach. If you want an overview of the steps and a "quick start" to creating a giving plan and legacy plan and reviewing your philanthropic activities, see the Quick Start Guide that follows this introduction. Appendixes on the attached CD-ROM include additional ideas on being an effective giver, more charts, sample letters, statistics, a section on considering making loans to friends, and an extensive resource section of useful materials and organizations.

You may want to make copies of the exercises as you go through the book and start a folder or binder for them. Your giving plan can also become a source for "our" family giving plan, and with this collaboration, more leverage. You might also want to consider working through the exercises with a group of friends or family members. Groups around the globe are using this book, one chapter at a time, to become more intentional. Many readers have found that working with others both broadens their perspective and maintains their momentum toward becoming inspired philanthropists.

Above all, have fun with your dreaming for the world and your planning. Giving money is one of life's great joys. You will change others' lives and you will change your own.

The following sections provide background on how philanthropy has changed and matured, along with a discussion of the difference between offering charity and creating change.

PHILANTHROPY—FROM TRADITIONAL TO TRANSFORMATIVE

People give for all kinds of reasons, from family tradition, a sense of obligation, or an expression of faith to a desire to act on passionately held beliefs, a drive to "pay it forward," or a feeling of abundance. Most giving falls into the charity model of responding to acute, immediate needs—blankets and food for flood victims, temporary housing for homeless families. The ability to respond to crises is one of traditional philanthropy's strongest assets. Traditional philanthropy is also very good at social maintenance giving: supporting the established institutions—educational, religious, social, and cultural—that maintain and improve society. Traditional philanthropy is based on responding to, treating, and managing the consequences of life in the existing social order as it is.

Transformational philanthropy, on the other hand, analyzes and responds more to cause than effect, seeking out the answers to questions such as these: What are the conditions that exacerbate or alleviate poverty around the world? How can health care be more equitable? What prevents food security for all? Transformational philanthropy supports what is called societal change—that is, actions that seek to address the root causes of disadvantage or the practices that threaten values such as equitable living for all or a healthy planet. For example, once warm and dry, flood victims may want to join together to advocate for effective yet environmentally sound flood control methods, including relocating businesses and houses out of the flood zone. For homeless people, over the longer term a sweat-equity program of home building and private-public partnerships for job training and education might provide more permanent solutions to their needs than do shelters and food kitchens. While the need for mainstream, crisis-healing philanthropy remains, there is also a need to go beyond the Band-Aids to the wounds themselves and their source.

Transformational philanthropy strives to fund solutions that are proactive rather than reactive, work that speaks to the underlying causes of people's distress. Its investment lies in challenging the assumptions that economic and social inequities are somehow unavoidable as the price of "progress" or "prosperity." We are living in a time of profound social, cultural, and economic change. It is important that philanthropy, long held as the means for alternative solutions to pressing problems, grows through each of us to better support the crucial issues of our time.

Table I.1 shows the differences in the effects of giving to charity and giving to change. Table I.2 gives some examples of ways to move from one approach to the other.

THE COURSE OF AMERICAN GIVING

Since institutional philanthropy's beginnings with the wealth created by the industrial giants of the late nineteenth and early twentieth centuries, the dominant public face of philanthropy in the United States has reflected the concerns of society's powerful elite. As activist and scholar Lisa Durán points out in the *Grassroots Fundraising Journal*, "Definitions of philanthropy have been dominated by a view that emphasized 'charity,' the detachment of professionalism, the benefits of tax deduction, and giving through charitable institutions."[1] At the same time, immigrant communities and communities of color, as well as those without enormous wealth, have a long history of giving traditions and philanthropic institutions.

Table I.1
Charity Versus Change Philanthropy: Characteristics

Charity	Change Philanthropy
Short-term fixes	Long-term solutions
Social services	Social change
Reactive	Proactive
Individual responses	Collective, organized responses
Dependent communities	Empowered, independent communities

Source: Changemakers, adapted from *Robin Hood Was Right: A Guide to Giving Your Money for Social Change* by Chuck Collins and Pam Rogers with Joan P. Garner, copyright © 2000, The Haymarket People's Fund.

Table I.2
Examples of Charity Versus Change

Charity	Change
Focus on individual needs	Focus on institutions and policies
Give to the fine arts museum	Give to an organization working to ensure National Endowment for the Arts (NEA) funding for the arts
Donate a dollar a day to help one child in Guatemala	Donate to development projects focusing on building up the local economy in Guatemala
Support shelters for battered women	Support conflict resolution and anti-violence programs for junior high and high school students to prevent battering
Fund Toys for Tots during the holidays	Fund organizing for a livable wage so parents can afford to buy toys for their kids
Give to a telethon for services for people with disabilities	Give to a group of disabled people and their allies pushing their elected officials to make public buildings accessible
Donate to cancer drug research	Donate to a group organizing to clean up the toxins in our environment and to pressure polluters
Send money to a shelter for homeless families	Send money to a housing coalition working for affordable housing
Give to a senior citizen center	Give to a senior action council working for home health aid coverage to enable older people to remain independent
Fund a scholarship for one high school student to attend college	Fund a student association organizing to ensure that higher education is affordable for everyone
Donate food to a food pantry to provide supplemental food for lower-income working families	Donate to a group lobbying to raise the minimum wage so people can afford to purchase the food they need

Charity is not a bad thing. But social change can ultimately eradicate the need for most charity.

Source: Changemakers, adapted from *Robin Hood Was Right: A Guide to Giving Your Money for Social Change* by Chuck Collins and Pam Rogers with Joan P. Garner, copyright © 2000, The Haymarket People's Fund.

Social changes of the past fifty years have brought changes to the world of philanthropy. In the United States, social and economic justice movements beginning in the 1960s worked for the rights of those largely ignored—including the movements for civil rights, student power, women's rights, and the rights of immigrants. All these movements helped to spread power beyond the wealthy elite and focused on a more democratic decision-making structure.

The changes in global communications wrought by widespread use of the Internet, along with the growth of the world economy, have further expanded our definitions of community and mobility and brought more attention to the links between the causes and effects of our actions.

These sea changes have also affected philanthropy, bringing a more democratic form of philanthropy that in many cases shifts the power to decide where philanthropic dollars go. Once these decisions were the sole purview of those giving the money; now, many foundations involve people from communities receiving funding as decision makers.

Many who inherited wealth in the second half of the twentieth century have also altered the course of philanthropy, developing alternative avenues for funding that would support groups seeking more fundamental social change represented by the social justice activities of their time. Toward that end, they started a number of public foundations across the country that are now dedicated to addressing some of the root causes of inequity and to broadening the traditional view of who gives to support fairness in America.

The democratization of philanthropy not only has brought the vast majority of Americans into giving and volunteering annually, it has also created new forms or vehicles for giving. Community-based foundations, giving circles, neighborhood funding, and the Internet offer people a way to share their giving process and decision making across a rainbow of personal and philosophical differences.

More than 91 percent of Americans give to charities during their lifetime. Globally, too, giving is filled with amazing generosity. Here are two stories from people who became inspired givers.

BECOMING AN INSPIRED PHILANTHROPIST
Tracey Minkin

Our early giving was to the Sierra Club because my husband was a member. Every time they called we'd give $25 or $35, but we had no idea how much we were giving over a year's time. One day I came across a brochure about giving that said that the people who earn the least give the most and that everyone should give 5 percent of their income. I went right home and suggested to my husband that we begin doing that.

The following year we made a list of our donations and noticed that, aside from gifts to our colleges, almost all our giving went to environmental groups. Although we were interested in social services, the environmental groups were the ones that had reached us. So we created categories of where we wanted to make donations—education, arts, environment, social services, and a slush fund—and earmarked 5 percent of our gross income to distribute.

As our income has risen so has our giving. We agree on what percentages to give to each category and research groups in those categories. The slush fund allows us to respond to other things that come up—friends who ask us to buy tickets for raffles or benefits, for example.

Each January we have what we call the Budget Summit. We used to have a bottle of champagne and have a party, just the two of us, to celebrate being thoughtful about our giving. That was before we had kids. Now we might sit down with a cup of tea. We review our previous year's giving and decide what we want to change in the year ahead. We keep track of our giving on a spreadsheet on the computer; with a few years all on one sheet, we can compare giving from previous years. We project how much the 5 percent is going to be, and we ask ourselves if we like the mix of groups we gave to last year. We talk substantially about how much to give to each group, trying to be realistic about the impact of the money. For example, $100 goes further at the local animal shelter than at a national environmental group, so we give a little more to the national group because we feel they're spending our money well. We're also interested in making a difference in our town, so we look for opportunities to give locally. We've decided to put human or social services over other concerns, especially work for the well-being of children, and we value local over national or international efforts. By the end of the summit, we've listed all the groups we want to give to for the next year.

When fundraising letters come from the groups on our list I write a check and note it on the spreadsheet. Some groups who are on our list never ask us. In December, I write checks to groups that haven't asked. If something comes up during the year—for example, if I see an ad for the Women's Center and it looks like they need the money right now—I'll send them a check.

Sometimes you have to swallow hard to do this. We made less money this year so it's tempting to cut back our percentage of giving. But we so firmly believe in philanthropy that we rely on our plan to keep us committed to our program. Giving should be that way. It's too easy just not to do it.

Miven Booth Trageser

My first giving plan was hopelessly ambitious and way too fragmented. I had been writing my will and decided that I wanted 60 percent of my assets to go to specific nonprofit organizations and 40 percent to specific individuals.

I looked at where I had been giving donations over the previous two years and decided that each of the three areas I had given most to—women's rights, community organizing, and alternative media—would receive one-third of the 60 percent. I designated ten organizations within those areas and the proportion I wanted each of them to receive. When it came to naming individuals, ten people came to mind to whom $100 to $1,000 would make a difference, and I named them in the will. Making this plan forced me to realize that I can't give to everything. I had to confront that feeling of not being able to do enough for the world, that I have limitations.

Then I thought, if I'm planning my giving for when I'm dead, what's stopping me from doing it now? That's when I decided to use my will as a blueprint for a yearly giving plan.

After a couple of years of trying to give according to the plan, I realized the plan included too many groups, which meant I wasn't focusing my giving in a realistic way. I discovered that there were three organizations to which I'd given more than $250 each year for several years; I had a good relationship with these groups and felt good giving to them, so I decided to simplify my giving plan by focusing on them, as they support a range of activities I care about.

I know that there are lots of organizations I'm ignoring. I can't even let myself read their literature because I feel too upset that I'm not going to give them anything because I'm committed to my plan. At the same time, there is something nice about saying no, I'm not going to spread myself any thinner.

I have never had a year where I followed my plan exactly the way I thought I would. I still find myself giving $30 to random phone solicitations or $10 at the front door. I thought the plan would arm me against that kind of spontaneous giving, because I would know I was being strategic. But my heart opens, and I'm glad I can give.

SOME BELIEFS ABOUT INSPIRED PHILANTHROPY

- Giving and sharing are universal human impulses for creating and sustaining culture and community.

- The Bible calls us to three main virtues—faith, hope, and charity—and declares, "The greatest of these is charity." At its root, giving is about hope, faith, and love.

- Everyone has a role in making the world a better place according to their idea of "better." One important way in which we each express our values and our citizenship in a democracy is by supporting the organizations and causes we care about.

- Philanthropy is a creative expression of that part of yourself that cares about and believes in the potential for change.

- The most effective philanthropy joins your interests and experiences with current needs and seeks desired outcomes for the public good, not for private gain.

- Creating a giving and legacy plan fosters more enjoyment, ingenuity, and effectiveness in personal philanthropy than does routine or re-active giving.

- Inspired giving ideas and solutions come from all generations and people of all walks of life. Community and family input in our planning makes for better giving.

- Coming into your own true place of giving is an evolving, definable, and developmental process.

- Allowing ourselves be moved by leaders, organizations, and those who seed hope is part of the great gift of inspired giving.

- Inspired philanthropy and service have transforming powers for all—givers and receivers.

QUICKSTART GUIDE:
TEN STEPS TO MORE INSPIRED PHILANTHROPY

Here is an overview of the process of developing a giving and legacy plan that is detailed in *Inspired Philanthropy*.

1. Begin with your values and passions: What do you care most about and what do you want to preserve or change during your lifetime and beyond? Ask mentors or leaders whom you respect what is needed. Choose two to five issue areas, populations, or approaches. Weigh these against what the community needs and your ideas of how change happens, and make adjustments. (Chapters One, Two, and Three)

2. Identify the mission, intention, or desired outcomes of your giving as specifically as possible. (Chapter Four)

3. Think about your immediate and lifetime giving: How much (as a percentage of your earnings, assets, or wealth) do you want to give now, or in the future? What will be your lifetime impact? (Support or guidance from mentors, financial or philanthropic advisors or coaches is helpful.) (Chapter Five)

4. Learn more about the areas you care about or what's needed through talking with others in the field and online research, and refine your priorities. (Chapter Six)

5. Research which groups match your mission and learn more about them through online research, their literature, their leaders, and their results. Evaluate the leadership of the organization, and its vision, budget, productivity, and partnerships or community ties. For groups in your highest priorities,

consider becoming more involved as a volunteer (board committee member, board member, program volunteer). (Chapter Six)

6. Returning to your mission and priority areas of interest, decide what percentage of your giving you want to direct to each area and the types of strategies you want to fund. Decide which groups you will fund, determine the amounts, and give the money with intention. At year's end or a time you designate, evaluate the impact of your giving and volunteering and review your process. (Chapter Seven)

7. Consider how you want to make your giving decisions: alone or with others through a giving circle, foundation, or created community of givers and activists (Chapters Eight and Nine)

8. Decide how you want to be involved with groups you fund and what skills you may need to learn to multiply your impact. (Chapter Ten)

9. Consider your lifetime contributions and leadership through legacy planning and an intergenerational dialogue about values and community needs. Engage your community and financial advisors and family to consider your giving capacity and larger or multiyear leveraged gifts during your lifetime and beyond. (Chapters Eleven, Twelve, and Thirteen)

10. Join with others to consider meta-level issues, such as global warming or economic development, education, electoral reform, or health care. Consider transformative giving with transpartisan partnerships. Engage donor peers and the next generation and those from community in your process of evaluation and revisions. (Chapter Fourteen)

Twelve Elements of Inspired Planning.

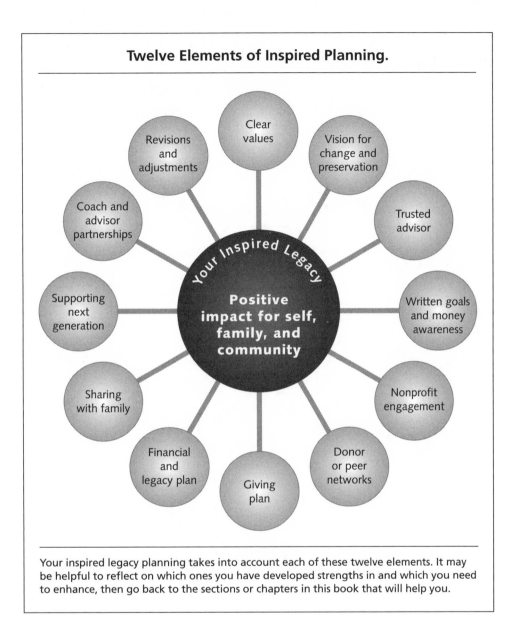

Your inspired legacy planning takes into account each of these twelve elements. It may be helpful to reflect on which ones you have developed strengths in and which you need to enhance, then go back to the sections or chapters in this book that will help you.

PART ONE

Creating Your Giving Plan

Giving and the Nonprofit World

"I got it, we had to help each other. We had to work together to get the power on and for things to be made right. We had to give to our neighborhood and to people who were in worse shape than we were. Then our faith and hope returned."

—Veronica, New Orleans survivor of Hurricane Katrina

In August of 2005, my family members and I were returning to Houston following my mother's funeral on the very night that more than two hundred buses arrived nearby with exhausted and traumatized people from New Orleans who had been evacuated from the devastation of Hurricane Katrina. As we watched the television news, we agreed that there could be no better recovery from our own personal grief than to extend ourselves to those arriving in need. The next morning, we signed up to help ease those first days of disbelief and fear among those survivors.

Like the people of Houston, people all over the country responded immediately. Book groups or social networks suddenly became shopping circles, forwarding diapers, underwear, can openers, backpacks for students, cell phones, and other items that local businesses in Houston had run out of. Members of churches, synagogues, mosques—peoples of all faiths, always the backbone of relief after disaster—were again devoted, diligent, and generous beyond their traditional service or areas of giving. It was a simply remarkable outpouring of love and concern.

Four years earlier, the world had seen a similar response. Within six weeks of the terrorist attacks on New York City on September 11, 2001, more than $1 billion had been donated to support the bereft families of the nearly three thousand victims of the attacks.[1] Americans throughout the country poured forth their help: donating blood, sending food and money, traveling to New York City to help sort through the wreckage of the collapsed World Trade Center buildings and counsel those who grieved and mourned. Within days, the nonprofit sector—the Red Cross; the United Way; and community, public, and private foundations—along with corporate America set up ways for their constituents, clients, and staff to express their sorrow and despair through compassionate action and gifts to nonprofit organizations serving those affected by the attacks. Giving online, a relatively new convenience that had accounted for less than 1 percent of dollars given, soared to 4 percent of dollars given in just two years.[2]

There are other examples of people reaching out to give. When only limited international relief came to the victims of the 2005 earthquakes in Pakistan, a group of U.S. medical students and young doctors packed up supplies and managed to push their way into the most devastated of the earthquake-ridden areas, where they spent months giving basic and essential medical care to families and victims, many from remote villages that had not seen doctors for years.

The nonprofit sector and volunteers like these are changing the world by filling—and even anticipating—needs that government and corporate services do not fully address.

In the face of global climate change, worldwide disease, and poverty, as well as natural disasters, can we find ways to learn to live sustainably and peacefully on this precious planet? Two weeks after Hurricane Katrina, former president Clinton launched his Global Initiative, attracting wealthy and highly connected participants who pledge to take a specific action—committing funds, donating needed supplies, or sharing expertise—on such issues as poverty, climate change, global health, and religious and ethnic conflicts. Clinton's advice to this elite set of corporate and foundation leaders was, "Don't wait for government and the bureaucracies to fix things. Get in there and decide what difference you can make. Figure out your greatest capacity to help or to leverage change, commit resources and yourself and your team and get working on it." By December of 2006, after the second Global Initiative Conference, pledges from this group totaled nearly $10 billion and benefited more than one thousand organizations.[3]

Although not everyone can create this kind of response, it shows that rolling up our sleeves—and working together—is not only the feel-better approach, it is the dependable way for recovery, change, and working proactively to avert future crises.

Can the nonprofit sector and each of us as more strategic donors and leaders be a new organizing force for good and for hope? Most of the groups and institutions that ask for our philanthropic dollars and donors who create the most impact are just that force.

NONPROFITS ARE AN ESSENTIAL LINK

Nonprofit organizations are the most common vehicle for distributing philanthropic funds in the United States, directing money and other resources to areas of need. Nonprofits provide services, education, and advocacy in a multitude of areas—from arts and culture, education, health, and public safety to religion, recreation, counseling, and community organizing.

Nonprofit organizations, sometimes collectively referred to as the *independent sector,* are legally incorporated organizations exempt by law from corporate income taxes because of their mission to accomplish a defined charitable, humanitarian, or educational purpose. No owner, trustee, or stockholder shares in any profits or losses of nonprofits.

A statistical view shows the enormous contribution of the independent sector to the country's economy:

- There are more than 1.5 million nonprofit organizations in the United States—schools, hospitals, human service agencies, arts and cultural organizations, and religious institutions.

- The nonprofit sector represents more than $700 billion in revenue,[4] accounting for 3 percent of gross domestic product.[5]

- About one-fourth of the U.S. population volunteers its time to an organization—representing 61 million people in 2006.[6]

- The nonprofit sector employs an astonishing 11 million people, making up 10 percent of the American workforce—more than all the employees of federal and state governments combined.[7]

Nonprofits of all types play a crucial role in the social, economic, religious, cultural, and community aspects of our lives.

THAT'S A LOT OF MONEY

According to *Giving USA 2006,* the annual yearbook on American philanthropy, donations of nongovernmental funds to nonprofit organizations totaled an eye-opening $295.02 billion in 2006, an increase of 5.7 percent from 2005. If you're like most people, you probably think that most of this money comes from corporations and foundations. You're in for a surprise. As you can see in Figure 1.1, more than 75 percent of the money given away in 2006 came from individual donors (and another 8 percent came from individuals in the form of bequests distributed after their death). Corporations contributed only 4.2 percent of the total and foundations only 12.4 percent. This general pattern has held true for a number of years. Individuals—like you—provide by far the greatest number of charitable dollars.

When most of us think of the philanthropy of individuals, we think of large gifts by very wealthy people. In 1997 Ted Turner's $1 billion pledge to the United Nations, followed in 1999 by Bill Gates's $24 billion endowment to the Bill and Melinda Gates Foundation and in 2006 by Warren Buffet's pledge of $31 billion to the Gates Foundation, have all set an enormously generous and even surreal standard of giving by the wealthiest Americans.

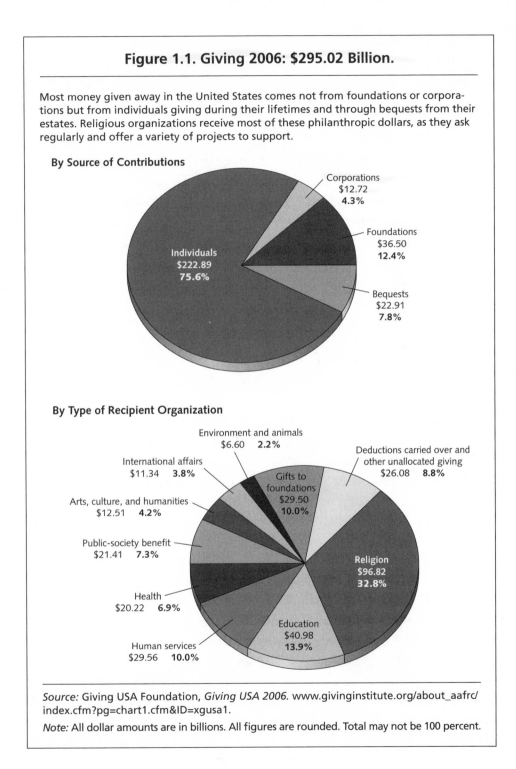

Figure 1.1. Giving 2006: $295.02 Billion.

Most money given away in the United States comes not from foundations or corporations but from individuals giving during their lifetimes and through bequests from their estates. Religious organizations receive most of these philanthropic dollars, as they ask regularly and offer a variety of projects to support.

By Source of Contributions

- Corporations $12.72 **4.3%**
- Foundations $36.50 **12.4%**
- Individuals $222.89 **75.6%**
- Bequests $22.91 **7.8%**

By Type of Recipient Organization

- Environment and animals $6.60 **2.2%**
- International affairs $11.34 **3.8%**
- Arts, culture, and humanities $12.51 **4.2%**
- Public-society benefit $21.41 **7.3%**
- Health $20.22 **6.9%**
- Human services $29.56 **10.0%**
- Gifts to foundations $29.50 **10.0%**
- Deductions carried over and other unallocated giving $26.08 **8.8%**
- Religion $96.82 **32.8%**
- Education $40.98 **13.9%**

Source: Giving USA Foundation, *Giving USA 2006.* www.givinginstitute.org/about_aafrc/index.cfm?pg=chart1.cfm&ID=xgusa1.

Note: All dollar amounts are in billions. All figures are rounded. Total may not be 100 percent.

But the wealthy aren't alone in their giving. Through an irrepressible spirit of generosity, people who toil all their lives at low wages manage to be major donors as well. Oseola McCarty spent a lifetime washing and ironing other people's clothes. In 1995, when she was 87, she gave $150,000 she had saved from her life's earnings to the University of Southern Mississippi for a scholarship fund to benefit African American students. Ms. McCarty became well known for her gift, but there are countless others who have given quietly from very modest means. Thomas Cannon, for example, a postal clerk whose top salary had been $20,000, had given by the time he died in 2005 more than $155,000 in the form of $1,000 checks, which he sent to individuals in need whom he read about in newspapers.

In fact, in relation to income, the most generous donors are those who are the poorest. According to INDEPENDENT SECTOR's *Giving and Volunteering in the United States, 2001,* 89 percent of American households contribute to charitable organizations. In 1998, contributing households with incomes of less than $10,000 gave an average of 5.3 percent of their household income to charity, while those with incomes of $100,000 or more gave only 2.2 percent. Contributing households with incomes between $40,000 and $50,000 gave on average only 1.4 percent of their household income. The 2005 *Giving and Volunteering in the United States* reveals $7.8 billion in giving from businesses and corporate foundations making up only a very small share of giving overall. Corporate philanthropy plays a much smaller role in the philanthropic field than the many individual donors collectively contributing in private philanthropy.

Whether you give a lot or a little, when you join the community of donors—to traditional, conservative, or progressive philanthropy—you join millions of other Americans who make charitable gifts and support nonprofit work as a way to express their caring and commitment to one another and the world.

THE ROLE OF PRIVATE PHILANTHROPY

For many years, government partnered with nonprofit social services and arts institutions by helping to support their work. During the past few decades, however, government support of nonprofits has diminished considerably. Extensive budget cuts have made the role of the individual donor increasingly important as more and more nonprofits lose the government funding they counted on. At the same time, institutions and services that have been the responsibility of government—from public schools, public parks, and public libraries to military supplies—have also seen such large decreases in government funding that they, too, have turned to private philanthropy to fill the gap. Of course, private individual giving can never completely offset the government's withdrawn funds, and we must continue to press for public money for the public good.

At the same time, as government funding has fallen off, the gap between rich and poor has widened. In 2004, for example, more than half of all income went to the top 20 percent of households, and the *average* CEO's paycheck was 431 times that of the *average* worker.[8] While the income of the top one-tenth of 1 percent of Americans more than doubled between 1980 and 2005, the earnings of America's bottom 90 percent fell.[9]

Inspired philanthropy poses an important question: Given the currently low and declining levels of government funding for social services and other nonprofit activity, and the increasing gap between rich and poor, what is each person's responsibility to make our society—and the world—more equitable? Most of us realize we could give more and that we are buying or wasting a great deal. Could we deliberately rethink the way we are living and giving? As citizens of the human community, we all have a responsibility to give as much of ourselves as we can. The widening gaps between the rich and poor beg us to consider whether such degrees or conditions of poverty should exist in a world with so much wealth. For those of us whose personal wealth or earnings have grown over the years, it seems only right to match our expanded financial resources or longer-term asset growth with equally strong community generosity.

THE POWER OF PHILANTHROPY

Philanthropy plays a critical role in America. Claire Gaudiani writes in *The Greater Good: How Philanthropy Drives the American Economy and Can Save Capitalism*: "Fifty-one percent of all hospital beds are funded by citizen generosity. Forty-nine percent of all two- and four-year institutions for higher learning are privately funded. Citizen generosity funds a little more than 20 percent of all students in institutions of higher learning, 95 percent of all orchestras, and 60 percent of social service organizations."[10]

More than that, without philanthropy, projects such as the airplane and space travel wouldn't have gotten off the ground. Philanthropy funds innovation before the market can support that innovation. If we need new thinking and new applications of solutions to complex problems, philanthropy plays a significant role—whether those are social or physical innovations. From civil rights to laws about drunk driving, from airplanes to medical innovations, philanthropy drives growth and change for our government and our for-profit markets. Here are some examples:

- Environmental Defense Fund—stopped the use of DDT, initiated the field of environmental law, birthed a movement that now constitutes hundreds of billions of dollars in products and services and employs millions of Americans

- MADD—changed laws across the land, created the idea of a designated driver, and surely has saved thousands of lives and billions of dollars in economic losses

- National Institute of Health—pushed by the funding and activism of Mary Lasker, now uses billions in government funding for medical and health research

- March of Dimes—funded by small donations from millions of people to fight polio, a disease now nearly extinct in the United States and fading worldwide

- Aeronautics—received significant funding from the Guggenheims for education, for technology development, and for the popularization of flying through the sponsoring of the Lindbergh flights and others; helped to catalyze a nearly $100 billion industry

Philanthropy has such a pervasive impact on our world, it is hard to imagine what our world would be like without its catalyzing effects. Many great initiatives start small, out of the basement or around the coffee table, and grow, with support from donors like you, to have far-reaching impacts on all of us.

Beginning with our own communities, we can see myriad nonprofit organizations that contribute to our benefit:

- Churches, temples, synagogues, mosques

- Cultural centers and community theaters, symphonies, and museums

- Zoos, community gardens, and farmers' markets

- Organizations offering counseling and legal defense for victims of domestic violence or rape

- Volunteer fire departments

- Local Girl and Boy Scout chapters

- Health clinics in rural and inner-city communities

- Organizations offering services for people with AIDS, alternative health services, and cancer research

- Homeless shelters and soup kitchens

- Organizations offering services for immigrants and refugees

- Groups working to protect our environment and endangered species

- Food banks, the Salvation Army, and Goodwill

These organizations and services depend on the generosity of donors inspired and compelled to contribute to improving our world. In the act of giving time, skills, and money, we all feel the spark of our original inspiration, which propels us to continue giving.

SOME GIVERS' STORIES

Here are some inspirational stories of donors with strong motivations and passions for giving and an organized, focused vision that has developed over time.

Beth and Amy: Social Venture Entrepreneurs

Beth and Amy were cofounders in the largest mid-cap IPO offering in the high-tech sector in 1999. Each of them walked away with a good-sized fortune while still in their early forties. Working with their financial advisor they put aside money for their future but also earmarked significant funds for a philanthropic or civic project. They learned about the various tools and techniques of estate planning and charitable planning. First they seriously considered starting a private foundation to advance their interest in helping children grow up to lead healthy and ethical lives as productive citizens. In the end, though, Beth and Amy realized that their greatest gift was not money, it was their own entrepreneurial skills and energy. So instead of giving money to a charity or putting it in a foundation for future grants, they started a new for-profit business with a double bottom line: financial return and social good. Their firm, MindOH (www.mindoh.com), has become a successful producer of programs on character education that are sold to schools; it also offers materials for parents, helping not only troubled children, but all children, find their way in school and in life.

Greg Garvan: Giving Back

Greg tells his own story:

> In the early 1990s I received an inheritance that presented my family with a number of questions: Do we give all or part away? Do we keep it for retirement? Save some for the kids? Will my wife have any special desires or needs?
>
> First we followed the age-old advice not to make any major changes for a year. We met with a financial planner to review our options. At the end of the year, we had made our decision: we would give 25 percent away outright and with the rest set up gifts to nonprofits through a vehicle called charitable annuities that would add income for our retirement.
>
> I decided I wanted to support small groups that others might not be funding and that would have some personal meaning to me. Since my family had roots in the South, in a town where we had owned a textile company for 120 years, we decided to give back to the people of that community.
>
> Through my travel and research I found small organizations not funded by larger regional foundations that help local minority farmers and new businesses. One was the South Carolina Farming Association's Seeds of Hope project, which links black farmers with local churches to set up farmers' markets. We provided money to buy a refrigeration truck they needed to transport produce to other area farmer's markets. In another philanthropic area, I convinced my siblings to join me in supporting the Black Historical Society and in honoring a black woman who had helped raise us by establishing the Carrie Kilgore Scholarship at the College of Charleston. This was a modest way of saying our thanks to someone who gave so much to each of us. My family and I also helped the Institute of Southern Studies, publishers of the magazine *Southern Exposure,* with a year of startup funding to hire a marketing and fundraising specialist.

Ruth and Abraham: Faithful Siblings
Giving Back and for the Future

Sister and brother Ruth and Abraham learned giving from their grandfather, uncle, father, and mother, who inculcated in them the notion of *tzedakah*—a Hebrew word meaning righteousness, justice, or fairness, which in many households is expressed through charitable giving, and is often considered by Jews to be a moral obligation. They were taught how important it was to listen and to simply be giving people.

Ruth says, "Giving to others is not only part of our lives, it is the thing we do as brother and sister to keep our bond, our joy, and our faith. We love creating plans and then surprising the next generation of leaders or family. We have set up funds for each of the younger generation in the family through the Jewish Endowment and the Jewish Fund for Justice. Beginning on their thirteenth birthdays, we give them the income from these funds to use in making tzedakah gifts of their own. They become responsible for healing the world (*tikkun olam*) through their actions and service for justice, just as we were. Teaching giving from the heart and soul feels more satisfying than buying or hanging on to material possessions. We say, pass it on with purpose!"

Harry and Melissa: Enabled to Do More

Harry is a successful business executive in Arkansas who has done well, though he would not call himself rich. He and his wife, Melissa, have been long-time supporters of their local community, giving to their church and to the local community foundation. They love giving and being active in the community, but they also sometimes say, "Charity begins at home," meaning that they have obligations to each other and to their children and grandchildren as well as to the causes they believe in and to their town.

Harry and Melissa have been working with a financial advisor who practices inspired legacy planning (for more on inspired legacy planning, see Chapter Eleven). The advisor, May Dickinson, spent hours talking with Harry and Melissa about their vision, values, hopes, and dreams for themselves, their heirs, their town, and even their county. Working with the couple's attorney and CPA, May made sure that their financial plans left Harry and Melissa well taken care of and that their children and grandchildren had "enough," by Harry and Melissa's own reckoning. But the advisor was also able to show the couple that they most likely had more than they could ever spend and more than they would want to leave to their heirs.

Harry and Melissa were excited to see that they had a pile of legacy dollars that they could devote, after all other needs and wants had been met, to doing something grand, something noble, something that would make a big impact on the wider community. Rather than waiting for death and letting their children have all the fun giving the money away, Harry and Melissa decided to put their stash of "extra money" and their personal time and energy into working with their church and with organizations supported through the community foundation.

Though not thinking of themselves as "philanthropists," Harry and Melissa are now known as leaders in their community and as admirable role models. What they are passing to their heirs is more than money: their example has already inspired their children to "step up" their own civic engagement.

John Gage: Living and Giving Simply

John tells his own story:

> I was trained in a religious order and in that role accepted a vow of voluntary simplicity. Although I am now out in the world, I try to live by my deepest beliefs, including living a life of simplicity, faith, and charity. My income is actually just below what the government considers the poverty level, but I still manage to give away 6 percent of it. In choosing which nonprofit organizations to donate to, I create a giving plan that includes setting a budget and establishing annual mission statements, what I call "hopeful goals." To fulfill those goals, I follow a number of practices: I sort direct mail contribution requests regularly in order to help groups eliminate duplications and to keep informed through their updates, I support investigative reporting in order to learn more about who is working for social justice, I favor low-profile groups that don't send elaborate or multiple mailings and whose communications are environmentally sensitive, and I initiate personal contact with at least half of the groups to which I give in order to ask them what they need in terms of money or support.

As you can see, givers come from all walks of life and from across the spectrum of wealth. What they have in common is a deep desire to extend themselves to do good in the world through being thoughtful about their giving. In the next chapter, you can begin that thought process for yourself.

You, the Philanthropist

My heart is moved by all I cannot save:
So much has been destroyed.
I have to cast my lot with those
Who age after age, perversely,
With no extraordinary power,
Reconstitute the world.

—Adrienne Rich

Whether you donate $25 to a nursery school raffle, $100 to a community health clinic, or millions to a new hospital wing, you've earned the right to call yourself a philanthropist. Philanthropy is not just the gracious giving of inherited wealth or the beneficent doling out of dot-com fortunes. The money can come from income earned and saved, a windfall at a bingo or poker game, or an inheritance. The three essential ingredients of philanthropy are giving, caring, and intention. When you give to needed programs or causes you care deeply about, your philanthropy develops special meaning.

The word *philanthropy,* derived from the Greek, literally means "love of humankind." *Inspired Philanthropy* defines as philanthropists people who exert themselves for the well-being of others, who engage in practical and heartfelt benevolence, and who donate money and time to causes they believe in so that the world may become a better place.

Another way to describe philanthropy is simply this: giving time, talent, or treasure for the public good.

If you don't do so already, calling any donations of time or money your "philanthropy" will give it the intention it deserves. Creating a giving plan is a process of becoming more intentional about your giving, identifying what you love and are concerned with, checking to see if your assumptions about those concerns are valid, and investing those issues with your own values, money, and time. Creating a giving plan means choosing initiatives, leaders, and nonprofits whose missions and strategies are working to make the changes or do the good you want to see.

You may still be having trouble thinking of yourself as a philanthropist. We all carry stereotypes of philanthropists, though we may not be conscious of them most of the time. Allowing ourselves to recognize these stereotypes and then contrast them with our actual experience helps to free us from long-held biases to understand how our actions make us philanthropists. Check out your own ideas about philanthropy in Exercise 2.1.

GRATITUDE

Many of us give because we feel grateful for something or to someone. Giving is sometimes an expression of that gratitude. We are all givers, and we are all receivers of gifts. Givers come from many walks of life: parent and relatives; teacher; scout leader; coach; mentor; policeperson; doctor or nurse; soldier; religious leader; author; friend; volunteer; Good Samaritan; blood or organ donor; giver of hospitality, kind words, time, money, love, or attention.

Exercise 2.2 may put you in touch with some sources of gratitude in your life and help you begin to think about how you want to give back—or, more accurately, "pay it forward"—to someone else. This exercise also gives you a chance to write down the ideas you have now about the legacy you'd like to leave. It's a topic we'll come back to in Chapter Eleven.

Here is how philanthropist Sally Gottesman links her gratitude with her wish to improve the world:

> Here is the truth: I am discontented with the world the way it is. This is a funny thing to write—I feel so lucky to be alive, to feel the heat from the sun falling on my arm, to look at the flowers sitting on my desk. I have the ability to read, to write, to breathe, to be filled with awe

Exercise 2.1
Stereotypes

10–20 minutes

Fill in the following sentences, allowing yourself to write whatever comes to your mind, uncensored. By getting at the ideas that are just below the surface we can begin to identify our stereotypes—and, if appropriate, discard them.

Typical philanthropists are:

(example: from old money; older than fifty-five; live in mansions, give millions)

a. _____

b. _____

c. _____

People I know who give are:

a. _____

b. _____

c. _____

As a giver I am

(example: generous, focused, scattered, impulsive):

a. _____

b. _____

c. _____

Reflection: What have you learned about yourself by doing this exercise? For example, you may have found that your stereotypes contradict your experience or that the terms philanthropist and giver elicit different reactions.

_____

_____

_____

_____

_____

_____

_____

_____

Exercise 2.2
Gratitude

15 minutes

What have you received, and how might you "pay it forward"?

A. The Greatest Gift You Have Received

Who has most deeply touched your life, or the life of your family, as a giver?

_____

_____

What did this mentor, hero, or heroine pass on to you that you most treasure?

_____

_____

What are you most grateful for?

_____

_____

B. What Have You Given

There are many ways to "pay forward" the gifts you have received by passing on your own gifts of yourself to others. Rate yourself below using a scale of 0 to 5, with 0 meaning you have no interest in that activity, 1 meaning you are not doing enough, and 5 meaning you are very active in the spirit of giving.

___ Parenting

___ Teaching

___ Coaching

___ Mentoring

___ Volunteering

___ Government service

___ Military service

___ Service through religious organizations

___ Committee work for a nonprofit

___ Service on nonprofit board

___ Artistic accomplishment

___ Spiritual assistance (meditation, prayer, observances)

___ Giving financially while living

___ Legacy gifts

___ Other _____

___ Other _____

(*continued on next page*)

Exercise 2.2
Gratitude, Cont'd

Looking at the ratings above, in what areas are you active and satisfied with your action?

_____

_____

What areas would you like to become more active in?

_____

_____

C. Giving While Living: What Do You Want to Do Now?

In the next three months I will extend my gifts to others in these ways:

_____

_____

_____

_____

_____

D. Leaving a Legacy

The one thing I want people to remember about me as a giver is:

_____

_____

_____

After I am gone, my hope is that my gifts continue in these ways:

_____

_____

_____

and humility for feeling at one with the Universe in the here and now. And yet, I am discontented. I want there to be peace. I want all children to have food to eat tonight and every night.

I fund to make change because I recognize that I can use my brain, my time, and my money to indeed make the world a better place. Two adages guide my efforts and give me energy as an activist and donor. The first is by Margaret Mead: "Never doubt that a small group of committed people can change the world, indeed it is the only thing that ever has." The second is from the Talmud: "You are not required to complete the task nor are you free to desist from it."

I choose to concentrate the majority of my efforts for change, both my financial resources and volunteer time, on a variety of organizations I am inspired by. I feel a passion for their missions, and to the core of my being, I believe they will help shape a world that is a better place for women and men, girls and boys.

I am blessed to have been raised in a family that values volunteerism and philanthropy. Early impressions guide me: my grandfather's stories of raising money for Palestine in the 1920s on the New York subway, my grandmother making me a life member of Hadassah; with my sisters, organizing a carnival in our backyard to raise money for multiple sclerosis when I was ten. Finally, there was the experience of my advocating for and becoming the first Saturday morning bat-mitzvah at my family's conservative synagogue. All these experiences imbued within me a sense of personal responsibility and proof that I could make a difference.

WHAT DO YOU CARE ABOUT?

It's important to begin with who you are and what is at your core. Knowing the sources of the inspiration of your giving will enable you to ground your giving and help you shape your choices. Inspired giving—giving that is sourced from your most deeply held values and concerns—means giving from your own and the communities' place of wisdom and hope.

Following are some examples of how philanthropists talk about their giving.

Sylvia M. Giustina has focused her giving on local and national projects. At the local level, she has found a way to share what she loves:

For the last ten years I have been giving monthly checks for charity. I started out giving a few programs $10 per month; now I give four organizations $25 a month each. At Christmas time I give more. In all, I give 2 to 3 percent of my total take-home income. My donations go to a domestic violence shelter called Raphael House, the Oregon Food Bank, the Red Cross, Northwest Medical Teams, Dogs for the Deaf, the Anne Frank Center, Oregon Heat, and the Brady Center to Prevent Gun Violence. I also tip really well. Once a year I give a non-tax-deductible gift to the Brady Center to Prevent Gun Violence's lobbying arm. Several of these charities are also in my will.

For Raphael House I also buy discounted music CDs and CD players and batteries. I like giving music because it's something I enjoy, and the people at Raphael House love it when I drop off music. I don't have a family of my own and I like to shop at Christmas time. I found a bookstore that sells remaindered books for $1 each. One year I spent about $50 there on books and brought them to Raphael House.

I decided I also wanted to give gifts for teenagers. After the shootings at Columbine High School I realized how vulnerable a lot of teenagers are. I bought some music and books for teenagers and gave them to the Salvation Army. A firefighters' charity called Toy 'n Joy collects things at Christmas for kids. When I heard they were having a hard time finding stuff for preteen girls, I did some research and found some really good books for that group. Books are not that expensive. I look for stuff that's quasi-educational, including *The Diary of Anne Frank* and also blank books.

One of my favorite gifts is ice cream. I mail gift certificates for Baskin Robbins to people I read about in the newspaper who are having a hard time.

You only have so much control, and so you do what you can in small ways. I know that I work better with concrete things than with abstracts. I've connected my head and my heart. I really love books and music and food. I don't think my gifts of music and ice cream are changing people's lives but they are lifting someone's soul.

Philanthropist Harriet Barlow describes the feeling she gets from giving this way: "Giving well requires that I listen to my inner self and be more conscious of who I am and what I want to express in the world. That's why giving is almost always satisfying to me—whether or not the projects I fund are successful."

Mary Lam, in contrast, discusses whether just giving from the heart is enough: "We Chinese give, but it's only from the heart. We need to use a little more mind behind our giving. Of course, coming from the heart is important. This is where it starts—a sense of gratitude, or a feeling of obligation to those we care about or who gave to us. But then we really need to find ways to extend our financial gifts and make them work for us with more impact."

Frank and Ruth Butler have found giving to be closely connected to their spiritual lives:

> Our giving has been and continues to be a great source of joy in our lives. It is grounded in our Christian faith. We have been blessed to learn from wise people, starting with our parents, who know how to incorporate sound values into all money practices. Every budget is really a moral statement highlighting priorities.
>
> Our mothers taught us that everything we have is a gift, and that the central theme of our lives should be an expression of gratitude to the One who created us. We were brought up to give away the first 10 percent of everything we earned and to save the second 10 percent. This ultimately enabled us to give even more.
>
> In our twenties, we got connected to three wonderful groups that continue to shape our thinking and lead us to other similar groups: Faith at Work, The Church of the Saviour in Washington, D.C., and Sojourners. We learned about "proportional giving," sharing much more than the first 10 percent as we prospered.
>
> Clarence Jordan, founder of Koinonia [a Christian Farm Community and birthplace of Habitat for Humanity] said that God created a world of abundance but that many people live with scarcity because the distribution system is messed up.

Knowing what you feel passionate about is the first step in determining where your personal contributions of money, time, and energy will feel most effective. Your financial resources are part of who you are. Giving money and time is about giving a part of yourself.

VALUES DRIVE DECISIONS

The next exercises ask you to look at what you value most and whether your funding choices to this point reflect those values. For many philanthropists, a giving plan is not only a way to express their values, it also helps them articulate what those values are.

Our values are characteristics we hold in high esteem, what we give worth to. We may value qualities of being, such as integrity and justice, or particular kinds of endeavors, such as working for justice for the disenfranchised, feeding those who are hungry, or elevating the status of women. Whether we are conscious of them or not, our values greatly influence our behavior as givers, including what we fund, how we evaluate projects, and how we relate to those we support. For example, if you value women's leadership, you may make it a priority to fund programs that give women opportunities to develop leadership skills. Even if a program you're interested in is not specifically oriented to women, you may want to know what percentage of their members and key staff are women. Exercises 2.3 and 2.4 will help you clarify your values as a giver.

MAKING CHOICES

Giving takes discipline. To be intentional means making choices—saying "yes" to some projects and "no" to others. Often in the face of so many choices of leaders and organizations we could fund, our decisions can seem arbitrary. At the same time, by making these choices we can also feel that we are taking on a great deal of responsibility and influence. (See Appendix F on the CD-ROM, "Breaking Barriers to Effective Giving," for tips on how to work with informational, emotional, and strategic barriers to giving.) Deciding to be a thoughtful donor means considering the kinds of questions presented in Exercise 2.5. Each of these topics is addressed in later chapters, but it might be helpful to jot down some of your thoughts on these questions now, then come back to them once you have worked through the exercises in the rest of the book.

WHAT DO YOU BRING WITH YOU?

Many donors also volunteer. Working with organizations is, for many, an unexpected source of satisfaction. Experienced donors report that one of the benefits of their work has been developing and sharing a wide variety of skills. Putting what you do well in the service of a cause you feel passionate about and being recognized for your contribution feels wonderful. In turn, you'll invariably learn more, which is another reward.

Exercise 2.3
Vision and Values

15–20 minutes

Put a check mark beside the values below that resonate for you. Then circle the *three* that are most important to you.

☐ Community	☐ Harmony	☐ Preservation
☐ Compassion	☐ Healing	☐ Respect
☐ Courage	☐ Honesty	☐ Self-Discipline
☐ Creativity	☐ Humility	☐ Self-Respect
☐ Determination	☐ Independence	☐ Service
☐ Diversity	☐ Innovation	☐ Simplicity
☐ Empathy	☐ Integrity	☐ Spirituality
☐ Equality	☐ Interdependence	☐ Stability
☐ Excellence	☐ Justice	☐ Teamwork
☐ Fairness	☐ Knowledge	☐ Thrift
☐ Faith	☐ Leadership	☐ Tradition
☐ Family	☐ Love of comfort	☐ Transformation
☐ Freedom	☐ Love of others	☐ Other: _____
☐ Generosity	☐ Loyalty	☐ Other: _____
☐ Good sense	☐ Patience	☐ Other: _____
☐ Hard work	☐ Peace	☐ Other: _____

Issue Areas and Concerns

Following are words or phrases that describe issue areas and concerns that you may care about as a contributor. The areas listed are only for inspiration. You may never have donated time or money to these areas of interest before; this exercise is simply to give you the chance to recognize what has meaning for you among things you could give to. Put check marks next to those that have the most meaning for you. Then go through the list again and circle your top three.

☐ Aging	☐ Catholic charities	☐ Death and dying
☐ Animals and species preservation	☐ Children or child care	☐ Demilitarization
☐ Anti-Semitism	☐ Civil rights	☐ Disability rights
☐ Anti-Racism	☐ Coexistence	☐ Disaster relief
☐ Arts and art institutions	☐ Community gardens	☐ Domestic violence
☐ Biodiversity	☐ Computer literacy	☐ Drug and alcohol abuse
☐ Boys	☐ Corporate responsibility	☐ Economic justice
☐ Business development	☐ Cultural heritage	☐ Education

(*continued on next page*)

Exercise 2.3
Vision and Values, Cont'd

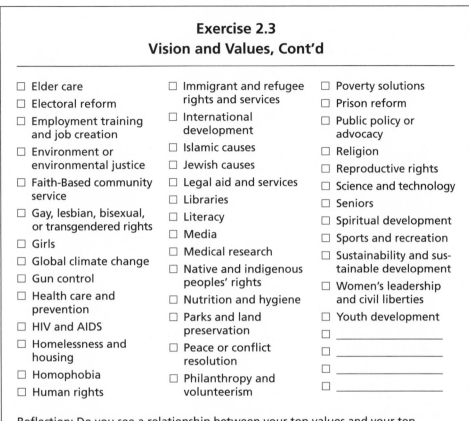

- ☐ Elder care
- ☐ Electoral reform
- ☐ Employment training and job creation
- ☐ Environment or environmental justice
- ☐ Faith-Based community service
- ☐ Gay, lesbian, bisexual, or transgendered rights
- ☐ Girls
- ☐ Global climate change
- ☐ Gun control
- ☐ Health care and prevention
- ☐ HIV and AIDS
- ☐ Homelessness and housing
- ☐ Homophobia
- ☐ Human rights

- ☐ Immigrant and refugee rights and services
- ☐ International development
- ☐ Islamic causes
- ☐ Jewish causes
- ☐ Legal aid and services
- ☐ Libraries
- ☐ Literacy
- ☐ Media
- ☐ Medical research
- ☐ Native and indigenous peoples' rights
- ☐ Nutrition and hygiene
- ☐ Parks and land preservation
- ☐ Peace or conflict resolution
- ☐ Philanthropy and volunteerism

- ☐ Poverty solutions
- ☐ Prison reform
- ☐ Public policy or advocacy
- ☐ Religion
- ☐ Reproductive rights
- ☐ Science and technology
- ☐ Seniors
- ☐ Spiritual development
- ☐ Sports and recreation
- ☐ Sustainability and sustainable development
- ☐ Women's leadership and civil liberties
- ☐ Youth development
- ☐ _____
- ☐ _____
- ☐ _____
- ☐ _____

Reflection: Do you see a relationship between your top values and your top interest areas? Here are two examples:

1. My top three values are dignity, equality, and opportunity, and my top three issue areas are education, economic justice, and youth development. I believe that the opportunity for a good education, particularly for young people who are shut out of their full potential early on because of poor schools, is vital to dignity, equality, and, finally, economic justice for everyone.

2. My top three values are community, justice, and respect, and my top three issue areas are seniors, poverty, and homelessness and housing. The relationship I see is that in order for everyone to live in a just community, all seniors must have enough financial support, including good housing, to lead their lives with respect.

Write down the relationships you see among your own values and interests:

_____

_____

_____

Exercise 2.4
Indicators of Your Values

15–20 minutes

In whatever way works best for you—free writing, quiet thought, or a conversation with a friend—explore one or more of the following questions that you find interesting. Write your answers below.

- What experiences and people have been key in shaping your core values and passions?

  _____

  _____

- What do you notice about your values when you consider your choices, such as life directions, career, free time, lifestyle, donations, and spending?

  _____

  _____

- When you hear of world events or witness an injustice, what moves you most? With what have you been most troubled? Most delighted?

  _____

  _____

  _____

DONOR DIVA

Although much of a giving plan focuses on financial contributions, inspired giving often comes from an integration of giving time, talent, treasures, or social connections. Volunteering with an organization provides intimate information about the needs and effectiveness of the organization. Some organizations need more volunteer time or social connection. Thinking beyond financial gifts can significantly increase the impact you make.

Exercise 2.5
Making Choices

20 minutes

1. How should I make the important decisions of where to allocate my philan-
   thropic dollars?
   - Should I get help from other family members or friends, or from people
     who may be more active in the community or knowledgeable than I am
     at this time?
   - Should I share the responsibility and privilege of decision making or giving
     with others who are from the communities I aim to serve?

   _____

   _____

   _____

2. How will I get the information I need? How much can I find out on the
   Internet, and how much time will I spend doing so? To answer any remaining
   questions, how much time will I allocate?

   _____

   _____

   _____

3. How much time overall will I devote to my giving: about the same as I do
   now? More than I have been? Should I give additional time to engage or
   partner with others?

   _____

   _____

   _____

4. How much money shall I give? Will this money come from income only, or
   could I raise or give more from other sources? Shall I discuss the options I
   might have with a trusted advisor?

   _____

   _____

What time, talents, and treasures do you bring to your passion? Find out in Exercise 2.6.

Exercise 2.6
Time, Talents, and Treasures

15–25 minutes

In the list below put a check mark next to each characteristic or item that is true for you. These may stimulate you to think of specific ways you want to share your abilities in the second part of the exercise.

☐ I can donate my professional skills to a nonprofit.

☐ My workplace has equipment or services or a meeting space I could offer to a nonprofit for their use.

☐ I'm good at organizing details and creating plans.

☐ I'm good at motivating people.

☐ I'm good at planning events and giving parties.

☐ I know many people in my community who might be good resources.

☐ I like to teach what I know.

☐ I am a good listener or writer.

☐ I have experience designing or administering Web sites.

☐ I am a supportive person to work with.

☐ I'm good with financial information.

☐ I like to raise money.

☐ I can translate or know people who can translate documents into other languages.

☐ I have graphic skills or artistic talents.

☐ I love kids or am good with elders.

☐ I am a passionate public speaker.

☐ I have ___ hours of time per week, or would be willing to take a day or more each month, to donate.

☐ Other:_____

Now look back at the top three values and issue areas you circled in Exercise 2.3. Think about the time, talent, and resources unique to you and your community that you can offer in working on those issue areas. For example, if you're a breast cancer survivor and one of your issue areas is breast cancer, you might write, "I have been through diagnoses and treatment and could help others know what to expect or simply provide support." Or, if you're passionate about electoral reform and belong to a civic group or business roundtable, you could invite a speaker on the topic to make a presentation.

Write a statement here of how you can offer your time, talents, and treasures:

_____

_____

_____

Developing Your System of Giving

*It is well to give when asked but it is better
to give unasked, through understanding.*

—Kahlil Gibran

Everyone has a system of giving. It may be as unsophisticated as the time-honored shoebox: throw every direct mail piece into it and once a week, once a month, or once a year, pull them out and write checks for the ones that appeal to you. Or it may be more spontaneous: write a check whenever an appeal strikes you as worthwhile, or someone asks, or an event seems like it might be important or fun. You may already be listing your contributions on a spreadsheet or using an advanced Web-based giving plan such as those at Newdea (www.newdea.com). Or your system may be as formal as directing the administrator at your community, public, or family foundation to send an annual check to the charity your family has been supporting for generations.

To develop more intention and consciousness about how you give—to whom, how much, when, and for how long—Exercises 3.1, 3.2, and 3.3 will help you see your current system. Even if you don't itemize your giving on your tax forms (only about 30 percent of Americans do), you may have a list of who you have given to during the past couple of years. Pull out whatever records you have—lists of your giving, receipts, checkbooks, or cancelled checks—to see your recent history of giving. These exercises will give you the chance to explore whether your giving has been a reflection of your values and interests and what changes you may wish to make now. In such an exploration, try to stay objective and not judge yourself for what you have done—or have not yet done. From here, you can begin to move clearly and intentionally toward what you want.

Exercise 3.2 will give you a bigger picture of where you have donated money recently, as you map the characteristics of the groups you've given to. Things to think about include the issue each group addresses, its size and age, and whether its scope is local, regional, national, or global. One interesting characteristic to consider is the strategies the group uses to create social change. The following list of strategies will help you fill in the column on strategies in Exercise 3.2.

Strategies for Change
- Advocacy
- Capacity building and leadership training
- Coalition building
- Culture, arts, and cultural arts
- Demonstrating, direct action, public education
- Disaster relief
- Economic development
- Education, training, resource development
- Empowerment
- Fundraising or leveraging funds
- Electoral politics (supporting candidates and initiatives; voter education and registration)
- Faith-based programs
- Grassroots community organizing
- Human or direct services
- Influencing public policy
- Media and media reform
- Meditation or prayer
- Problem analysis and research
- Public interest law or legal reform
- Research
- Shifting consciousness
- Systems change

Exercise 3.1
Review of Your Recent Giving

15–20 minutes

The next two exercises build on this one. First, write a short statement about how you are feeling about your giving now. (For example, do you feel you are giving enough? Too much? Is it directed in the ways you want?)

_____

_____

Now, on the following chart, list organizations you've given to in the past two years. In the next exercise, you'll have a chance to uncover the patterns in your giving. Feel free to copy this page or use the download on CD enclosed.

Organizations Donated to in the Last Twenty-Four Months	Amount Given	Why I Gave

Exercise 3.2

Characteristics of the Groups You Support

Beginning with your list of organizations in the previous exercise, map your top ten groups on the following chart to see the patterns of your giving. To spark ideas for the strategies column, see the list of strategies for change prior to Exercise 3.1.

Organization	Issues It Addresses (refer to list)	Strategies It Employs	Size by Budget*	Age**	Scope***

*Small: Less than $250,000; Medium: $250,000–$1,000,000; Large: More than $1 Million

**Start Up: 0–2 Years; New: 2–5 Years; Established: 5–10 Years; Sustained: 10-Plus Years

***Local, State/Regional, National, International

Exercise 3.3
Reflections

A. Characteristics of the Groups You Supported
Thinking about the characteristics of the groups you've donated money to in the past two years, answer the following questions.

1. Within each set of characteristics, was your giving focused on certain categories or varied? Were these choices intentional? If they were, what were the reasons behind your choices?

   _____

   _____

2. What do you see as the pros and cons of the pattern your giving has taken within each category? (For instance, your dollars may have great impact on small, start-up organizations, but start-ups sometimes fail. Giving locally offers you personal connection, yet some solutions require a regional, national, or global approach.)

   _____

   _____

3. Looking at the characteristics of the groups you've funded, is there anything different you would like to do next year? What? Why?

   _____

   _____

B. Your Relationship with Groups You Supported
Look again at the groups you listed in Exercise 3.2 and take stock of the relationships you have with them.

1. With what number of organizations are you a

   ___ Recipient of the organization's services

   ___ Past recipient of the organization's services

   ___ Volunteer

   ___ Member

   ___ Board member

   ___ Staff member

   ___ Other: _____

(continued on next page)

Exercise 3.3
Reflections, Cont'd

2. With how many do you

    ___ Know people in the organization

    ___ Know people who have been affected or helped personally by this or similar organizations

    ___ Know other donors

3. With how many did you learn about them through

    ___ Direct mail

    ___ Family, friends, social club, association, or work colleagues

    ___ Local public or community foundation or workplace giving

    ___ Media or the Internet

    ___ Other: _____

4. With how many do you

    ___ Want your donation to be completely anonymous

    ___ Want your donation held in confidence (only one or two people in the recipient organization know)

    ___ Don't care whether your donation is known

    ___ Want people in the community to know you made a donation

5. With how many did you stay informed by

    ___ Reading newsletters, e-news, Web sites, or annual reports

    ___ Attending events

    ___ Meeting one-on-one with staff or board

    ___ Other: _____

IMAGINING A BETTER WORLD

The information you generated in the exercises so far in this chapter describes your present giving practices and something about how you operate as a giver. When looked at as a whole in this way, your giving choices may surprise you—both in where your priorities have been and in what characterizes the groups you have given to. The strategy, size, age, and scope of those groups reflect how they make an impact on the issues they address. How you give—how often, how much, and how you leverage your gift or support your areas of greatest interest or concern—reflects how you make an impact on the groups you give to. Now is your chance to take a new look at how you want to be part of creating more significant change.

A first step is to reflect on societal or cultural change in a broader sense. You have the chance to affect the problems that most concern you on two levels: responding to immediate needs and looking beyond those needs to the sources of the problems, where social change happens (for a discussion of charity versus change, see the Introduction). To get at where change can take place on the issues you care most about, it's helpful to begin to develop your own ideas about how you might be involved in creating change. Some people call this process development a "change strategy." Your change strategy defines how you live and the choices you make with your time, your money, and your relationships with those you might influence. It involves aligning your practices with your principles. For instance, if you think of yourself as an environmentalist who cares about global warming, but you are driving a gas-hungry SUV or you are invested in a company with a poor record of environmental safety, then your actions are likely out of alignment with your values. Having a change strategy can help you to put your values into action (for example, take steps to reduce global warming).

Having a change strategy is one part of understanding a *theory of change*. A theory of change defines all the building blocks required to bring about a given long-term goal. It is a specific, focused way to get from the current situation to a desired outcome. (For more resources on how to build a theory of change, see Appendix I, "Resources," on the CD-ROM.)

One way to begin to define these things for yourself is to consider the questions in Exercise 3.4.

Though these questions probably aren't unfamiliar, realistic answers are usually complex. Nonetheless, it is worth trying to articulate answers, even at the risk of oversimplifying, because you will learn more about what you want to be giving to.

Exercise 3.4
Thinking About Change

As best as you can at this point, answer the following questions to begin to develop a theory of change.

- What is it that you hope to change or preserve during your lifetime? (You may want to refer to the issue areas listed in Chapter Two.)

  _____

  _____

- Has your past giving been a reflection of those hopes?

  _____

  _____

- What are some of the causes behind the problems that concern you?

  _____

  _____

- What do you wish were different, and what might help change the situation?

  _____

  _____

CREATING YOUR VISION AND A THEORY OF CHANGE

The exercises that follow present ways of creating your vision for change. If Exercise 3.5 seems daunting at first, you can skip to Exercise 3.6 for another way to envision what you might create. Like most of the exercises in this book, these may spark you to begin exploring why change is needed on issues you care deeply about, what changes could be most useful, and how you can contribute.

Following these exercises are more ways of thinking about and building a comprehensive giving strategy.

Exercise 3.5
Imagining a Better World

Part 1: 30 minutes

Part 2: 30 minutes

This exercise is in two parts—one cerebral, the other imaginative. The first part asks you and a supportive, interested friend or friends to think deeply about an issue, how things came to be the way they are, and what might help create positive change regarding that issue. The second part calls on your imagination to move beyond the rational thought process to an imagined state of an improved world. The two parts do not have to be done together. Again, detachment can help you move forward to intentional choices. What emerges here can be very personal and emotional, which will be useful later in using your personal connection to an issue to make change in that sphere. Allow yourself to explore issues fully and from many different angles and perspectives. An example of doing this exercise using the topic of homelessness follows.

Choose one topic that is of significant concern to you—something you'd really like to have an effect on in the world (you may have identified a topic in the questions above or you can refer to the list of issues in Chapter Two).

Topic: _____

Part 1: How did things get the way they are? What might help them to change?

With your friend who shares your interest or concern, brainstorm about what you know about this issue and present some of your main questions. You may want to consider the effects of key historical events, public education and opinion, and the interests of proponents and opponents of various actions that could address the issue. This part of the exercise may lead you to do some research to inform yourself more fully about the issue. When you've completed your thinking, list some of the ways the issue has been dealt with in the past and possible ways to address it in the future.

Part 2: Imagining a better world

In some quiet time alone, or with your companion of Part 1, imagine a world in which the issue you discussed in Part 1 has been completely changed for the better. For example, imagine an end to discrimination, or all endangered species flourishing. Daydream about the specific circumstances that would be different in this new world. What had to happen to make your vision possible?

When you're finished, reflect on your vision the way you would if you were thinking about a dream from which you had just awoken. Choose one piece that strikes you. Look for what is most exciting, intriguing, or surprising in your vision, something you would love to see in your eyes-open, real-life world. Brainstorm with yourself or your friend about ways this piece could inspire a new area to fund or a new approach to your giving.

(continued on next page)

Exercise 3.5
Imagining a Better World, Cont'd

An Example of Imagining a Better World
Topic: Homelessness

**Part 1: Why is there homelessness in the United States?
What might help this to change?**

Key Historical Events, Public Opinion, and Interests

- Federal policies have cut back on resources and services for the poor and the mentally ill, leaving many of them on the streets without the community services they need.

- Other federal cutbacks have severely reduced funding for subsidized housing.

- The real value of wages for many working people has decreased as costs of living have escalated.

- The millions of Americans without health insurance are only an illness or an accident away from using all their savings on health care.

- Widespread corporate downsizing and relocation to other countries have left many low-wage workers without jobs.

- After many years of widespread, visible homelessness, the general public has become hardened to it and concerned about their own safety; many cities have instituted "panhandler" laws prohibiting homeless people from asking for money.

- Many city governments seem more concerned about keeping homeless people out of downtown areas where they disrupt commerce than with trying to meet these people's needs for food and shelter.

- Continuing trends include the isolation of individuals and the dissolution of communities.

Questions

- What is involved in people becoming homeless right now?

- What impact has welfare reform legislation had on homelessness? On immigration and homelessness? On migration and homelessness? On the increases in the prison population?

- What are the characteristics of different populations of homeless people (women with children, substance abusers, and so on)?

(continued on next page)

Exercise 3.5
Imagining a Better World, Cont'd

- What role does addiction play in the lives of homeless people?

- What are the specific needs in my city? For example, are there enough shelters? Do they stay open year-round?

- What is my city doing to integrate people of diverse economic status and reduce isolation?

- What helps people to find homes and jobs again?

- Can philanthropy help find an effective, long-term solution to the gap between the homeless and those who are not homeless?

Possible Actions and Keys to Change

- Proactive and humane government policies

- Job training for jobs that are actually available

- Subsidized housing programs

- Establishment or development of multiservice centers

- Recovery programs and better education about addiction

- Government enforcement of shifting handouts helping people get into stable programs that have longer-term impact

- Public education that emphasizes how close many families are to homelessness

- Community development groups that connect people around shared community interests

- Expanded and improved government assistance systems that provide minimum financial security, basic health care, and mental health services, especially for families in distress

- "Living wage" campaigns, affordable housing campaigns, small business loans, and tax reform—all of which would contribute toward a more equitable distribution of wealth

Part 2: Imagining an end to homelessness. What characteristics would our culture have in order to eliminate homelessness?

Our culture would place a high value on everyone's quality of life. Communities of caring would support all of their citizens. Nonprofit organizations, religious

(*continued on next page*)

institutions, and governments would support the infrastructure that provides services such as job training, career counseling, and apprenticeships. There would be enough safe, clean shelters for people who needed them, including adequate facilities for women with children. People who lost their jobs or suddenly had their income threatened for some other reason, such as family illness, would have access to friendly and forthcoming government welfare programs, including housing, food, and transportation vouchers, and health care. There would be multiservice centers that help those in need with support, referrals, and training all in one place.

How to begin to help

One piece that might strike you is the need for job training and career counseling programs available to anyone who needed them. You could begin by phoning your local church, synagogue, mosque, homeless shelter, or city hall to find out what programs exist. You could then contact some of the programs to find out what they need most. They may need volunteers to help job seekers go through the newspaper's classified section and phone employers, or they may need interview clothes and voicemail services for people looking for jobs, or bus and taxi vouchers for people going to interviews. You might host networking events to help connect individuals so they can share skills, experiences, and opportunities. You might see a way that you personally could begin to make a difference in the lives of some of the homeless people in your area. Beyond such immediate help, you may hear about campaigns to change laws or regulations affecting homelessness and how to become involved at that level.

DONOR DIVA

Work backward. Inspired change making often comes from releasing the preconceptions you have about what is possible. Create a vision unrestricted and unlimited by what is. Then, assuming that is possible, work backward to see what would make it possible. Assume that a spaceship can land on the moon and then figure out how to do it. Start from the vision.

Exercise 3.6
Million-Dollar Visioning

30–45 minutes (This exercise is also great to do with your family or a group once each person has chosen his or her values and issue areas.)

Here's your chance to play Monopoly for the public good. Instead of hoarding your money and buying up all the properties, use this exercise to reflect on your vision of how you would give the money away to help create the world you want.

1. From the list of values and issues you care about, choose one problem in society you would like to help resolve:

   _____

   _____

2. Now imagine you have just been given $1,000,000 to give away or invest in solving that problem, with no strings attached. What would you do, who would you convene or hire to support your efforts, and what institutional partners would you choose?

   _____

   _____

3. What outcomes would you hope for and in what time frame?

   _____

   _____

4. How would you be involved to maximize impact?

   _____

   _____

5. How would you share your vision with others?

   _____

   _____

6. What is holding you back from starting some of this work, even without $1,000,000 or more currently in hand?

   _____

   _____

THE WHEEL OF INTEGRATED CHANGE MAKING

Figure 3.1 shows a way of looking at the various aspects of making change—the wheel of integrated change making. As you continue to evolve your thoughts about how to help and about your giving plan, consider the partners and collaborators who can assist you, how you will evaluate and revise your giving, and what experimentation you want to explore. Having a clear approach will help you bring about a well-defined long-term goal. You will have the chance to continue to refine your answers to these questions and more as you develop your giving plan in the next chapters.

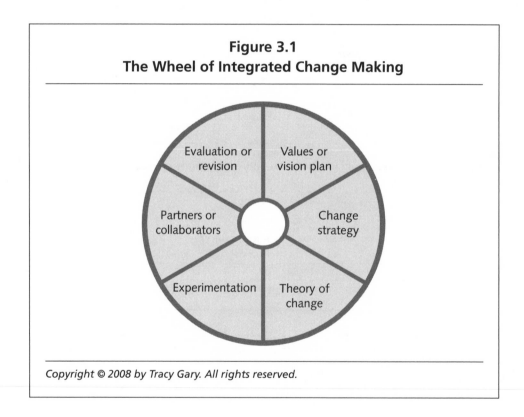

Figure 3.1
The Wheel of Integrated Change Making

BUILDING A COMPREHENSIVE GIVING STRATEGY

With the wheel of integrated change making in mind, use Exercise 3.7 to begin to build a comprehensive giving strategy.

Exercise 3.7
Steps for Building a Comprehensive Giving Strategy

20 minutes

What is the problem you want to address?

_____

_____

What is your goal or the outcome you hope for? What would you like to see changed in the long term?

_____

_____

What are some short-term outcomes or achievements that could be first steps toward a long-term outcome?

_____

_____

What are the ideas, systems, practices, policies, behaviors, and so on that will need to change in order to achieve these outcomes?

_____

_____

What activities and strategies will create the outcomes you want to see?

_____

_____

What people need to be involved or influenced?

_____

_____

What are the resources needed to put toward achieving these outcomes? (people, time, money, materials, partners)

_____

_____

(_continued on next page_)

Exercise 3.7
Steps for Building a Comprehensive Giving Strategy, Cont'd

Write two or three statements representing the beliefs you have about how change happens:

_____

_____

_____

_____

EVALUATING YOUR IMPACT

If impact is the record of change, then how do you determine whether you are having the impact you want with what you want to change in your community or the world? How will you document that change?

These are the tools that can help you:

- A giving plan, including leadership and volunteering (see Chapter Seven)

- A legacy plan (See Chapter Eleven)

- A community of donors, investors, activists, and community leaders

- Time for reflection and consideration of "spiritual call"

- Due diligence and spirit of inquiry, and willingness to change course

- Personal coaching and mentorship along the way

- Measurable objectives and stated outcomes and a way to evaluate learning

- Rigorous evaluation and reworking of your planning and leadership or your own intuitive analysis

- Willingness to balance passionate interests with evidence of community need

LEARNING MORE ABOUT SOCIAL CHANGE

Thinking about what you want to change may stimulate you to want to know more about what really creates change. What kinds of actions have meaningful impact toward shifting harmful practices to create a better world? A lot of innovative theory has been published about social change, and moving case studies of specific issue areas exist as written documents, films, plays, and visual art (see the "Social Change" section of Appendix I, "Resources" on the CD-ROM).

You may want to take advantage of some of these resources and find others. Before you know what you want to fund, develop your own ideas about how to evaluate the approaches various organizations take. In Chapter Six and in the "Resources" appendix, you'll find lists of organizations that can help you find and evaluate nonprofits that are in alignment with your vision.

In the next week, take some time to locate some resources on an aspect of societal change that you would like to see happen. For example, find books on the topic in a library or bookstore, look into a history or sociology class at an adult education center or local community college, identify one or more people you could interview who have been effective at making change in an area you care about, watch a video or film on the topic, think of others you could talk to who have focused on an area that concerns you. You might interview a leader, another donor, or a staff person at a foundation that is making the kind of difference you hope to. Ask yourself what strategies have seemed to produce the greatest result in the giving area of your greatest concern.

In answering these questions you are developing a key piece of your toolkit for giving: you have established your values and interests or concerns and now you are developing your ideas about how change happens. Both will continue to be refined over time and as you gain experience.

Stay curious about what it takes to make positive change. Curiosity will bring forth new information and options for you.

When you've laid out some options for what you want to look into and how, choose one or two of them and schedule time for them in the next month or two. What you learn may affect your giving now or thinking about your legacy as you prepare for the transfer of some of your assets to the next generation, to your spouse or partner, or to a foundation or groups you may want to support during your lifetime or beyond. Think of your process as one of experimenting and refining your approach to change as you learn more over time.

YOUR GIVING PORTFOLIO

Just as with developing an investment strategy, it takes trial and error to evolve your giving strategy. Think of the groups you fund as a kind of mutual fund of strategies or approaches. On one end of the menu of a giving portfolio might be tried-and-true "blue-chip-like stocks": larger nonprofits that have been in existence for years with stable leadership and a record of results. At the other end you may want to reserve 10 percent of your giving for high-risk nonprofit ventures that carry the possibility of high reward. Consider your tolerance for risk and what you have noticed about your past giving. Think of constructing your giving portfolio or plan much like a multipronged investment strategy as one way to be assured that you are diversifying and trying multiple ways to solve problems and to help make needed changes. Often in a family one person will give to one predominant type of strategy while another person will give to a different strategy, balancing the mix. In later chapters you will be able to explore how you might mix your giving portfolio or plan for better results, but for now, your task is to get clear on the framework and underlying principles of your giving strategy.

Increasing your knowledge and experience will greatly increase your effectiveness as a citizen and a donor and help you refine your philanthropic mission. The next chapter brings together what you've learned about yourself and your giving so far and takes you to the first step of creating your giving plan: your philanthropic mission statement.

Creating a Mission Statement

*If you do not change direction, you may
end up where you are heading.*

—Lao Tzu

All of the information about what you value and how you'd like to give that you've considered in the previous chapters will be useful in the next step, creating a philanthropic mission statement. This statement summarizes and focuses the purpose of your giving. It will serve as a guide as you create your giving plan in the next chapters.

Your mission statement should be a brief answer to the question, "What do I want to do with my giving and my time, and why?" Mission statements can be followed by action steps that will carry out the mission during a certain period of time, which will then be evaluated and refined to meet the mission more effectively. Once created and refined to your satisfaction, your mission statement will guide you in developing your Inspired Philanthropy Giving Plan in Chapter Seven. If your family is giving together, now is the time to articulate a collective vision. Once you have your vision and a refined mission for your giving, then matching your mission with organizations' missions, strategies, and programs becomes easier.

WRITING YOUR MISSION STATEMENT

A personal or family philanthropic mission statement provides a clear way to express what you are trying to do with your giving.

The most effective mission statements are usually no more than two or three sentences—something you can easily remember and others can easily understand. Though a mission statement is brief, it needs to pack a lot of information, so it will take some work to get it to say just what you want.

To begin, review what you learned about yourself from the exercises in the previous two chapters. With this information, you're ready to use Exercise 4.1 to try your hand at drafting a mission statement.

When drafting your philanthropic mission statement, include the following elements:

- Your passionate interests

- What you think can help improve or change the issues that you care most about

- What you are doing to support improvement or change (some action steps)

- The time period during which these philanthropic actions or gifting will occur

Before you begin, you might want to look at the examples on the following pages of mission statements that others have written (the mission statement is in italics, followed by some of the action steps the writer is taking to make progress on his or her mission and a sense of the time period for its implementation).

Exercise 4.1
Writing Your Mission Statement

25 minutes

Draft your own philanthropic mission statement here. Room is provided for a couple of drafts and a final statement.

First Draft:

- What I'm passionate about changing in the world:

  _____

  _____

- What I think can help improve or change the issues or problems I care most about:

  _____

  _____

- What I am doing through my giving to support improvement or change:

  _____

  _____

- The time period for my actions ahead:

  _____

  _____

Second Draft:

_____

_____

Final Statement:

_____

_____

_____

_____

INSPIRED MISSION STATEMENTS FROM
INDIVIDUALS AND FAMILY FOUNDATIONS

1. *I seek to reduce the amount of violence within families in my community.* I do this through the following actions: donating money to family violence prevention programs, volunteering ten hours a month on parent telephone hotlines that seek to reduce stress in families, continuing my ten-year commitment as a Big Brother, and advocating for laws that punish crimes of violence against families and that protect victims of violence. These actions will continue to be my priority for the next three years.

2. *We as a family are strengthened and sustained by our shared faith in God.* Our financial giving centers on our church, particularly its commitment to the religious education of children here and abroad. We will prioritize giving in this area for the next ten years.

3. *I want to help immigrants to this country.* Everyone in my family from my grandparents' generation was an immigrant, and the country has been good for us. I fund groups that give immediate support to immigrants and help them obtain free or low-cost legal aid. I commit to this approach for at least five years.

4. *The Brown Family Foundation gives back to the communities in Wisconsin in which our company does business.* Our mission is to promote the economic and social vitality of rural communities. The Brown Family Foundation serves as a hub connecting farmers, the food industry, government, and academics to understand and address the issues that are critical to Wisconsin farmers.

5. *The Seed Fund exists to provide seeds to low-income communities for gardening and soup kitchens.* We are a group of organic farmers who believe that healthy food and hands-on growing and cooking of food can change the health and well-being of any community. We make contributions of money, seeds, or both to schools and projects that distribute seeds, and we establish community gardens and teach sustainable gardening.

6. *I believe that summer camp should be an experience available to all kids.* I've seen children gain enormous self-confidence, skills, and new friends through summer camp experiences that have helped transform their lives. Our family has established the Campers Fund to give camp scholarships to low-income and disabled children who have never been to camp. It is our family goal to pro-

vide scholarships beginning in 2007 for two to four kids per year for three years to the summer camp of their choice.

7. *The two areas in my life that I have a strong passion for are music and work against racism.* I donate monthly and serve on the board of a local music program that provides music training for inner-city kids who cannot afford lessons and for schools and communities whose music programs have been cut. I am using my professional knowledge on the finance committee, and I'm managing the endowment fund. I have also arranged for the organization to receive a bequest through my will.

8. *The Mission of the Abraham Fund is to foster empathy, understanding, peace, and coexistence between Muslims and Jews and diverse people worldwide.*

9. *As long-time community members, we believe in supporting and the sustained economic and cultural development of our community.* Through our donor-advised fund at the local community foundation, we make multiyear grants to groups that provide job training programs and micro-enterprise loans to individuals. We will evaluate our progress every three years.

10. *The mission of our family giving is to assist those throughout the world who are poor, ill, or otherwise suffering.* Our mission bears witness to Christ's teaching of faith, love, and hope. Our giving mainly supports our church's worldwide missions.

11. *I believe that nothing can positively affect a person's life more than a good education.* Therefore I devote whatever extra money and time I have to helping students get scholarships and access to the best educational opportunities available. For the next three years, my specific actions in this area will be to help two high school students every year get the scholarships they need to continue their education.

12. *Our family's goal is to bring creative expression to our community.* We fund art and photography classes for inner-city and rural young people, and have established a summer community arts program that works with more than two hundred young people in our town each summer. We are committed to continuing the arts program for ten years, then evaluating whether there are other areas we should become involved in. In addition, we buy art from emerging artists for personal investment and enjoyment.

13. *We aim to link youth around the world and enable them to collaborate on social change projects.* We do this though the development of a Web site, online chat rooms with multilingual translation, and periodic in-person convenings. Our goal is to promote international collaboration on one new project each year and to host one convening every three years.

14. *We support the reduction of global warming by funding grassroots projects around the world, including media tools, that will shift behavior to more conscious conservation and global cooling.* In the next three years, we will fund at least ten projects worldwide as well as align our giving portfolio and conservation commitment.

15. *Our family believes in libraries and literacy as a means of strengthening community.* We contribute to libraries and reading programs, especially those that are bilingual and that bring the community together. During the next five years, we will fund 20 percent of the costs of our community's English as a Second Language program through the local libraries.

MISSION MATCHING

Your mission is a great tool for matching your values, vision, goals, and objectives with those of nonprofits and other donors who care as you do or have similar strategies or hopes. We call this "making a mission match." Once you have a working philanthropic mission statement, you have a new tool to help attract and find partners for your work and your funding ahead. Your task is to match your mission with those of other nonprofit leaders and nonprofit organizations. Having a clear statement of purpose enables you to find groups you may want to fund—and will ultimately help similar funders or groups find you. Chapter Six discusses how to research and locate groups to give to.

Here are several examples of mission matching, from a family foundation, public foundations, corporate foundations, and individual givers, showing some of the organizations that they have found to fund and how they found them.

The Jacobs Family Foundation

Values: risk taking, entrepreneurship, self-reliance.

Vision: stronger communities through economic development.

Mission: "Exploring new philanthropic roles and relationships for strengthening under-invested neighborhoods, making grants that support innovative, practical, and sustaining strategies for community change."

Grantee sample: The Jacobs Center for Neighborhood Innovation in the Diamond District of Southeastern San Diego.

How they found the grantee: A year-long community-based needs assessment.

Global Greengrants

Values: conservation, diversity, community.

Vision: stronger grassroots organizations worldwide building greater education and advocacy for societal change for the environment.

Mission: "We believe that grassroots groups are a key to solving the intractable problems of poverty, powerlessness and environmental destruction. Our experience has shown that there is no better investment than supporting passionate people with great ideas."

Grantee sample: Mauj Community Center and the Rural Development Policy Institute in Pakistan, to ensure that fair water, human, and cultural rights policies are enacted in their area.

How they found the grantee: an open web-based grant application process, with staff evaluations and a global advisory board's recommendation, then board approval.

The Women's Fund of Greater Milwaukee

Values: empowerment, equity, justice.

Vision: stronger organizations serving women and girls and tools for families and communities to encourage a new generation of funders of women and girls.

Mission: to advance access, equity, and social justice through woman-focused philanthropy, grantmaking, and advocacy.

Grantee sample: Girls Mean Business, to publish a new book on girls' giving and entrepreneurship.

How they found the grantee: encouragement by a board member and staff person for the group to apply to the Fund's twice-yearly grants process.

The Humana Foundation

Values: we are committed to serving the needs of children, families, and seniors in their quest to build healthier lives and communities. We embrace health as a balanced state of well-being, recognizing an interrelationship between mind, body, and spirit.

Mission: the Humana Foundation supports and nurtures charitable activities that guide others toward decisions promoting healthy lives and healthy communities.

Sample grantee: the DePaul School's program for learning disabilities and dyslexia, through a grant to enable the school to meet the needs of its Kentucky-area students by upgrading their computer lab.

How they found the grantee: a grant application form on the Humana Foundation's Web site and a referral from an employee of the Humana Foundation.

Marie Stewart

Values: education, fairness, opportunity.

Mission: to provide partial scholarships for low-income African Americans to go to college or religious seminary in North Carolina.

Sample grantee: Bennett College scholarship.

How she found the grantee: Marie's niece had gone to Bennett.

The Animal Health Foundation

Values: the companionship of a dog or cat, communicating with a horse, and observing the fascinating behavior traits of wild animals are all priceless gifts. While we appreciate the value of animals on earth, animal lovers also share their concerns for pets, wildlife, and for the people who appreciate animals.

Mission: to help animals and the people who care about them.

Sample grantee: The Delta Society—The Human Animal connection, for its Pet Partner's program and its goal to improve human health through service and therapy animals.

How they found the grantee: through a veterinarian involved with each, and through Internet research by the grantee.

Jamie Erickson

Values: family, community, empowerment, independence, and generosity.

Mission: to engage my family in giving our time to help elderly people do their taxes and to support financial education in homeless and battered women's shelters.

Sample grantee: Transforming Communities, for its financial education programs for battered women and their families.

How she found the grantee: Erickson's daughter met the head of the training program at a nonprofit training program and picked up their brochure and offered it as a possible grantee to the family.

HOW TO FIND POSSIBLE MISSION MATCHES

Here are some ways to find groups that might match your funding mission:

- Conduct Internet searches on your own and through links at inspiredlegacies.org. (See Chapter Six for more Internet resources.)

- Talk with people who share your values or who may know groups or funders with shared interests.

- Involve people from the constituencies that you are seeking to fund in your grantmaking or program evaluation.

- Attend issue-related regional and national conferences.

- Read the paper, subscribe to a clipping service on your issue of choice, or seek out research about your field or population of interest.

- Engage someone to do formal outreach and PR about your work.

- If you are a private funder with a donor-advised fund or a direct funder giving more than $100,000 per year, develop a Web page with details of your vision, mission, and goals, and potential grantees will find you.

- If you are a foundation, be sure the Foundation Center Library has a copy of your funding guidelines, annual report, and updated grantees list.

- If you are a nonprofit organization or have a foundation, complete and update your www.guidestar.com information for your IRS 990 form.

- Invite a panel of community leaders, donors, and activists to share their perspectives on what to fund or how to do so.
- Trust your instincts and keep your eyes and ears open. Serendipity will bring funders and projects together sometimes, but it's best to be proactive and ask for referrals.

Exercise 4.2 will help you get started on mission matching.

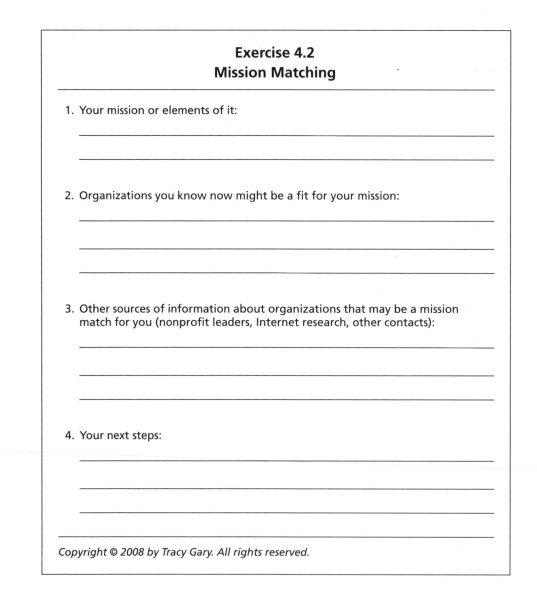

Exercise 4.2
Mission Matching

1. Your mission or elements of it:

_____

_____

2. Organizations you know now might be a fit for your mission:

_____

_____

_____

3. Other sources of information about organizations that may be a mission match for you (nonprofit leaders, Internet research, other contacts):

_____

_____

_____

4. Your next steps:

_____

_____

_____

Deciding How Much to Give

*Giving and sharing are simply life's greatest joy.
I endeavored to raise my children, as I was raised, so
that they understood and saw from us that engaging
with community is the best way not only to make
change, but to be changed for the greater good.*

—Patricia Murrill de Bary

The tradition of expressing compassion through giving and service is present in all religions and cultures and celebrated as acts of benevolence to bring peace, justice, and a sense of prosperity among people. Giving of your time and money is more than simply doing good. It is acting in a conscious and intentional way to weave yourself into a caring culture and to express your deep concern for justice or for preserving or changing people, places, or the planet.

Giving part of your income or assets, whether it is easy to do or a financial stretch, and giving a portion of your time out of a desire to share and help, are gifts that extend not only to the recipient but back to the giver as well. Giving is one of the most powerful and joyful things we are blessed to do. Moreover, if society is to reflect the real pluralism that exists around us, it is absolutely critical that we share our good fortune through compassionate action.

This chapter looks at the philosophy of different giving practices and invites you to explore some of your beliefs about your ability to give. The giving practices offer values-based approaches that may help you decide how much you want to give of your financial resources. You might want to share your thinking with your family and your financial, philanthropic, or legacy advisors. They too need to know your thoughts about giving and your intentions so they can support your desired directions. Sometimes asking the simplest of questions during your time with your accountant or financial planner can unleash more money for your giving or legacy. (See Chapter Eleven and Appendix A on the CD-ROM for more on how to work with advisors for more inspiring outcomes.)

Before you decide how much you want to give, it's useful to get some perspective on how much you truly have.

HOW MUCH MONEY DO YOU THINK YOU HAVE?

People's attitudes toward their personal resources of money and time are formed early. The level of financial safety and income your family did or did not have as well as messages you received while you were growing up about how to use money and time become both conscious and not-so-conscious beliefs and attitudes when you are grown. The socioeconomic class in which you were raised, the class backgrounds of your parents and extended families, and the class that you would currently describe yourself as falling within all exert enormous influences on how you think about money.

For example, if you grew up in a household in which there wasn't always enough money for essentials like food and clothing, you may still be anxious about having enough of these basics, regardless of how much income you have now. Even if you don't feel lack, you like many people may feel that you do not have enough money.

One way to reduce anxiety around money is to unearth the beliefs you hold about it. Do you feel, for example, that you have more or less than your share, or do you worry that you may not have enough in the future? Do you believe that you can or do earn enough money to support yourself and any dependents who may need your help?

Most of us have a distorted idea of where we fall on the economic scale. The following statistics may bring some perspective: According to the United Nations, if you earn any money at all, you have more money than one billion people in the world. Moreover, half the world—nearly 3 billion people—lives on less than $2 a day.[1] One billion children live in poverty (of the 2.2 billion children worldwide, that is nearly half of all children).[2] The combined wealth of the three richest people in the world is greater than the combined gross domestic product of the forty-eight poorest countries in the world.[3] In the United States alone, 12.6 percent of the population—37 million people—live in poverty.[4]

Although trying to grasp these differences might be overwhelming, just seeing where you are on the spectrum of wealth in the United States might help you think differently about both what you own and what you give.

Table 5.1 shows age and wealth disparity figures for 2004. Find your age and look at how you compare, given your household net worth.

Table 5.1 Age-Wealth Disparity		
	Median Net Worth by Age Group	Median Income for Head of Household
20–24	$3,900.00	$19,511.00
25–29	$12,030.00	$33,887.00
30–34	$42,800.00	$47,236.00
35–39	$48,940.00	$48,263.00
40–44	$98,000.00	$52,371.00
45–49	$136,190.00	$62,639.00
50–54	$152,101.00	$57,505.00
55–59	$249,700.00	$62,639.00
60–64	$244,000.00	$49,290.00
65–69	$179,000.00	$36,968.00
70–74	$207,400.00	$28,753.00
75 and older	$163,100.00	$23,618.00

Note: All numbers in inflation-adjusted 2004 dollars.
Source: "Age-Wealth Disparity: 2004 Figures." *USA Today*, May 21, 2007, p. 2A.

Exercise 5.1 offers another way to think about how much money you have.

MAJOR GIVING PRACTICES

Another way to address your feelings about how much you have and how much you want to give is to articulate your values and beliefs about living compassionately in the world. Some of us were raised with or now follow a religious tradition that clearly spells out the role of giving money and time within a set of spiritual values or practices. Others create their own tradition.

All major religions have traditions of giving to help the poor or needy among them. In many Christian faiths the form is tithing (literally giving one-tenth of your earnings); in Judaism, the obligation to give is expressed as *tzedakah,* Hebrew for "righteousness, justice, or fairness." In Islam, the practice of *zakat* requires giving a certain percentage of income and assets.

A contemporary view of tithing, from the national organization the New Tithing Group (www.newtithing.org), urges wealthier donors to include their assets, and middle-income donors to consider their own needs, when determining what percentage of their wealth to give away. "If the bulk of a donor's wealth resides in investments (or real estate)," they say, "tithing even 10 percent of their income may fall short of their actual giving capacity. Although we ask people to factor income and investments into their charitable choices, for those with moderate incomes new tithing is often more conservative than old tithing because it takes into account their living expenses and need to save for future costs like tuition, healthcare, and retirement."

Finding the right balance, given our wants and true needs and the needs of human and planetary security around us, is key. Giving less than we are able leaves us feeling isolated and often afraid for the world. Giving beyond what's safe for our own security may make us popular, but often leaves us feeling empty and afraid for ourselves. Lifestyle guides and new ways of balance have proliferated on the Web. New American Dream (www.newdream.org), Your Money or Your Life (www.your moneyoryourlife.org), and Simple Living (www.simpleliving.net) all have ideas for lifestyle choices that might permit more giving and leisure time. See also Class Action (www.classaction.org) and Responsible Wealth (www.responsible wealth.org) if you'd like to get more support or attend a workshop about class and privilege.

Some people base their giving not on a religious tradition but on a belief in stewardship. Many people believe they are merely shepherds or stewards of the money they earn or inherit and that they have a responsibility to use their money for the public good. Similar to tithing, but without the notion of giving a particular percentage, this philosophy is based on the belief that claiming personal ownership of wealth reinforces the unequal power structures that enable just a few people to accumulate large amounts of money. Some who subscribe to this philosophy keep only enough money to cover their basic living expenses and give the remainder away. Notably, a number of people who inherited large amounts of money have given away all but enough to live an average, comfortable life. For some inspired reading about these donors, see *We Gave Away a Fortune* by Christopher Mogil and Anne Slepian (see Appendix I, "Resources," on the CD-ROM), the excellent magazine *More Than*

Money, archived at www.civicreflection.org/resource_library/mtm_archive, and "Inspired Stories" at www.50percentleague.org. The Bolder Giving initiative of the 50% League has some truly wonderful questionnaires and coaching available for those who are considering their giving potential and what more they might give. Inspired Legacies and the 50% League are two donor-centered national organizations that sell only goodwill for the community. They partner closely to provide support to wealth holders considering how best to redirect their resources.

HOW MUCH SHOULD YOU GIVE?

On average, individual Americans give away only about 2 percent of their income to charity (average household annual contribution for most Americans is $1,620.)[5] It's well known that those with less income give away a greater percentage of their income than those with more. Even the wealthiest Americans, those in the top 1 percent of income and assets, who have more than $6.5 million in assets and $1.1 million in pretax annual income, give on average only 4.4 percent of income (or about $48,000 of that $1.1 million of income) when they could be giving so much more.[6] The question is, Do you want to be "average" or a leader in giving and helping others? If you had $500,000 in pretax income, how much would you want to give?

If we want to see true change nationally and globally, we must consider how to give more and give more effectively. To start, consider what giving at least 5 percent of your income and five hours a week of volunteer time would do to boost your well being and that of your community. For some, giving 10 percent is their

---

DONOR DIVA

Percentages and dollars make up a portion of the giving you can do. However, inspired gifts involve more than money. What other forms of "capital" can you use to leverage your financial giving? In addition to the financial capital you offer, how much do you want to contribute from your social, intellectual, talent, or courage and leadership capital? You may be quite surprised by the amount of value you have to offer.

---

faith commitment. For others of great wealth, giving 20 percent of income and 1 or 2 percent of assets will be more in line with what feels appropriate. There are also donor leaders who commit to giving 50 percent of their earned income. (For more on giving from greater wealth, see Chapter Thirteen.)

Giving effectively is not about giving from guilt or acting from a position of noblesse oblige but about understanding that voluntary giving is a key method of creating a world we want to see and one way to work to rebalance inequality. For an excellent analysis of how philanthropy has contributed to the success of capitalism and the outstanding way these systems are woven together, see *The Greater Good: How Philanthropy Drives the American Economy and Can Save Capitalism*, by Claire Gaudiani.

Figure 5.1 shows the levels of giving and consumption in the United States over the past several years. Clearly, our personal and material consumption have risen while our giving has decreased as a percentage of expenses.

Thinking anew about how much you have and how you want to participate in creating change, use Exercise 5.2 to consider how much to give.

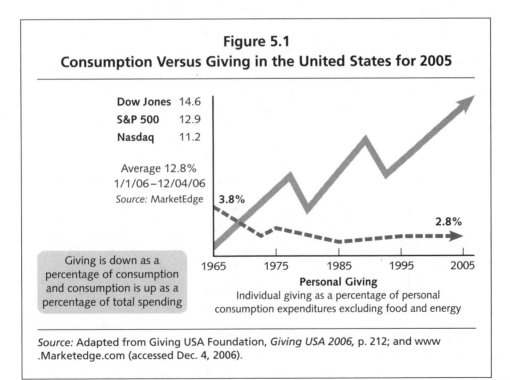

Figure 5.1
Consumption Versus Giving in the United States for 2005

Dow Jones 14.6
S&P 500 12.9
Nasdaq 11.2

Average 12.8%
1/1/06–12/04/06
Source: MarketEdge

3.8%

2.8%

Giving is down as a percentage of consumption and consumption is up as a percentage of total spending

1965   1975   1985   1995   2005

Personal Giving
Individual giving as a percentage of personal consumption expenditures excluding food and energy

Source: Adapted from Giving USA Foundation, *Giving USA 2006*, p. 212; and www.Marketedge.com (accessed Dec. 4, 2006).

Exercise 5.2
How Much Should You Give?

10 minutes

Part A

First consider this question:

Given our enormous privilege—whether courage capital, wisdom capital, creative capital, or financial capital—what more can we do, while staying in balance ourselves, for humanity or our communities now? What are you uniquely called to do on the question of how much and how best to give? (Most people give from their income, but some more wealthy donors give from their assets as well. When planning for giving after death or when making multiyear gifts, people often give some from assets and some from income. For more on giving from assets see "Giving Principal" later in this chapter and Exercise 13.1 in Chapter Thirteen.) Write your thoughts here:

_____

_____

_____

Part B

In thinking about what percentage of income you want to give away, you might start by looking at the following chart. Find your income level, then look across the row until you see an amount that feels right to you as an amount to give away. You may need to check your capacity with your family or advisor, but for now just identify what you'd like to be giving. Now look at the top of the chart to see what percentage that is. Do both the amount and the percentage feel right to you? If not, where is the disparity? If you have given in the past, what percentage of your income does your past giving represent? How does it compare with the amount or percentage you chose on the chart?

If your income* is	and you want to give					
	2%	3%	5%	10%	15%	20%
$30,000	600	900	1,500	3,000	4,500	6,000
$40,000	800	1,200	2,000	4,000	6,000	8,000
$50,000	1,000	1,500	2,500	5,000	7,500	10,000
$60,000	1,200	1,800	3,000	6,000	9,000	12,000
$75,000	1,500	2,250	3,750	7,500	11,250	15,000
$100,000	2,000	3,000	5,000	10,000	15,000	20,000
$150,000	3,000	4,500	7,500	15,000	22,500	30,000
$200,000	4,000	6,000	10,000	20,000	30,000	40,000
$250,000	5,000	7,500	12,500	25,000	37,000	50,000

*You may choose your level of giving based on your pretax or post-tax figures.

(continued on next page)

Here's another way to think about your giving potential, suggested by donor leaders Anne and Christopher Ellinger of Bolder Giving:

> Your full giving potential is whatever money you decide that you don't need personally in your lifetime. Imagine, finally determining "how much is enough"!
>
> How much of your income and assets do you actually need:
>
> - To have the lifestyle you want?
> - To enable what you wish for in the lives of your children and other loved ones?
> - To provide for illness and old age?
>
> The remainder is your "giving potential"—money that you could reasonably invest in building a better world, including to help those who are far from meeting even basic needs.
>
> Engaging your full giving potential includes taking leadership: inspiring other givers by being a mentor and role model. No matter how great your wealth, your leadership could unleash far more resources toward addressing the world's problems than any amount you give personally.

Giving from a Family Foundation or Donor-Advised Fund

The law requires private and family foundations to give at least 5 percent of their total assets annually. However, foundations could be doing much more. Returns on investments of foundation assets over the past twenty years have averaged 12 percent.[7] Going beyond the mandated 5 percent of giving means the opportunity

SOME FACTS ON NET WORTH IN THE UNITED STATES

- Americans with incomes of $14,768 or less (the bottom 20 percent) have, on average, assets of –$7,075 (they are, on average, $7,075 in debt), whereas the top 20 percent (making $68,015 or more) have, on average, assets of $871,463.*

- Those with the top 20 percent of assets control 84.7 percent of the wealth in the United States.**

- The wealthiest 1 percent of Americans have more wealth (38.1 percent of the total wealth) than the bottom 90 percent combined (29.1 percent of the total wealth).**

Sources: *Michael E. Davern and Patricia J. Fisher, "Household Net Worth and Asset Ownership: 1995." Washington, D.C.: Census Bureau, 2001.

**Edward N. Wolff, "Recent Trends in Household Wealth in the U.S., 1983–2004," Table 2, Jerome Levy Economics Institute, June 2007, www.levy.org/pubs/wp_502.pdf.

to foster greater change. If you are giving from a family foundation or donor-advised fund, think about what amount will be truly meaningful. (For more on these types of giving vehicles, see Chapters Eight and Nine.)

GIVING PRINCIPAL

Although not a giving philosophy per se, "never touch principal" has been such a time-honored belief among people with inherited or earned wealth that it deserves some attention here. In addition to the people already mentioned who have given away most of their assets, others who have inherited or earned wealth are choosing to give a portion of their assets during their lifetime. These assets can include stocks, bonds, real estate, insurance policies, and works of art.

Given the intricacies of tax benefits for gifts of cash, appreciated assets, and planned gifts, you should work with a financial planner or estate or tax professional to consider just how much is possible or advantageous for you to give. Keep in mind, however, that many asset managers or trust companies make their living from fees on managing your assets, so don't be surprised if you encounter some resistance to this idea of giving from principal.

Giving some or even most of your principal, if you have planned for your own safety net, can be exhilarating. Donors who have done so have found that it inspires them to live more simply or to make money to replace these assets. For some, that action can be normalizing amidst having wealth that sometimes feels stagnant, staggering, or simply burdensome.

Chapter Eleven goes into detail about working with financial advisors to make the best decisions about what to save and what to give. When you do, you can try various projections to see how your assets might grow over the course of your

---

TAX DEDUCTIBILITY

Here are a few things to consider about the benefits of charitable giving to your tax situation.

- Donations to public charities that are designated as tax exempt under section 501 (c)(3) of the tax code are tax-deductible to those who itemize contributions of $250 or more. Donations to nonprofits that are designated as 501(c)(4), which are formed in order to participate in lobbying, political campaigns, and legislative advocacy at a greater level than public charities, are not tax-deductible.

- Some volunteering expenses may be tax-deductible. Check with a tax advisor regarding out-of-pocket and travel expenses and which receipts are required.

- Gifts of appreciated stock, property, and cash have various beneficial tax advantages; check with a tax advisor.

- No one will benefit more from your IRAs upon your death than a nonprofit (because, unlike individuals, they will not have to pay taxes on the money received). Consider listing your favorite groups as beneficiaries of this part of your estate. (Check carefully with your tax professional, as rules change. For example, there are greatly increased benefits to giving from IRAs to nonprofits in the 2007 tax year, which may or may not be extended.)

Regardless of your financial situation, spend time with your financial planner or your own trusted advisor to learn about new options and ways to plan for and use your resources and assets.

lifetime and then think through how much will enable you to achieve specific goals. When you've considered how much you actually need and what amount you want to leave or gift to your loved ones and for what purposes, the answers can sometimes greatly free up your giving.

Here's how philanthropist Peter Lew considered the issue of giving away more from income or principal:

> I am considering a change in the way I handle my annual giving. I have always heeded the advice of my father to conserve principal whenever possible and spend only income. My income from investments has remained static over the years, but the value of the principal has ballooned. If I decided to give away a small percentage of principal annually, say 1 to 4 percent, I would be able to increase the amount of my giving tenfold at least. My investment advisors tell me I would be better off with this strategy than taking a portion of my portfolio and investing for extra income to donate.

THINKING A LITTLE BIGGER

Imagine a twenty-eight-year-old who gave $3,000 each year until she died at age ninety-one. In sixty-three years of lifetime giving, she would have given $189,000, not including any gifts that came from her estate after she died. Use Exercise 5.3 to calculate your potential lifetime giving.

Now reflect again on what you noted in Chapter Three that you want to change or preserve during your lifetime, and on your philanthropic mission statement from Chapter Four. If properly focused, you can see that your own resources are a big start on that effort. Collaborating or raising money and influencing others or working on policy changes are other ways to move your mission even further. In Part Two you'll find more on how to help leverage your contribution.

Exercise 5.3
How Much Will You Give During Your Lifetime?

10 minutes

First, note how much money you gave to nonprofits last year or, if you prefer, start with the figure you decided to give in Exercise 5.2. Multiply that amount by the number of years you expect to continue to live (for example, if your life expectancy is eighty-eight and you are forty-eight now, multiply your giving by forty years). The total represents your future giving.

$_____ × _____ = $_____
Your giving last year   Years left of life expectancy   Future giving

Add to that an estimate of how much you've given up till now. The result shows your total giving during your lifetime:

$_____ + $_____ = $_____
Future giving   Giving to date   Lifetime giving

Now consider what percentage of your assets (for example, 10 to 50 percent) you will direct to be given to nonprofits you care about after your death. Estimate the value that percentage will translate into and add that amount to your total lifetime giving.

$_____ + $_____ = $_____
Lifetime giving   Value of gifts from estate   All gifts during life
and after death

Finally, consider how much giving you might influence in your lifetime through your own fundraising and by inspiring other givers by your example and add that to the total to get a truer sense of your total impact.

$_____
Lifetime fundraising

Where to Give

Philanthropy is commendable, but it must not cause the philanthropist to overlook the circumstances of economic injustice which make philanthropy necessary.

—Martin Luther King

his chapter covers the first steps of developing your giving plan, including how to find information about specific groups to give to and how to decide which are worthy of your time and dollars. The giving plan that you will complete in Chapter Seven will lay out the elements to accomplish your mission and focus your volunteer time, money, and ideas.

CHOOSING WHERE TO GIVE

With more than 1.5 million nonprofits in the United States alone,[1] how many do we really know about? Do you only know about the big national groups or those that get your attention with their direct mail appeals, Web advertising, public service ads, and community billboards? What if you've decided you want to support groups responding to a specific local problem in your community? Perhaps you've heard about some regional, statewide, or global groups that sound interesting. Maybe you're wondering if the groups you already give to are really the ones you want to continue to support. Or perhaps thinking about your areas of interest has led you to think about how problems relate to each other and what larger-scale solutions to them might be.

One of the benefits of creating your giving plan is taking the time to think seriously about where your financial contributions will have the greatest impact on the issues you care most about.

For most people, a percentage of their donations goes to support cherished or honored obligations and civic responsibilities. Most people fund projects they have been involved with or that their friends tell them about or ask them to support. Beyond those, how much of your giving do you want to direct to more strategic or transformational efforts for your community or the world at large? We want also to have enough flexibility to be able to respond to a chance to fund a great leader or support something innovative. It takes discipline and additional time to find leaders and groups that can accomplish your goals or who are reaching for a vision similar to yours. Investing that time will bring the satisfaction of moving beyond familiar terrain to supporting work you feel more passionate about—a move that can be both life-changing and world-changing.

A first step in thinking about which groups you want to include in your giving is getting clearer on where you want to allocate your donations. Exercise 6.1 walks you through this step.

SOURCES OF INFORMATION

Now that you know the problems, opportunities, or issues you want to address with your funding and what percentage of your donations will go to each, do you wonder if there are groups working in your top interest areas that you don't yet know about? And what about the scope of your giving—are you thinking only about funding local groups? Would donating to statewide, national, or international organizations achieve additional important strategic goals?

Finding out which groups address the issues you care most about will take some research. You might start by asking friends, family, and colleagues which organizations they support. Beyond that, here are more options (also see Appendix I, "Resources," on the CD-ROM).

In the human service field, the nearest United Way office or local alternative workplace giving fund or federation (see www.choiceingiving.org) can give you a list of groups they fund (for more ideas beyond those mentioned in this section, see "Resources"). For issues outside of human services, your local or statewide community foundation, Funding Exchange member fund (www.fex.org), or women's

Exercise 6.1
Your Funding Areas

---

20 minutes

Step 1. Write your mission statement from Exercise 4.1 in Chapter Four.
Mission Statement:

_____

_____

Step 2. Look at your priority areas from Exercise 2.3 in Chapter Two. Do they match up with your mission? If not, revise your priority issue areas and write them here:

_____

_____

_____

_____

Step 3. Compare these areas with where you have given money away recently, from Exercise 3.1 in Chapter Three, and review your analysis of creating a better world, from Exercises 3.4 and 3.5. Note what you have learned from this comparison:

_____

_____

Step 4. Given your interest areas, where you have been giving, and how you think change will happen, list a maximum of five areas in which you would now like to concentrate your funding:

Areas of Funding

1. _____

2. _____

3. _____

4. _____

5. _____

_____

(continued on next page)

Exercise 6.1
Your Funding Areas, Cont'd

Step 5. Now think about whether prioritizing your choices will make your strategy more effective. If so, rewrite your list in priority order.

Areas of Funding

1. _____
2. _____
3. _____
4. _____
5. _____

Step 6. From the total amount of money you've decided to donate (see Exercise 5.2 in the previous chapter), allocate a percentage to each area based on your assessment in Step 5 of the importance of each to your mission. Then translate each percentage into a dollar amount. (The sample giving plans in Chapter Seven show how some donors have allocated percentages of their giving according to their priorities.)

Area of funding	Amount	Percentage
1.		
2.		
3.		
4.		
5.		

foundation or federation (www.wfnet.org) can provide information about groups serving your community.

The Internet provides many sites devoted to the conscientious donor wanting to research the size, effectiveness, and legitimacy of nonprofits (see Exhibit 6.1). Other sites also offer online resources for donor education. These span a wide range of topics, including planned giving (www.pgdc.com/usa), social ventures (www.svn.org), and giving globally (www.gwob.net or http://globalgiving.org).

Exhibit 6.1
Online Giving Resources

The following online sites offer information about nonprofits in many fields, some with links to donate directly. See Chapter Eight for a listing of sites for making donations online.

www.AllCharities.com—Provides a comprehensive list of charities (more than 800,000) to which individuals can donate, with detailed descriptions of all the charities listed.

www.charitynavigator.org—Evaluates the financial health of America's largest charities.

www.GrantMatch.com—Grantmakers and seekers can tell each other who, what, where, when, how, and why they exist in the nonprofit world. Grant-seekers register their organization and list proposals or donation requests by categories. Grantmakers list their funding interests and create a request for proposals.

www.GuideStar.org—Free database offers information on the operations and finances of nonprofit organizations, including 990-IRS forms and the forms of foundations.

www.Helping.org—Helps people find volunteering and giving opportunities in their own communities and beyond, to donate time, services, or financial support. Includes access to online resources to organize, recruit, raise funds, and publicize.

www.JustGive.org—Connects people with the charities and causes they care about.

You can also learn more about specific nonprofits from a growing number of private monitoring groups, such as the Better Business Bureau's Wise Giving Alliance (now merged with the National Charities Information Bureau) (www.give.org), and the American Institute of Philanthropy (www.charitywatch.org). These groups review the financial and fiduciary performance of nonprofits.

A fun way to go about these explorations is as part of a giving circle or network of friends who talk about giving. (See Chapter Eight for more information on giving circles and www.venturesingiving.org for a report on giving circles.) If you give $10,000 or more per year or are considering doing so, you could investigate being part of a donor network (see www.donorleaders.org) or find others through a religiously affiliated organization or community or public foundation. Perhaps there are discussions about giving organized through your workplace. Learn what others know on the issues that interest you and take notes.

Philanthropic and legacy advisors can direct you to specific nonprofits. These advisors can be found working as program officers of public or community foundations, in United Way branches and alternative workplace funds, or in independent offices. Appendix I, "Resources," contains a list of philanthropic advisors you can hire to help you find groups that match your values and vision.

Of course, mission matching goes beyond just online research. It's key if you are determined to make an impact that you do your due diligence in speaking with professionals or donors who give in the areas you care about to find the best nonprofits and leaders for your goals of creating a better world.

GATHERING INFORMATION

Once you have the names of some organizations working on your issues, one of the best ways to learn about what they're doing is by getting information directly from them. The expertise, information, and perspectives of these groups and leaders will expand your knowledge and help you make giving choices that are most appropriate for you.

First go to the groups' Web sites to see how they talk about their work and contact them for newsletters or annual reports. For some small groups that may not have Web sites, call them directly for more information. When available, an annual report will describe the agency's mission and its goals and objectives for the previous year and how they were met; it will also convey the agency's perception of its impact and effectiveness. By law, you may also request a group's tax report, called a "990 Form," which will reveal the percentages of the organization's budget spent on administration, program, and fundraising. Guidestar (www.guidestar.org) makes available the 990 tax forms of more than one million nonprofits. This information gives you one way to evaluate effectiveness: Do they seem to be using their money wisely? Though the rule of thumb is that not more than 25 percent of an organization's budget should go to the combination of expenses in fundraising and administration, start-up agencies or those doing work that has never been done or work that is highly risky or complex may initially need to allocate a much greater percentage of the charitable dollars they receive to building infrastructure (staffing, administration, operating expenses, and the like). National organizations or agencies with multimillion-dollar budgets, such as the United Way, are able to keep fundraising and administration costs quite low, often less than 20 percent of their total budget. But for smaller groups, keep in mind that it does take money to cover outreach and development costs. Focus first on the content, leadership, constituency, and quality of the work and then look at the group's budget and finances.

Here are some of the questions to keep in mind when gathering information about a group:

- What is the leadership or management style of the organization or its leaders?
- Do you admire the staff and leadership? Are they working in alignment with your giving goals and objectives in some important ways; are they a "mission match" for you?
- Do the staff and board leadership work well together?
- What is the impact or effectiveness of the organization, or its results?
- How well does it collaborate and with whom?
- Are diverse constituents involved and helping to guide outcomes?
- Is the organization financially stable? (How much income does it bring in from fundraising or earned income? Does it have any cash reserves?)
- What are its strengths and challenges?
- What is the organization working on now, and what does it need?

A Web site and printed materials will focus on the successes or positive stories about an organization and its work. To answer some of these other questions will require talking with someone who is more closely involved as well as reviewing the group's annual report if they produce one. You may know the leader or someone who is a donor or friend of the project. Give them a call or drop them an e-mail with a few questions.

Most of us can't evaluate in depth most of the organizations we give money to. There simply isn't time. But especially if you are considering a group to receive one of your largest gifts it would be beneficial for you to do some review of their work. It is in the nonprofit's interest to have you giving to them for the content, delivery, and analysis of their work and not only for their leadership or because you got a referral from a friend. Deeper research will engage you more and encourage you to learn along with the organization about what makes lasting change.

Worksheet 6.1 provides a more comprehensive way to evaluate if a group matches your own values and mission and where you might want more information to make a thoughtful decision. You may not want or need to find out about every category in the chart, but they will give you an idea of the various organizational characteristics that go into how an organization meets its mission.

Worksheet 6.1
Evaluating a Group for Possible Funding

Name of organization: _____

Contact: _____   Location: _____

E-mail: _____   Web address: _____

Phone: _____   Date of assessment: _____

Assessment Area	Strengths (✓ or rate)	Challenges (✓ or rate)	Notes or Next Steps
Values and culture match			
Mission match			
Strategy alignment			
Program effectiveness			
Leadership (ED or board chair)			
Board (#) plus key leaders			
Staff (#) and quality			
Board, staff, and volunteer teamwork			
Number of volunteers			
PR, marketing, or messaging			
Web presence			
Location and feel of office			
Geographic reach of organization			
Commitment to and evidence of diversity			
Key organizational collaborators			

(*continued on next page*)

Worksheet 6.1
Evaluating a Group for Possible Funding, Cont'd

Assessment Area	Strengths (✓ or rate)	Challenges (✓ or rate)	Notes or Next Steps
Accessibility and transparency			
Impact and evaluation standards and measures			
Outcomes or results communicated well			
Accountability standards			
Staff benefits			
Financial reporting clear			
Balance sheet			
Cash flow			
Financial need			
Fundraising process			
Donor systems and thanks			
Development plan			
Development committee			
Donor engagement programs or evidence of commitment in past			
Structure of the organization and power dynamics			
Other or overall rating			

DONOR DIVA

Trust yourself. Through all the number crunching and research, certain organizations and leaders may resonate for you. This is your giving. Does thinking about giving to an organization evoke a smile? Does your gut feel right about it? Your brain is processing more than the data on the page. Do internal "due diligence" and trust what does or does not feel right to you. It will make a big difference to the energy you are willing to contribute toward an organization.

For groups that seem worth your further attention, you might want to attend one or more events they sponsor. Or you can volunteer with a group that particularly interests you and is based locally to get a sense of its program and leadership, the strength of the executive director and other staff, the board and their experience, and the size and structure of its volunteer corps. If you become a major donor to a group (defined variably by the size of the donation; for some groups, a $250 gift is considered major, for others, only gifts of $5,000 or more), it's likely that a board or staff member will call or want to meet with you to give you updates about the group's work. If you are considering making a substantial donation, it would make sense to review the organization's current and projected budgets. You may also want to conduct a site visit. Guidelines for reviewing budgets and making site visits are presented in Chapter Thirteen.

LEVELS OF PHILANTHROPIC INTERVENTION

Organizations approach issues from a variety of perspectives and structure their work around various goals. Even organizations working on the same issue may work differently. Table 6.1, Levels of Philanthropic Intervention, revised for this edition by consultants Mark McDonough and Tesa Silvestre, presents a detailed introduction to various levels at which groups and organizations work. Just as business people often have business plans, having a giving plan with a multipronged or varied "mutual fund" of approaches enables more precise outcomes. Different strategies result in different activities to create change. Use the chart and its accompanying text to find strategies that seem the best choices for meeting your personal mission statement and that you feel most comfortable giving to, given the funding considerations discussed here. Using multiple strategies over a five- to twenty-year period is often the best way to see and create change.

PHILANTHROPIC INVESTING

In financial markets, investors seek to build a balanced portfolio of lower risk/lower return assets (typically bonds and blue chip stocks) and higher risk/higher return assets (high tech, small cap, and international stocks). The current practice in the field of philanthropy amounts to investing nearly 90 percent of one's resources in the equivalent of bonds (called "Needs Philanthropy" in Table 6.1). Here are some things to keep in mind when considering how to invest one's philanthropic resources across levels:

1. *Focus.* Higher levels focus on "upstream" root cause solutions; lower levels focus on symptom reduction.

2. *Popularity.* Lower levels currently get many more donations because they tend to be issues that pull at the heart. Higher levels tend to appeal more to our rational understanding of what will solve the problem. Lower levels are more immediately satisfying.

3. *Time Horizon.* Lower levels address pressing needs. Higher levels also address those needs but do so by working through the causal chain. They take more time to get to the symptoms but have more permanent effects.

4. *Tangibility of Impact.* The lower the level, the clearer the impact of your giving can be. Example: Giving $50 to the Children's Hunger Relief Fund will feed X children for a month. Higher-level impacts (changes in legislation for instance) are broader in scope and have longer-lasting effects. It is much harder if not impossible to measure the tangible and quantifiable results of individual giving. It is also harder to measure the effects of value shifts such as eating less beef or driving more fuel-efficient cars, but the results are long lasting and pervasive.

5. *Risk and Return.* The higher the level, the more risk you must take about the final impact of your giving. For example, giving to the Environmental Defense Fund will fund research and advocacy to change laws and corporate practices that adversely effect the environment, but one can't be sure that the laws and practices will change.

Table 6.1
Levels of Philanthropic Intervention

	Funding Focus	Merits	Limitations or Challenges
Level 1: Needs Philanthropy *Addresses immediate and recurring needs*	Relief efforts (disasters, hunger, wars) Care programs (day care, shelters, refugees) Cultural activities Religious services	Alleviates urgent and critical needs Responds quickly to unforeseen events Takes care of vulnerable populations Draws attention to key social issues Offers simple and accessible ways to relieve donors' urge to "do something" Gives donors opportunities to build civic muscles (generosity, solidarity, and so on)	Focuses on symptoms (tip of iceberg) Relief effects are typically short-lived Often amounts to a drop in the ocean Relief efforts are rarely synergized Can disempower people through dependency and perpetuate the problem Can easily feed donors' propensity to guilt-based and reactive giving
Level 2: Empowerment Philanthropy *Empowers individuals to take care of themselves*	Education and mentoring Job training and skills Personal growth and spirituality Tool acquisition (books, computers) Living infrastructure (building homes, wells)	Builds people's assets to help them become more effective in directing their lives and meeting their own needs Encourages self-responsibility rather than dependency Has more lasting effects	Receptivity to training varies Disempowering effects of training if based on "we know better than you" attitudes rather than partnering with target population to find optimal solutions Limited way of dealing with root causes

Level 3: Capacity-Building Philanthropy *Expands groups' ability to serve the commons*	Leadership and management training Developing systems for IT, fundraising, and so on Strategic planning Capital campaigns Building alliances Creating needed organizations	Empowers organizations and communities Minimizes waste and inefficiencies (doing more with less) Maximizes beneficial impact (doing more of the right things) Improves accountability, building trust with donors Fosters collaboration through networking and coalition-building	Finding organizations ready and willing to learn to be more effective Possible negative side-effects of sustainable funding (endowments can make organizations less responsive) Current bias against allocating philanthropic money to administrative costs
Level 4: Systemic Philanthropy *Develops systemic solutions to collective problems*	Research think tanks Policy or legal reform Shifting consciousness Civic engagement Media reform Collaboration among key stakeholders	Deals with the root causes of problems Targets most effective change strategies (replicability or tipping point effects) Most lasting and comprehensive impact if successful (for example, campaigns to stop smoking; support use of organic food, and so on) Highest leverage of philanthropic dollars	Hard to identify and implement comprehensive solutions Current strategies are often polarizing (conservatives versus progressives) Takes time to create visible impact Harder to mobilize donors Highest risk of failure May be best chance for breakthrough

There is no ideal portfolio of philanthropic investments that fits everyone. Just as in the financial markets, one should build a portfolio that reflects one's values and interests and combines elements across the spectrum of risk and return to get an optimum balance.

Philanthropy seems to be evolving through the four levels. Philanthropists unhappy with charity's lack of residual value have pushed for investments in empowerment. Most lay people have become familiar with the catch phrase for empowerment philanthropy, "Give a man a fish and he eats for a day; teach a man to fish and he eats for a lifetime." The latest generation of philanthropists, steeled by the discipline of venture capital investors, are pushing philanthropy's leading edge with a call for capacity investments—especially ones that measure and increase effectiveness of mission delivery. Others, particularly women donors, who are featured in Chapter Fourteen, which is on transformational philanthropy, are for making sure the whole lake is clean and productive for all. So as you can see, our expectations of how to leverage our giving are growing!

GIVING INTERNATIONALLY

Many of the compelling and challenging issues in philanthropy today are global in nature and scope. Charity may begin at home, but it doesn't end there. As private investment capital profits from "emerging markets," so private philanthropic capital discovers "emerging opportunities" when it goes abroad. Because of the strength of the dollar in less developed countries, small donations can sometimes yield big results. Funding a program in South America, Africa, or Asia may require less money to support the staff or office space or to fulfill their mission. Some funders or foundations fund all over the world. As of 2006, only 3.8 percent of U.S. giving was directed internationally. We could be offering much more.

Giving internationally can be a valuable way to help remedy some serious problems in other countries, particularly poverty; impeded economic development; the negative results of globalization; limited access to schooling; poor health care; and economic, racial, and gender inequalities.

Consider how you might help accomplish any of the goals established in 2000 through a thorough international process of many community leaders and experts led by the United Nations (see Figure 6.1). Imagine if all of us worked locally, regionally, and globally to accomplish these goals. Perhaps the most ambitious millennium goal is to cut in half the level of poverty worldwide by increasing the daily

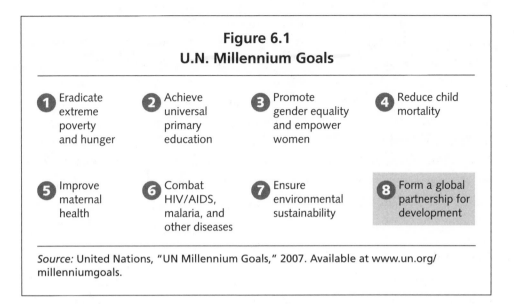

Figure 6.1
U.N. Millennium Goals

1 Eradicate extreme poverty and hunger

2 Achieve universal primary education

3 Promote gender equality and empower women

4 Reduce child mortality

5 Improve maternal health

6 Combat HIV/AIDS, malaria, and other diseases

7 Ensure environmental sustainability

8 Form a global partnership for development

Source: United Nations, "UN Millennium Goals," 2007. Available at www.un.org/millenniumgoals.

income of those living on $1 per day to $2 per day through jobs and economic development. Here is an integrated strategy that has the advantage of sound research and the thinking of many experts. You can read the full U.N. Millennium Goals for further inspiration and consideration at www.un.org/millenniumgoals.

A number of international agencies direct donations to worthy overseas projects. Many have offices or staff in the United States, as well as advisors, partner organizations, offices, or consultants overseas. Onsite intermediary organizations, such as the Global Fund for Women (www.globalfundforwomen.org), Global Greengrants Fund (www.greengrants.org), American Jewish World Service (www.ajws.org), the International Development Exchange (www.idex.org), and Oxfam (www.oxfamamerica.org), are well connected and full of great information about local politics and strategic ideas about what needs funding. Another resource is Grantmakers Without Borders (www.gwob.net), where you can find extensive information and resources about international giving.

ALTERNATIVE HOLIDAY GIVING

In 2006, the average American shopper spent $900 on holiday gifts, including about $100 for gifts for themselves as they shopped for others. Many people have become disillusioned with the excessive materialism that has become associated with holiday giving. Instead of the day after Thanksgiving being the largest shopping day of the year, groups now encourage us to think of it as "Buy Nothing Day" (see www.buynothingday.org). Many churches and temples also promote more giving to charities during this season.

These kinds of gifts are gaining in popularity in the United States; many people start giving internationally through holiday gifts to a global nonprofit such as the Heifer Project (www.heifer.org) or Oxfam (www.oxfam.org). Organizations such as Ten Thousand Villages, Seva, and the Heifer Project reported that the 2006 holiday season saw a great increase of these expressions of global connectivity and sharing (see also www.changingthepresent.org).

MAKING DECISIONS

Two remaining factors involved in your decision making are risk and trust. Like good decision making about a lot of things, a certain amount of the actions you will take in funding nonprofits involves daring to make decisions that either might not turn out as you hope or that may yield more than anyone could have imagined. If your tolerance for risk is low, think about challenging yourself. Since what's at stake can potentially change lives, the returns can be huge.

After global catastrophes such as 9/11 and Hurricane Katrina, the best work is often done by trusting that those on the ground know what they need. For example, the Ms. Foundation and the Twenty-First Century Foundation were applauded for their help in the Gulf Coast because they asked what local nonprofit leaders needed and made funds available for those needs. Without electric power, local grantseekers lacked computers to type proposals and fax machines to send them;

DONOR DIVA

Consider cutting your holiday consumption costs by half during the next holiday season, then adding that amount to your giving plan or alternative gift shopping. Now there's a true gift.

these exemplary funders took information by phone and filled out the applications so that groups could get started on rebuilding.

Risk and trust involve recognizing that philanthropy is a collaboration. The act of giving money, time, or attention engages us with others and creates community. You may not need to know everything about an issue you care about or about the organizations working on it in order to make a thoughtful funding decision. For many donations, as a donor you may be satisfied having a general sense of trust in an organization's effectiveness and leadership, perhaps based on examples of constituents that serve to illustrate impact and results. For others, you may want to have an in-depth working knowledge of the group. A combination of these approaches brings a lot of understanding about an organization and will propel communities—donors, community leaders, and activists who know what's needed to find solutions to the critical problems we face.

Creating a Personal Giving Plan

*We cannot live for ourselves alone. Our lives are connected
by a thousand invisible threads, and along these sympathetic
fibers our actions run as causes and return to us as results.*

—Herman Melville

You have now reached the heart of Inspired Philanthropy—writing a Personal Giving Plan. Now that you have been doing some thinking about how you want to direct your giving, you're ready to begin planning how, where, and when to distribute the funds you've decided to contribute. (You may create your giving plan alone or with family members.)

Even if you don't have a formal budget, Exercise 5.2 in Chapter Five will have given you a sense of how much you want to give, either as an absolute figure or as a percentage of your annual income. You might also check with your financial advisor to determine the maximum amount you could give that would benefit your taxes or the world while keeping your financial life in right relationship with your commitment to your own balance. As fortunate as many of us are, it's a good idea to take this extra step to be sure that we are neither undergiving nor overgiving. In fact, working with your financial advisor and family to create a financial plan, a philanthropic plan, and an estate plan (as discussed in Chapter Eleven) is a key tool for the journey of your legacy and for shaping the world we want to live in and leave for future generations (see Figure 7.1).

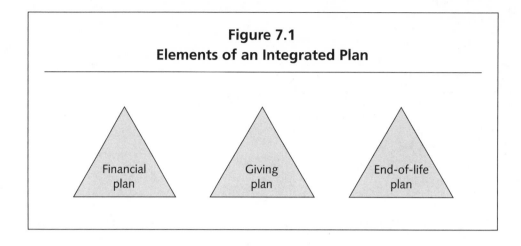

Figure 7.1
Elements of an Integrated Plan

Financial plan

Giving plan

End-of-life plan

Too often financial plans and estate plans are created without attention to or articulation of core values. We need to keep at the heart of our planning what really matters, why we are planning, and for whom. Too often financial plans are created with only our own financial security and tax reduction as objectives. Likewise, estate plans are predominantly created to avoid or reduce taxes, or to pass money, meaningful objects, or lessons on to our families or friends. Little, if any, support is passed to the nonprofits we have cared most about. Establishing a philanthropic or giving plan may tie together and lend added meaning to your other planning. Having or making money for others, not just for ourselves, gives added significance to doing good for the greater community. With a giving plan in place, your financial plan and your estate plan are likely to shift. In Chapter Eleven we will discuss how to create a fully integrated legacy plan using the elements of your financial plan and the giving plan that you are about to construct.

In this chapter, you'll draft your giving plan and create your funding cycles, deciding when during the year you want to make—and make good on—funding decisions. This chapter also includes tools to assess the results and impact of your giving. The next two chapters explore the many different vehicles for giving beyond personal checkwriting, including giving circles, donor-advised funds, and family foundations—a choice you can make once your giving plan is established.

When you've created and tried out your giving plan you'll find that it not only helps you manage your planned contributions, it also allows you to anticipate unexpected requests and engage in spontaneous acts of generosity or demonstrations of caring. A personal giving plan can also help you organize your time, so that you spend it in ways that reflect your values.

GETTING ORGANIZED

Chapter Six gave information about researching the nonprofit groups you might like to give to. As you get your giving plan organized, this would also be a good time to begin—or improve—your database of groups you are interested in or already give to. People devise various systems for this task, from Rolodex cards to Excel-based spreadsheets or bookmarked Web sites. You might check out the systems available from Web sites such as www.newdea.com or your community foundation. If you have a family foundation or an advisor, they may have a system that simplifies this process for you. You can also find Web-based forms at the Inspired Legacies Web site (www.inspiredlegacies.org).

How to Plan and How Often to Give

Think about how often you want to do your giving. Is it realistic for you to set up a monthly giving program, or would you be more comfortable doing your giving on a quarterly, semiannual, or annual basis? Because it can be daunting to hold on to all the requests from nonprofits and the research you do on nonprofits for a full year, it's best to make some decisions at least quarterly on who to keep on your list of possibilities and to make some contributions at least twice a year.

Most donations are made during the "giving season" between November 15th and January 5th, but keep in mind that nonprofits need money all year long. For those of us among the small percentage of Americans who earn or inherit enough to itemize their taxes, timing on giving can matter, and we need to work within family obligations and with our financial advisors to be sure we are not sacrificing important income or assets by poor planning. Early on in your giving year, ask your advisor what the maximum estimated amount is that you can afford to give to nonprofits while maximizing the tax benefits. Ask again near the end of the year when you are more sure of your income and deductions, as you may be able to give more in December.

If you have more than you need regardless of your level of income, you may want to give from assets or give property (donating, for example, a used car, a piece of art, or a second home during your lifetime or at death). If you are in a position to give more than your income permits, as discussed in Chapter Five, you may want to give from both income and assets—if even a small percentage of assets, perhaps 1 percent annually.

The key is to be intentional about your commitment and your process and to have fun with your giving, even to be inspired with it and the people who are helping you build the world you want. Recently, high-end or asset-wealthy donors have said, "Why should I buy something for myself when I could help someone in a hurricane-ravaged part of New Orleans rebuild their church or their home for the same amount?" Such thinking represents the new level of consciousness that has begun to set in for those of great wealth. Giving from assets or as much as 50 percent of income may seem a choice for only the ultrawealthy, but you will see in Chapter Thirteen that giving to one's greatest potential is a growing trend.

If you are in such a position and want to be part of a new wave of people who are choosing to live more simply or if you want to transform communities and the world by extending more of what you have financially, you may consider several other leveraging strategies, such as working to advance the following initiatives:

- Adequate taxation or incentives for equitable economic development

- Effective use of tax dollars

- Conscious consumerism, local and organic food advocacy, and recycling

- Shareholder activism

- Election activism

- Living wages and reasonable benefits (including affordable health care)

- Waste reduction, including addressing global warming

- Improved educational, housing, and medical services for the poor

- Devoting more time and money to organizations that match your giving strategies

Having a giving plan supports the use of your most effective and directed time and money to ensure a more secure world. Human security is not just about preventing nuclear war or a terrorist attack; it is about waking up to care about others and choosing through our actions to provide opportunities for more people. In short, human security is best attained through building community, which is exactly what philanthropy that is based in and guided by community does. The real enjoyment of giving is in the community and in the change we get to make.

Giving to address our social structure and to truly partner with the beneficiaries of our giving requires thinking and may require action beyond your own or your families' wants if not needs. Choosing to dedicate more to our philanthropy and acting on choices that are less wasteful or less about increasing our prestige, comfort, or personal convenience is committing to make the world better for others as well as ourselves.

Integrating Your Plan

Worksheet 7.1 gives you a template for making your giving plan. In Exercise 7.1, you can bring together your values, your vision, your issue areas, and your mission statement, which you established in earlier chapters, to create an overview of your giving plan. You may want to make a few copies of the blank worksheet to work from or create one for yourself on a spreadsheet so you can generate copies as you need them. Following the exercise are several samples of completed giving plans. Refer to the sample giving plans to see how others at various income levels and with various funding interests have created their plans. Spend some time looking at these samples, then try filling out a worksheet yourself, guided by the steps outlined in Exercise 7.1.

This is one of the most important exercises, so give it as much time as you need. The first time through, do it *just* as an exercise, without necessarily committing yourself to the results. Try to fill out every column in one session. By doing so you'll find out where you need more information or which decisions you are not yet ready to make. You may find you need to refer back to earlier chapters or do more research on your own.

Once you've filled in any gaps in your thinking as best you can, fill out a clean copy of the giving plan, creating a working document you can use. The plan you create should cover one year, starting now.

When you are done, give yourself a pat on the back—you have completed your first year's giving plan! Look at it again and see how it feels. Make any adjustments you want before you start implementing it, and then make a commitment to yourself to follow the plan for the next year. Try it out for the whole twelve months and then evaluate and refine it as necessary.

Worksheet 7.1
Your Giving Plan

Mission and values statement: _____

Year of plan: _____

Financial donations: $ _____

Volunteering (total hours): _____

Funding Area	Percentage	Organization	Amount	When	Volunteer Hours	Notes, Contacts, Previous Gifts
TOTALS:			$	____ HRS.		

Exercise 7.1
Your Giving Plan

30 minutes or more

This exercise will help you create an integrated giving plan using Worksheet 7.1. Or, if you prefer, translate these questions into a drawing, chart, or spreadsheet that works for you. These questions draw on the exercises from previous chapters. Once you have completed integrating the answers here, Worksheet 7.1 consolidates the information, providing a big-picture view of your plan. (To see what a completed giving plan looks like, see the sample giving plans that follow these instructions.)

Name: _____

This plan is for the following year(s): _____

Step 1.

A. List the values that shape your giving plan.

   (Refer to Exercise 2.3 in Chapter Two and your mission statement in Chapter Four.)

   1. _____

   2. _____

   3. _____

B. State your overall vision, goal, or hope for humanity (from the reflecting you did in Chapter Three):

   _____

   _____

C. List your main areas of funding (from Exercise 6.1):

   1. _____

   2. _____

   3. _____

   4. _____

   5. _____

(*continued on next page*)

D. Identify the strategies you prefer organizations use (refer to "Strategies for Change" in Chapter Three, or you may want to choose a philanthropic level at which to give, from Table 6.1 in Chapter Six):

1. _____

2. _____

3. _____

4. _____

E. Identify the geographic areas you want to give in:

Local _____%

Regional _____%

National _____%

Global _____%

F. Note the organizational sizes you plan to give to:

Small _____%

Start-ups or those under three years of age _____%

Medium _____%

Large or established _____%

Step 2. Using Worksheet 7.1, list your funding areas from the previous step in the first column (copy and expand the chart to accommodate as many organizations as you wish to include). Leave the other columns blank for now. You will come back to them in the next steps. If there are other funding areas you want to include, such as gifts to family and friends and tickets to fundraising events and dinners, add them here. You may also want to include a miscellaneous category, to give yourself room to make donations that don't fit in any named category, and in which you can respond to good work and urgent needs that may require a quick reaction. This category can be called "donor's whim" or "opportunities," or some choice of your own to enable your spontaneous generosity. There are moments in history when we are simply called to consider different approaches or engage in acts of heartfelt (inspired) giving.

(*continued on next page*)

Exercise 7.1
Your Giving Plan, Cont'd

Step 3. On the basis of the research you did in Chapter Six, designate in column three of Worksheet 7.1 specific groups you want to give to within your funding areas. If you haven't decided on all the groups you may want to include in a particular funding area, place a question mark where you need more information. Look for mission matches: the goals of the groups you choose should help accomplish your own giving mission.

Step 4. If you did not indicate the percentage of your giving you wish to go to each funding area in Exercise 6.1, do so now and add it to the worksheet in the second column. Choose first which area you are most committed to, placing your largest percentage of the total amount you will give there. Then follow with the percentages for your other issues or areas of funding.

Step 5. In the fourth column fill in the specific dollar amounts you will give to each of the organizations listed. If there's more than one group you want to give to in a given area, think about how you want to distribute the amount of money you've allocated to this area among the groups you've listed. A strategic point to consider for each organization is whether a large or small gift would be most effective. (On one hand, if you can do so, making a large gift of $250 to $5,000 may be crucial to the survival of some fledgling organizations. On the other hand, a local group may do more with $100 than a national organization can do with $500. For some colleges and high schools with multimillion-dollar capital campaigns, alumni participation at any level may be more important than the size of your gift in one year.) Experiment with different amounts and give yourself permission to make mistakes with gifts. If you learn that something you did wasn't right, you'll find out more clearly what does suit you.

Step 6. Decide on your funding cycles. When are you going to make your funding decisions and write your checks—will you do it once, twice, or four times a year; in the spring, the fall, at the New Year, on your birthday? Or will you decide whenever asked? In choosing your giving cycles, consider times of the year when you have a tight cash flow, tax time, heavy request times, and times when dinners and events seem to cluster. Once decided, give yourself permission not to make any gifts outside of your giving cycles. In the "When" column in Worksheet 7.1, write in when you plan to write a check or otherwise give to a group, based on the funding cycles you have established.

Step 7. Worksheet 7.1 contains a separate column for volunteer time. Your volunteer time may go to organizations you do not support financially. If you're going to volunteer time actually working with an organization, will you do so on a regular basis—perhaps a weekly stint answering phones or attending a monthly board meeting—or a seasonal basis—say, planning a fundraising event or helping write grant proposals at certain times of the year. Indicate how you will be involved and how much time you will spend for each organization.

(*continued on next page*)

SAMPLE GIVING PLANS

Here are three giving plans that real donors have made. You will see that there are lots of different possibilities for what personal giving plans can look like. The first plan is in narrative form only. The others use the chart format just presented.

Sample Individual Giving Plan: $3,250[1]

Values that inform my giving: equality, community, and justice: I want to find ways to distribute resources more equitably to individuals and organizations. So, for example, I am just as interested in corporate social responsibility as I am in individual efforts.

I am also interested in organizations that bring together people who would otherwise not come in contact with one another—particularly people of various races and classes. I believe that social change happens primarily on two levels—either on a large-scale, systems level or at a very local, even interpersonal, level. Many stereotypes seem to melt away when people get to know one another as humans rather than as members of a preconceived group. When those stereotypes disappear, people are more likely to come together to create social change across lines of race and class.

Therefore, I am interested in working with organizations that foster community, particularly across lines of racial and socioeconomic difference; strive to distribute economic resources more justly; and support young people who are involved in these efforts. Because my philanthropic resources are limited, my giving is focused primarily in my home city.

Organizations to which I will give in the next year: During the next year, I intend to make contributions to the following organizations:

- Common Impact/Harbinger Partners ($1,000)

- Casque and Gauntlet at Dartmouth College ($700 payment on a pledge to the endowment fund)

- Responsible Wealth ($300)

- Resource Generation ($150)

- The Boulder Community Foundation ($500)

- Peace Games ($100)

- LISTEN ($200)

- BELL Policy Center ($100)

- Discretionary funds to support other organizations or individuals who are doing good work ($200)

Total giving: $3,250, or 10 percent of my income of $32,500

DONOR DIVA

Filling out Worksheet 7.1 will immediately help you to deal with the many requests that come in the mail or on the phone. If a request would fit in your funding area, consider it. If it doesn't but it still speaks to one of your values, consider whether you want to give to it through your miscellaneous, "donor's whim" category. If neither is the case, throw it away or pass it on. Letting go of what isn't important to your mission and goals frees up your energy for giving.

Sample Family Giving Plan: $10,300

This family's giving plan is also presented in worksheet form on the next two pages.

Mission: Our family seeks to be stewards of the resources entrusted to it for the benefit of our community through those we serve with our time, talent, and treasure. We make this giving plan as a way to bring more order and communication to our giving and to engage our teenage children in giving and service.

Values: Community, service, faith, and diversity

Total deductible giving for 2007: $10,300 (10 percent of combined income plus 25 percent of the kids' allowances)

Nondeductible giving:

- Political campaigns (local and national): $1,500
- Gifts to family: $2,000
- Income from our revolving loan fund for family and friends: $2,500

Volunteer hours (family commitment of 500 hours per year: 125 hours per person, or about 2 to 3 hours each on Saturdays)

Interest areas:

- Religious/faith: 30%
- Economic development and job training: 30%
- Environment and saving animals: $25%
- Education: 10%
- Cultural arts: 5%

Geographic reach:

- Local: 80%
- National: 10%
- Global: 10%

Methods of giving:

- Weekly church pledge
- United Way, payroll deduction, and Black United Fund
- Youthgive.org (via kids' giving cards)
- Direct donations

Sample Family Giving Plan: $10,300

Mission and values: Steward our resources in the service of community, service, faith, and diversity

Year of plan: 2007

Financial donations: $10,300

Volunteering: 500 hours total for all family members

Funding Area	Percentage	Organization	Amount	When	Volunteer Hours	Notes, Contacts, Previous Gifts
Faith	30%	Abundant Life Missionary Baptist Church	$2,500	Weekly $50	200	
		Interfaith Workers' Justice Fund	$500	June 1st		
Economic development and job training	30%	Jobs for Youth	$750	9/07	100	Family volunteering
		21st Century Foundation, New Gulf Coast Fund (via the Black United Fund)	$2,000	4/07		
		Lambi Fund of Haiti	$250	June 1st		
Environment, animal, and species survival and health	25%	Healthy Children/ Healthy Planet (via YouthGive.org)	$500	Nov. 15th		
		The Green Job Corps	$1,000	Nov. 15th		
		Global Greengrants (via YouthGive)	$250	Nov. 15th		

(continued on next page)

Sample Family Giving Plan: $10,300, Cont'd

Funding Area	Percentage	Organization	Amount	When	Volunteer Hours	Notes, Contacts, Previous Gifts
Cultural arts	5%	National Black Women's Health Project	$750	Nov. 15th		
		African American Arts Alliance	$400	Nov. 15	100	On Ex. Comm.
		National Public Radio (via YouthGive) (International desk)	$400	Nov. 15		
Education	10%	Evanston Public School	$150	Nov 15	50	Kids' classrooms
		Nu Lamda Nu International (African education)	$100	Nov. 15th		
		Bennett College	$500	Nov. 15th	50	On Alumni Board
		Kid's & friends raffles, and events	$150	as needed		
		Remaining opportunities:	$100	by 12/31		
TOTALS			$10,300		500 hrs.	

Sample Couple Giving Plan: $45,000

Mission and values: To preserve cultural heritage through the arts, education and technology, philanthropy and volunteerism

Giving Plan for 2007

Financial donations: $45,000 (15 percent of family pretax income of $360,000)

Volunteering: Three hours each week, both of us (three hundred hours per year)

Funding Area	Percentage	Organization	Amount	When	Volunteer Hours	Notes, Contacts, Previous Gifts
Cultural arts	50%	Asian Arts Museum	$5,000	November	100	Docent
		Asian Cultural Center	$5,000	November		
		Public Library	$2,200	March		
		Asian Elders Oral History Project	$10,000	March	100	Co-founder
Education and technology	25%	Educational Fund for Bilingual Teachers	$5,000	March		
		Stanford University	$1,250	November		
		The International Forum on Globalization	$5,000	November		
Philanthropy and volunteerism	25%	The Seattle Foundation	$2,500	March	100	Giving Circle
		Women's Funding Alliance/Seattle	$2, 500	November		
		Catholic Campaign for Human Development	$5,000	November		
		Family neighborhood giving—Bread for the Journey	$1,550	March		
TOTALS			$45,000		300 hrs.	

Sample Family Giving Plan: $500,000

Mission and values: To support and expand the field of philanthropic giving, projects related to education, fair elections, and a balanced world

Total giving for 2008: $500,000
Financial donations: $500,000
Volunteering (total hours): 250

Funding Area	Percentage	Organization	Amount	Volunteer Hours	When
Family	10 percent $50,000	Atlanta Community Foundation	$50,000 for Family Fund		October
Community	30 percent $150,000	Atlanta Women's Fund	$50,000	100	Nov.
		Rotary Club	$50,000	100	Dec 1
		The Algebra Project	$25,000		Oct.
		Scholarships to five schools	$25,000		June
World	60 percent $300,000	The Carter Center—election monitoring	$25,000	50	Oct.
		The Global Fund for Women for TEWA Nepal	$100,000 (50 percent each)		Sept.
		Reuniting America	$100,000		Oct.
		Oxfam	$25,000		Nov.
		iearn.org	$25,000		Nov.
		YMCA Internships	$25,000		Nov.
TOTALS			$500,000	250 hrs.	

MULTIYEAR GIVING

A multiyear giving plan can be a simple and helpful way to look at what you've been doing and plan ahead. Use Worksheet 7.2 to record your giving over several years.

Worksheet 7.2
Multiyear Giving Record

Area of Funding	Organization	2006	2007	2008	2009	2010	2011
		$	$	$	$	$	$
		$	$	$	$	$	$
		$	$	$	$	$	$
		$	$	$	$	$	$
		$	$	$	$	$	$
		$	$	$	$	$	$
	Total donations:	$	$	$	$	$	$
	Total donated goods or clothing:	$	$	$	$	$	$

CLARIFYING YOUR INTENTION

Worksheet 7.3 gives you a quick way to ground yourself even further in your intentions for giving. Knowing what your intention is will also help later when you evaluate whether the gifts were effective. Make a copy of the worksheet for each gift that you intend to evaluate and file it as a reminder of your intention at the time of the gift giving.

Worksheet 7.3
Giving Intention

Name of organization: _____

Date of gift: _____ Amount of gift: $_____

With this gift/donation, I want to participate in

_____ The spirit of generosity and faith

_____ Supporting someone I trust or respect

_____ Sustaining the mission of an organization I believe in

_____ Working with other donors or nonprofit leaders

_____ Increasing the financial capacity of an organization

_____ Helping to leverage more resources through a challenge gift

_____ Advancing leadership capacity within an organization through money or time given expressly for trainings or expansion

_____ Providing support for direct services to constituents

_____ Helping to provide specific outreach or support to a targeted population or a specific geographic area

_____ Assisting to ensure that the issues being addressed by this organization or leaders get media or PR exposure

_____ Providing tangible goods (clothes, computers, desks, food)

_____ Ensuring public policy or advocacy linkages

_____ Designating money for research or documentation

_____ Helping a group or community do better planning, visioning, or collaborating

_____ Contributing to public education options

_____ Funding an artistic presentation, interpretation, or expression

_____ Attaining visibility or recognition for our family or business

_____ Other: _____

_____

(continued on next page)

Worksheet 7.3
Giving Intention, Cont'd

For gifts of more than $5,000   Name of organization _____

1. The organization and I have set detailed goals or agreed on the expected impact of my gift: _____ Yes _____ No

   Comments or notes:

   _____

   _____

2. At the time of my gift I specified how and if I wanted to be recognized.

   _____ I was specific with _____ (person's name) at

   _____ (name of organization) about my wish to remain

   anonymous; we spoke on _____ (date) in person/phone/in writing

   (attach letter to file).

   _____ I do not wish to remain anonymous.

   Comments or notes:

   _____

   _____

3. I spoke with _____ (person's name) in the

   organization on _____ (date) about reports I do and do not want

   to receive on the organization's work.

   Example: "I spoke with Niki Newago on July 16th about the fact that I only wish to receive the annual report and one call or visit a year."

   Comments or notes:

   _____

   _____

REVIEWING YOUR GIFTMAKING FOR
YEARLY RESULTS AND IMPACT

There is much to learn by implementing your giving plan. Once you've completed your year of giftmaking, or as often as you want to do so, reflect on how well your money was used and how well you feel you did as a donor. Worksheets 7.4 and 7.5 provide questions that may be useful in your review. (The questions in Worksheet 7.5 on how you made your giving decisions and other ways you expressed your values will become clearer as you read the chapters that follow.)

EXPANDING YOUR GIVING HORIZON

Having a giving plan is one step in responding to the enormous problems that create inequality, violence, and illness for millions of people every day. It's hard to conceive that your donations, whether $500 or $50,000 a year, will really make much of a dent in the vast web of those problems. Yet through conscientious, thoughtful responses, and through leverage, the donations of each person contribute to positive change. Here is what some experienced donors have said:

> I know that my donations combine with thousands of others to make change and help people daily. Given my privilege, that is enough. My job is to admit my place in society's current order and to do my part to share what I can. Of hundreds of contributions I have made, fewer than three percent have, I think, been spent without adequate care or expertise. Trusting others to know what needs to be done and giving them the chance to do so is my task.

> It's really all about just listening to what communities say they need and checking in about their competency. A giving plan takes time, but it is such a great tool for having more impact.

> I see that the steady and intentional gifts I have made over time have built organizational stability and leadership savvy.

> Having a giving plan has opened my eyes to what is around me and through the choices it requires me to make, has made me more reverent of the multitude of worthy needs.

> I have learned never to resist my own generous impulses.

Worksheet 7.4
Results and Impact

If you gave large gifts that you want to evaluate before giving again, answer the following questions about the impact of your donation:

1. What were my intentions and goals and were they reached? (Have I reviewed the organization's finances or received a report about how the money was spent? Was my donation spent as it was intended, designated, or originally requested? If not, was I informed along the way?)

_____

_____

_____

2. What do I perceive is the organization's progress and what tools can I use for evaluation? What other organizations collaborated or worked on this issue? What feedback could I get from them about the effectiveness of the group I gave to? (For large gifts: Do I want to hire someone to do a more formal evaluation or do it myself?)

_____

_____

3. How stable does the leadership seem now? Is it stronger? Weaker?

_____

_____

4. Is the organization more, or less, financially stable now?

_____

_____

5. Were there strategic outcomes—programs, products, or services?

_____

_____

(continued on next page)

Worksheet 7.4
Results and Impact, Cont'd

6. Did the gift leverage other money or results?

   _____

   _____

7. How do I feel about administrative costs versus program and fundraising costs at this organization now? Are they different from what I expected?

   _____

   _____

8. What learning went on for me and for the organization through this gift, if any?

   _____

   _____

9. How well did the organization inform me of its progress or engage me in its work?

   _____

   _____

10. Were there anticipated results or impact and were they achieved?

    _____

    _____

Notes about future gifts or about concerns or feedback to share with group or leader:

_____

_____

_____

Worksheet 7.5
How You Did as a Donor

Take a few minutes to recall your giving and volunteering over the past year. Check any of the items below that describe your activities. Then go through the checklist again and put a star next to anything you would like to do differently in the coming year.

Volunteering

I volunteered each week or month (check one)

_____ 1–2 hours

_____ 3–5 hours

_____ 6–10 hours

_____ 11–16 hours

_____ 17–20 hours

_____ 21+ hours

I volunteered with the following organizations and did the following activities:

_____

_____

I increased my ability to assist the nonprofit sector by

_____ Taking a class (for example, on how to be a board member, on fundraising, or for other skills)

_____ Reading about nonprofit or community issues

_____ Other: _____

Fundraising

I leveraged my ability to support organizations by

_____ Learning about fundraising

_____ Fundraising from individuals

_____ Hosting events for nonprofits or politicians

_____ Cohosting large events (for example, buying a table of seats and organizing friends to come)

_____ Speaking as a donor at events to motivate others to give

_____ Speaking to media about my giving

_____ Other: _____

(*continued on next page*)

Giving

I gave

_____ Small amounts to many groups

_____ Larger amounts to several groups

_____ A balance of the two

I gave to

_____ Too many groups

_____ Enough groups

_____ Not enough groups

As a percentage of income or assets I gave

_____ Adequately

_____ Less than I could have

_____ More than I could really afford

I collected mail requests and gave to selected ones

_____ As they came in

_____ Monthly

_____ Quarterly

_____ Yearly

_____ Not at all

I attended fundraising events

_____ Once or twice

_____ Quarterly

_____ Monthly

_____ More often

_____ Not at all

I generally gave

_____ Anonymously

_____ Using my name

(*continued on next page*)

Worksheet 7.5
How You Did as a Donor, Cont'd

_____ Publicly if asked

_____ Through a foundation or donor-advised fund where I won't be identified personally

I gave to the following number of issues or populations:

_____ 1–2

_____ 3–4

_____ 5–6

I evaluated where to give by

_____ Checking their info on the Web or their e-newsletters

_____ Reading annual reports, funding proposals, or direct mail pieces

_____ Going on site visits or talking to staff

_____ Attending briefings on the issues I give to

_____ Talking to other funders and activists

_____ Reading through groups' proposals

_____ Checking with groups that evaluate nonprofits

_____ Listening to my heart

_____ Other: _____

Planning

I followed an overall giving plan that identified how much I would give of

_____ Income

_____ Assets

_____ Time

My giving plan specified

_____ My areas of focus

_____ The types of organizations and strategies I want to support

I reflected on my overall giving

_____ At the beginning or end of the year

_____ On a regular basis during the year (how often?)

(_continued on next page_)

Worksheet 7.5
How You Did as a Donor, Cont'd

_____ Through drawing, writing, or talking with others

_____ Through a formal evaluation process

I talked or consulted with the following people about my philanthropy

_____ A financial planner or investment manager

_____ An estate attorney

_____ A friend or fellow donor

_____ A mentor or philanthropic advisor

_____ A development director

_____ Foundation staff

_____ An activist involved in the areas I give to

_____ A donor support network

_____ A wealth coach or personal coach

_____ Other: _____

Identity and Community

I let others know I am

_____ A donor, giver, or philanthropist

_____ A volunteer or activist

_____ A donor activist or donor organizer

I made some of my giving decisions

_____ With others (partner, family, friends)

_____ By talking with other donors who give to what I do

_____ With other activists or community leaders at the decision-making table

_____ Informed by other leaders and activists or donors or news

_____ With support of a donor network or giving club

_____ Other: _____

Integration of Values

In addition to giving and volunteering, I expressed my values by

_____ Loaning money to nonprofit organizations

(continued on next page)

THE PHILANTHROPIC LEARNING CURVE

Becoming an inspired philanthropist takes time. Every philanthropist enters the process of giving from a different point. Your approach to giving depends on your enthusiasm and focus, how much time you have, your understanding of the issues that interest you, and your comfort with analyzing information and making decisions. Like any new skill or role, it follows its own trajectory, from exciting periods of rapid learning to frustratingly slow plateaus and times when it all just feels too hard. During the early months, it is particularly helpful to share your experiences with other donors with whom you can commiserate and who can coach and cheer you on.

There does, however, seem to be a progression common to all philanthropists. H. Peter Karoff of the Philanthropic Initiative has dubbed this progression "the philanthropic curve," and has described it as consisting of the following six levels.

Level One: Becoming a Donor

A complex combination of influences, which can include personal and religious values, family background, business and social pressures, ego, and heartfelt response to the world around you, motivates you to become a donor. Giving becomes part of your way of life, your position in the community, your yearning to be a good person. Over time, giving becomes less satisfying and requests increase. For the most part, you give small amounts to an ever-growing number of groups.

Level Two: Getting Organized

You have enough experience as a donor to be able to analyze your giving patterns, what really interests you, and which gifts have awarded you the most satisfaction. You begin to develop priorities and criteria for your giving, learn to say no, and make fewer but larger grants.

Level Three: Becoming More Strategic

Knowing what issues really interest you, you now realize that you don't know enough about them. So you do research, talking to other donors, talking to experts in the field, reading, consulting with your community foundation, making site visits to organizations addressing those issues. Your giving becomes more focused, and the groups you support reflect your top priorities.

Level Four: Focusing on Issues and Results

At this stage, you become more interested in results and evaluation. It is important that you maximize your giving and increase the possibilities that it will make a difference. Rather than responding to effects, you begin to investigate underlying causes, focusing on building the capacities of the organizations of the most talented and effective nonprofit leaders. You are more proactive, searching out the best people and organizations to support rather than waiting for requests to come to you.

Level Five: Leveraging

At this stage, your giving supports the development and funding of programs designed to meet specific programmatic objectives. You enter into collaborations with other donors and participate in public-private partnerships. You have become increasingly knowledgeable about the issues you fund, about what works, and about what can really make a difference.

Level Six: Harmony and Congruence

You experience a satisfying alignment between your most deeply held values and your giving interests. Your philanthropy is one of the most exciting and fulfilling aspects of your life.

Here's how two donors discussed their development as a donor:

Harriet Barlow

I'm learning over the years what I need to stay energized and optimistic as a giver; some of my funding needs to nurture things I can literally see and touch—murals in my neighborhood, community gardens, projects that affect people I know. Some of my money needs to go to projects shaping the larger political and economic picture, touching the lives of people I will never meet, perhaps taking longer than my lifetime to bear fruit. For instance, during the Mississippi flood disaster in 1994, I didn't give blankets and canned goods, but instead supported projects that would help people rethink how to build on flood plains.

I also need a balance between funding creative startups that get my adrenaline going and directing my money to projects I'm confident will bring results. High risk and low risk—like a good stock portfolio! When I evaluate my giving, I am not judging whether others have done right by me, but rather assessing my own thought process, how I might become more strategic, more deeply attuned to what I need as a giver at this stage in my life.

Pilar Gonzales

My philanthropy has evolved over the many years I've been a donor. First and foremost I identify with my communities of origin. Because my grandparents, my father, and I were farmworkers, from a poor background, I continue to give money to organizations working on behalf of farmworkers, indigenous people, and other marginalized peoples.

I found that being a philanthropist can give you power, whether perceived or actual. Sometimes by making a large gift, you find yourself invited to join committees, to join a board, or to give advice to nonprofit executives. In order to challenge the classism of gala events,

I've bought tickets to high-dollar events just so I could sit at a table with someone influential I needed to talk with about a political issue important to me.

My giving has evolved into a giving plan which includes upstream, strategic giving and giving to direct services, putting me in touch with people experiencing poverty. I've been doing my own "Glove Giveaway" for more than seven years. I buy hundreds of work gloves, ball caps, and gallons of coffee throughout the year and take these provisions to street corners where immigrant day laborers stand waiting and hoping to be hired for a few hours. I visit them on those early mornings, hand out the stuff I've bought, and thank them for their hard work.

For ages, I resisted giving to environmental issues because I felt the issues of farmworkers were invisible to that movement. I know that people will give fish and trees, but somehow rural families were not seen as part of the *movement* to save the earth. But if I were to have an impact in my communities of origin, I needed to challenge my own assumptions about environmental organizing, so I decided to give money and time to several environmental nonprofits. I've always been pleased with that decision.

It's safe to say I wouldn't be a philanthropist if I didn't give to people outside my familiar cultures. Giving to predominantly white organizations has been crucial to being a philanthropist. It allows me to exercise my widest compassion and unbiased humanity toward others—not just for my people. As a donor of color I would like white donors and activists to know that I am motivated to give money and time by the same things that motivate them. For example, if we have children we may prioritize giving to education or health care. We also give to what we enjoy and what attracts us—for example, to museums or to our places of worship or to scholarships for students and professionals.

As for accumulating wealth while being the executive director of a foundation, I was shocked at how few solicitations were made to me. I would be overlooked when organizations were asking for large gifts. It seemed that people did not consider me a potential donor to their causes! Did they still see me only as a grantee, I wondered? Sometimes, white people don't want to solicit people of color, even those with money, because they think there's something special they have to do, or perhaps the asker feels some guilt. As a Native American Mexican woman who is a donor in the larger community, I like to be asked for money! And I'll make my decisions they way you do: based on personal compassion, economic ability, and financial savvy.

The Many Ways to Give

Philanthropy flows from a loving heart,
not an overstuffed pocketbook.

—Douglas M. Lawson

Now that you have a plan for where you want your donations to go, you can consider some of the many ways to move your financial gifts to the nonprofits you've chosen. This chapter covers common ways people make philanthropic gifts. In Chapter Nine, there is more detail about setting up and giving through institutions, including family and corporate foundations.

If anything, the average giver may feel overwhelmed by how many choices there are. Aside from established structures such as giving through bequests and directing your donations through donor-advised funds, there are quite a number of new strategies for giving, new methods of donor involvement and education, new structures for decision making, and new decision makers.

To learn a lot more about any of the ways described here that sound interesting to you, check with associations of nonprofits (listed in Appendix I, "Resources," on the CD-ROM) or local public, community, or women's foundations for seminars they may offer on ways to give and on legacy planning for donors. (For inspiration, see Appendix C on the CD-ROM for a number of creative ideas for giving that individuals or groups of donors have come up with, and Appendix D on the CD-ROM to learn about the giving choices of a number of celebrity philanthropists.)

All of the giving models discussed here apply to any giving budget. Although donor-advised funds, venture philanthropy, and donor circles usually involve gifts of more than $2,000, many people take advantage of these options by pooling donations.

For any form of giving, the work you've done so far on clarifying values, defining a vision, and creating a giving plan are the building blocks on which to base your actions and strategies.

DEFINITIONS OF COMMON VEHICLES FOR GIVING

The variety of avenues available for personal giving are defined here. The next sections contain more detail on frequently used ways to give and some of the newer ways people are directing their giving. Different methods provide different results, both for you and for the organizations you contribute to. Professionals can help you make the most informed choices about the vehicles that can work for you. You can help them by being very clear about what you want to accomplish and why. (Appendix H on the CD-ROM, "Comparison of Giving Options," contains a detailed summary comparison of financial characteristics of some of the major types of charitable giving options covered in this chapter and the next.)

Bequests. Leaving a stated sum of money or a percentage of your estate to nonprofits, family, or friends by naming them in your will. You can also structure a trust that will benefit charitable organizations or individuals during or after your lifetime (such as a charitable remainder trust and or charitable lead trusts—a planned giving specialist or your financial advisor can tell you more about these vehicles). You can also name one or more nonprofits as beneficiaries of an insurance policy or as the recipient of your IRA or retirement funds.

Community Development Financial Institution (CDFI). A lending institution (including community loan funds, community banks, and credit unions) whose mission is to reinvest in targeted, underserved communities. CDFIs are supported by institutions as well as individual investors and donors who preserve capital while these lending agencies make that capital accessible to a community of organizations and individuals.

Community Foundation. A public foundation that receives donations from a broad base and whose charter is to serve its community or issue-specific population. There are nearly one thousand community foundations throughout the United States and a growing number internationally. Community foundations vary in length of time in existence, asset base, level of service to donors, political orientation, and level of community involvement.

Community-Based Foundation or Federation. A public foundation or workplace-giving alliance of organizations that receives donations from a broad base of donors. The aim of community-based foundations, led by teams of activists, donors, and community leaders, is to identify problems in their communities and then to address or solve them or advocate for changes together. The impact of these funds is to democratize philanthropy as well as to share power in decision making and community building. There are now more than 250 of these funds or federations in the United States and a growing number worldwide.

Corporate Foundation. A private foundation established by a business or corporation as a means of carrying out systematic programs of charitable giving. The board of directors of such a foundation is usually composed of senior executives and directors of the company. In most cases funds are received and distributed each year from current profits of the parent company. Giving committees or staff are sometimes hired or designated to determine where management and employees would like gifts directed as well as community need. Workplace or payroll-deduction options such as Choice in Giving or the United Way are often partners with business (and government) giving. Some corporations link with named nonprofit organizations in cause-related marketing agreements whereby the corporation donates to a specific nonprofit a portion of its profit for specific items purchased or services used. (See Chapter Nine for more on setting up and giving through a corporate foundation.)

Donor Circle or Giving Circle. Types of pooled funds (see Pooled Funds, further on). Donors make a commitment of one to five years to share in studying, donating funds, and becoming advocates around a specific issue, region, or population. They usually work with a community of peers or a group of people with expertise in a specific issue or interest, often because they want to give in a particular geographic area. Increasingly, friends and families are starting giving circles to include the younger generation, and neighbors or groups of friends are forming giving circles to deepen their collective learning.

Donor-Advised Fund. A fund established by an individual donor or group of donors at an existing community foundation, public foundation, or federation, or through a philanthropic program at a financial services institution. Donors make recommendations about where they would like their contributions to go; the fund handles the administrative details, IRS reporting, and investment management for a defined fee.

E-Philanthropy. Online nonprofit and philanthropic activity, including Web-based giving, volunteering, advocacy, and organizing.

Family Foundation. A private foundation involving family, extended family, and sometimes community advisors. There are more than 36,700 family foundations in the United States alone. Families with less than $100,000 to give annually or with less than $2 million in assets may not want to set up a formal foundation. Instead, they can create a donor-advised fund at their local community, public, or women's foundation. See Chapter Nine for more on setting up and giving through a family foundation.

For-Benefit Corporations. A new wave of companies that have been formed, in the spirit of Paul Newman's company, Newman's Own, for the primary purpose of generating profits to be contributed to nonprofits as grants. Some examples are Peacekeeper (www.imapeacekeeper.com) and Annie's Homegrown (www.annies.com). For a discussion of the theory behind for-benefit corporations, see the article, "The Blended Value Proposition: Integrating Social and Financial Returns," by Jed Emerson (available at www.blendedvalue.org/media/pdf-proposition.pdf).

Pooled Fund. Individuals pooling any amount of money together to gain philanthropic leverage. Friends, service clubs, graduation classes, and, most recently, a proliferation of giving clubs have created pooled giving funds.

Private Foundation. An organization whose function is to give away money; generally supported by a small number of private donations.

Supporting Foundation. Also known as a Supporting Organization. A tax-exempt organization, usually with at least $10 million in assets, that is closely tied to at least one other public charity. Supporting foundations are alternatives to establishing a private foundation; they minimize the administrative burdens of managing a private foundation and have fewer limitations on charitable deductions. Check with your financial advisor, as new regulations for supporting foundations appear from time to time.

Trusts. A variety of vehicles that can offer lifetime income or tax advantages to you, your family, or your favorite charity. Planned giving specialists and attorneys are knowledgeable about the various forms of trusts (which include charitable remainder trusts, charitable lead trusts, qualified terminable interest property, life estates, unitrusts, annuity trusts, uniform credit trusts, generation-skipping trusts, and qualified personal residence trusts).

Venture Philanthropy. The application of the investment and management practices of venture capitalism to philanthropic giving (for more on venture philanthropy, see www.svpseattle.org or www.robinhood.org).

CONSIDERING HOW TO GIVE

Exercise 8.1 is designed to help you think about the different ways there are to give and which of them are right for you.

FREQUENTLY USED WAYS TO GIVE

This section goes into more detail about commonly used vehicles for giving: online giving, workplace giving, giving circles and donor circles, donor-advised funds, and venture philanthropy.

Online Giving

The Internet enables remarkable new opportunities for philanthropy. Whether as a way for businesses to offer a portion of profits of online sales to nonprofits; a connecting resource where people can join funds, talents, and knowledge; or an information portal on good giving, the Internet increasingly creates opportunities for better-connected and better-informed philanthropy. At one end of the spectrum, for-profits such as Amazon.com are channeling numerous small gifts to nonprofits that link with Amazon to receive 4 percent of sales of their books or other merchandise. At another Internet giant, eBay, auctions can be used for selling items from which the money paid goes to nonprofits. See Exhibit 8.1 for a number of groups that enable you to make donations online. (For online resources for researching nonprofit groups, see Chapter Six.)

Most organizations have Web sites and online giving capacity to facilitate giving. Here are some other sites using the Internet to raise and give funds:

- www.pledgebank.com: A place to challenge others to join in an activity or make a gift conditional on the participation of a set number of others. It can be used to challenge others to take actions, such as pledging to mentor a child, or to give, such as "I will give $1,000 if ten people will give $100 to a specified cause." Originally devised for the United Kingdom, Pledgebank now serves a global constituency in eleven languages.

Exercise 8.1
Giving Methods

5–10 minutes

	I have used this method	I want information on this method	Not applicable to me or not interested
Financial Gifts			
Written a check	☐	☐	☐
Given cash	☐	☐	☐
Donated by credit card	☐	☐	☐
Given stock	☐	☐	☐
Given real estate or other holdings	☐	☐	☐
Setup charitable estate planning	☐	☐	☐
Designated insurance policies or IRAs to a nonprofit beneficiary	☐	☐	☐
Other: _____	☐	☐	☐
Non-Financial Gifts			
Given house or space for fundraising events, activists' or artists' retreats, or issues briefings	☐	☐	☐
Written a letter or placed a phone call of recommendation (leverage)	☐	☐	☐
Given equipment	☐	☐	☐
Given skills	☐	☐	☐
Other: _____	☐	☐	☐
Decision Making			
By self	☐	☐	☐
With partner	☐	☐	☐
With family (all ages)	☐	☐	☐
With groups of other people from similar incomes	☐	☐	☐
With mixed-income group	☐	☐	☐
With group of co-workers or friends	☐	☐	☐
Gave decision-making power to group of professionals in the field, or representatives of constituency groups or activists	☐	☐	☐

(*continued on next page*)

Exercise 8.1
Giving Methods, Cont'd

	I have used this method	I want information on this method	Not applicable to me or not interested
Gave decision-making power to a staff member, program advisor	☐	☐	☐
Gave decision-making power to someone else to decide	☐	☐	☐
Other: _____	☐	☐	☐
Mechanism			
Public community foundation or federation	☐	☐	☐
Donor-advised fund	☐	☐	☐
Donor circle	☐	☐	☐
Giving circle	☐	☐	☐
Online donation	☐	☐	☐
Venture philanthropic fund	☐	☐	☐
Loan to a nonprofit or individual	☐	☐	☐
Investment in a community loan or micro-enterprise fund	☐	☐	☐
As part of a mixed group of low-income and wealthy activists	☐	☐	☐
Workplace or payroll deduction	☐	☐	☐
Family foundation	☐	☐	☐
Supporting foundation	☐	☐	☐
Other: _____	☐	☐	☐
Designation of Donations			
Operating expenses	☐	☐	☐
Capital expenses (such as for building or equipment)	☐	☐	☐
Grantmaking funds	☐	☐	☐
Leadership sabbaticals	☐	☐	☐
Endowment gifts	☐	☐	☐
Matching or challenge gifts	☐	☐	☐
Technical assistance	☐	☐	☐
Scholarships	☐	☐	☐

(continued on next page)

Exercise 8.1
Giving Methods, Cont'd

	I have used this method	I want information on this method	Not applicable to me or not interested
Loans	☐	☐	☐
Existing debt reduction	☐	☐	☐
Time frame			
One-year gift	☐	☐	☐
Multiyear gift	☐	☐	☐
Gift with no amount of time attached	☐	☐	☐
Planned gift (during lifetime or upon death)	☐	☐	☐

Reflection:

1. What is your analysis of your methods of giving?

_____

_____

_____

_____

2. What methods do you want to learn more about?

_____

_____

_____

_____

3. What information do you need and who or what resource can best answer your questions?

_____

_____

_____

_____

- www.dropcash.com: A way to post a fundraising campaign anywhere online. Posting a dropcash box shows a bar to reveal the progress of a campaign as well as links to more information.

Higher-end donors may want to check out these sites:

- www.10over100.org: Created by Internet entrepreneurs James Hong and Josh Blumenstock as a way to commit to giving and to challenge peers, the site offers a place where a donor can pledge to give 10 percent of income over $100,000.

- www.donorleaders.org: Offers information about and links to donor networks for high-end donors.

- www.newdea.com: A Web site for high-end donors to organize and evaluate giving.

You can also find many volunteering opportunities on the Web. Here are a few sites to get you started:

- www.networkforgood.org: Information and connection to opportunities to volunteer.
- www.onebrick.org: Helps connect local volunteers to local projects, rewarding volunteers with social activities.
- www.CharityFocus.org: An organization of and for volunteers, connects people to opportunities to serve, especially opportunities related to technology.

Philanthropic Conversations

The Internet provides a wealth of information from and for foundations, nonprofits, and other organizations involved in philanthropy. Blogs offer individuals a voice for sharing their perspective on giving and causes. More blogs come online every month, some sticking around for a few posts or a few months and others sticking it out with a growing readership. Here are some current starting places for dialogue:

- www.worldchanging.com: Share ideas and information about making the world a better place.
- www.Idealist.org: Information and a connecting space for volunteers and nonprofits.
- www.nextbillion.net: A site to identify and discuss sustainable business models that address the needs of the world's poorest citizens.
- www.gifthub.org: A prominent blog on developing a conversation about a wide range of issues within philanthropy.
- www.philanthromedia.org: Offers discussion for the high net worth donor and professional philanthropist and advisors.
- www.gayleroberts.com/blog: Offers discussions about fundraising for nonprofits
- philanthropy.blogspot.com: Offers "provocations on the future of philanthropy."
- www.thephilanthropicenterprise.org: Seeks to understand "the role of voluntary action and philanthropy."

- www.onphilanthropy.com: A global resource for nonprofit professionals.
- www.globalfundforwomen.org: A site about women's philanthropy worldwide.

Virtual Worlds, Real Philanthropy

Perhaps the most unusual site offering an avenue into philanthropy is Second Life (www.secondlife.com). In this virtual world avatars interact with each other in a wide range of activities in what appears at first to be a videogame environment. Increasingly, however, the space takes on serious efforts. Nonprofits open virtual doors and hold fundraising events. Better World Island, a virtual land in Second Life, offers a meeting place for people striving to create a better world. With organizations such as the American Cancer Society holding virtual Relays for Life in the world of Second Life, Second Life clearly offers some serious opportunities for philanthropic efforts.

Workplace Giving

Many donors participate in workplace giving campaigns whereby charitable donations are deducted regularly from employees' paychecks. The system is most often administered by a federation of nonprofit agencies that are the recipients of the donation. Contributions can be made to a general pool or designated for specific member organizations or for particular issue or interest areas. The United Way has had the largest and best-known workplace fundraising appeal. Its funding focuses primarily on human service needs. Over the past few decades, community-based workplace funds entered this arena. These new funds—with fifty charitable federations and funds serving more than two thousand nonprofits nationwide—not only have built good track records, they are also raising money at a higher rate of growth than the United Way.

Funds solicit for their member agencies or grantees, which include health agencies, community development organizations, neighborhood groups, environmental protection projects, organizations working on nonviolence, arts and cultural organizations, women's groups, and a multitude of identity groups, including African Americans; Hispanics; Native Americans; Asian Americans; and gay, lesbian, or transgendered people. They also build community dialogue across sectors through the use of shared networking and sites to better collaborate campaigns and marketing and capacity building.

This movement is growing rapidly. According to *Giving at Work 2003,* by the National Committee on Responsive Philanthropy, employee contributions to the progressive community-based funds—which include Black United Funds, environmental funds, social action funds, and women's funds—made up 11 percent of pledge dollars from traditional donors in American workplaces from 1996 to 2001.[1]

If your workplace doesn't have giving options through payroll deduction, contact your local community-based workplace fund or federation or United Way about initiating a campaign. Inquire whether the fund you give to includes groups that match your values and perspectives on social reform. If not, ask for more choice in the programs being offered. The National Alliance for Choice in Giving (www.choice ingiving.org) can give you more information about your local or statewide environmental funds, Black United Funds, women's funds, the Native American Rights Fund, United Latino Fund, and social action funds. Independent Charities of America (www.independentcharities.org) is another resource for workplace giving.

Public foundations and community-based workplace funds are among the most effective methods for donors to ensure that their money is being distributed democratically. Funds are pooled and redistributed based on a thoughtful and ethical process through committees that include representatives of the communities being served.

Giving Circles and Donor Circles

A report from New Ventures in Philanthropy chronicles the emergence of thousands of giving circles across the United States and the globe (www.givingforum .org/givingcircles).

Giving circles and donor circles have taken off as new models of giving. Both involve groups of people pooling some philanthropic dollars and making joint decisions on the use of those funds. The difference is in institutional affiliation. Giving circles generally have no institutional affiliation (except sometimes for fiscal sponsorship, such as locating a giving circle at a local community foundation). They consist of groups of people with some common interests and values who seek to make philanthropic gifts through collective giving. Donor circles, on the other hand, are programs developed by established giving institutions, often for the benefit of their grantees or their own programs. (For example, a group of donors to a hospital might want to join together to fund at a higher level collectively and give to prevention projects in the community or buy new equipment for local health clinics in their neighborhood. The hospital would start a donor circle and donations would be made through the hospital's special donor circle fund account for that purpose.)

Giving Circles

Giving circles are a kind of social investment club, with the funds invested in nonprofits. Like-minded donors explore and collaborate with one another to make focused social investments with impact. By acting collectively, giving circle members have the chance to infuse the nonprofits of their choice with financial and intellectual capital, resources, and contacts.

A giving circle often begins when an individual brings together a small, informal group of individuals whose members share the following desires:

- To leverage the impact of their charitable contributions with shared expertise and volunteerism

- To connect meaningfully with the communities and causes they care about

- To participate in a social network of people who share similar interests and values

- To learn more about philanthropy as a vehicle for social change

Among the many advantages of forming giving circles are the following:

- Pooled dollars invested toward a key issue can have a far greater impact than smaller individual gifts.

- Collective "know-how" of a group adds value and impact to volunteerism and charitable investments.

- Creating partnerships with a smaller number of charities creates a deeper level of involvement and gives a better chance to gauge your return on investment.

Giving circles have become a popular community-building and collaborative learning experience. In a relatively short time, the impact of pooling money and distributing it in one's community can provide enormous satisfaction. It is also fun to participate with others and share in learning new information.

In her book *Creating a Women's Giving Circle*, Sondra Shaw Hardy describes the common elements of giving circles:[2]

- Membership is broad, diverse, and inclusive.

- The amounts of money contributed may or may not be the same from each member and are given at least annually; philanthropy is an activity in which anyone may be involved.

- The money is pooled and members determine how it will be distributed.

- The money is used to help address specific community or institutional needs.

- There are educational opportunities within the giving circle to learn more about philanthropy and finance.

- The membership is proactive and participatory.

- There is a minimum of donor recognition other than personal thanks.

- Volunteers provide most of the circle support.

Examples of Giving Circles

Here are two stories from donors about forming giving groups: the Friday Night ShoeBox Group of Berkeley, California, and the Boston Women's Tzedakah Collective.

Mila Visser't Hooft: The "Friday Night Shoebox"

We started the Friday Night Shoebox in 1998. As people have moved away we've invited others into the group. Now eleven people regularly attend. We have among us doctors, lawyers, nonprofit workers, a geo-chemist, a journalist, a biologist, and a potter. Each meeting we give what we think we would spend on a Friday night out. The amount we each put into the "shoebox" is not known to the rest of the group: we want to make sure people are equal partners, whether they give a bur-rito's worth or the equivalent of a three-course dinner with wine and theater tickets. The money is held at a donor-advised fund at the local community foundation. This lets our donations be tax deductible. The foundation directs our money as we advise.

Our first year was spent primarily on procedural issues and learning what the group considered important to fund. Even now a difference of opinion still exists within the group: some like to give more locally, others more internationally. Exploring various topics (suggested to the group by individual members) has provided us with the chance to have a number of very interesting discussions and develop our decision-making process.

So far, we have raised $23,000 and given away $18,000. Over the years we have increased our grant size and have started to make repeat grants. We don't know if our philanthropic interests will change substantially over time, but we're enjoying learning from each other and seeing how much more we can do with our collective contributions than any one of us could have done alone.

Sarah Feinberg: Boston Women's Tzedakah Collective

The Boston Area Women's Tzedakah Collective is a group of ten young professional women who work and study in the Boston area. Though we have economic, religious, sexual, and cultural differences, we hold a common belief that we receive a great deal from the community in which we live and want to give back to that community. In giving collectively, we overcome our individual differences, knowing we can contribute more than any of us could individually. Our mission is to bring together women who have limited means but enormous passion to make the world better. We want to uncover and explore our essential values. Our goal is to have an impact on our lives and the lives of others.

Since our level of giving is small, we feel that our impact is greater at the local level; we can see it more easily, and we have the chance to become involved with the organizations we donate to.

At the beginning of each giving year, we spend three meetings developing our collective values and becoming informed about issues we are interested in. The first year we chose to focus on domestic violence as an area that could affect each of us. The second year we decided that working on economic justice would challenge us to focus on money in a socially productive way, to push ourselves in an area in which we felt less comfortable, to focus on some of the root causes of societal problems and enter an area of funding we don't address in our private giving.

Our group meets each month for about two hours. There are four official volunteer positions: two cotreasurers, a premeeting e-mail person, and a note taker. Everyone has an equal stake and voice within the group. We have each committed to participate in at least two community service projects with one or two other members of the collective.

For the first two years, each person contributed $10 per month to the collection. At the end of the second year, as most of us were graduating and entering the working world, we changed the dues structure to be unlimited, but also anonymous, so that everyone will continue to have an equal voice.

In the first year, since we spent so much time learning about philanthropy and our individual ideas and beliefs, we made our funding decision with little information. In the second year, we created a curriculum to learn about the area we were interested in funding and to get hands-on experience through site visits. Groups of no more than three people made a site visit to each organization we were considering and made follow-up phone calls to get more information. Our grant-making decision felt better since we were basing it on data (budget size, constituent size) and other information (how the organization interacts with the rest of the community, structure of the organization and its compatibility with our mission and goals).

By the time we had to make a decision, we understood and trusted each other, and we were able to communicate in a productive way. We decided to fund a smaller organization, and focused on issues of need, sustainability, and fit with our interests. Ultimately, we created a pros and cons chart for the top three organizations we were considering for a donation.

Each member has her own reasons for joining the Tzedakah Collective: some want to meet other women who are committed to giving on a limited income and to be able to make more of a difference than when donating alone. Many want a structured way to donate time and money to causes they believe in. Others join for the social aspect. The collective gives us a way to think constructively about what issues matter to each of us individually and collectively and a way to learn more about issues in the area that we might otherwise not think about. It enables us to take the time to research the best place for our money, which we don't have the time to do on our own.

We like to think of our money helping affect the life of at least one other person, such as helping one extra woman deal with abuse or go to job training, or one extra child have a good place to go to school. This feeling of impact gives us great satisfaction.

Donor Circles

In the 1990s the Ms. Foundation for Women and the Global Fund for Women pioneered a model called Donor Circles. In these programs the organization creates significant pools of money for specific projects or interest areas with gifts of $5,000–$1 million each from major donors. The donor circle is often staffed by the sponsoring agency or foundation, which uses 20 to 35 percent of the income to manage overhead and expansion of the circle. In addition to administrative tasks, these costs support a high level of donor engagement to deepen donors' expertise in giving through site visits or in-service trainings. Such long-term donor education has resulted in donors' expanded commitment to an area of funding or to their partnership with the sponsoring agency.

Donor circles generally consist of ten to twenty-five donors or their representatives who meet three to five times a year to deepen partnerships and collective knowledge among themselves, staff, and advisors. After two years of being a member of a donor circle affiliated with an abused women's center, one donor commented, "I feel as though I am now a donor activist on this issue. In fact, not only will I give more to the battered women's shelter that sponsored the circle, but I will be a champion of this cause in getting friends and more of the community involved. I also have been so moved that I have decided to make a legacy gift in my will to the organization."

Donor-Advised Funds

Donor-advised funds offer an alternative to establishing your own private foundation. Individuals, families, groups, and corporations can establish a donor-advised fund. A donor-advised fund enables a donor to make an outright, irrevocable contribution of cash or securities to an organization that acts as fiscal manager of the fund and distributes the fund's income or assets to nonprofit organizations on the donor's behalf. Donor-advised funds have been available through public foundations, Jewish Federations, and the United Way for many years. In the past five years, financial-services companies such as Fidelity, Vanguard, Schwab, and American Express have also established donor-advised charitable giving programs so that customers' dollars can easily be transferred within an institution for charitable purposes. Where the granting areas are in alignment with their missions, public foundations (such as women's funds and some other community-based foundations) also handle limited numbers of donor-advised funds. It is estimated that nearly $1 trillion is now held in donor-advised funds and family foundations, and the amount of money that has been donated through these funds in the past decade represents a huge area of growth in American philanthropy.

Typically, a minimum of $5,000 to $10,000 is required to open a donor-advised account. The donor or donors may make periodic recommendations to the board of directors or overseers of the account regarding distribution of the fund's income, but these recommendations are not legally binding. In theory, this means that a donor relinquishes ultimate authority over the fund in return for the convenience, tax deductions, and potential cost savings of having a larger institution manage his or her charitable contributions. In practice, however, such institutions rely substantially on donor input to direct how the funds are distributed. Simply put, donor-advised funds allow an individual to exchange ownership of assets for tax and administrative benefits while still maintaining influence, just short of control over how the assets are used.

Among the most commonly marketed benefits of donor-advised funds are the following:

- They are easy to establish.
- There is no need to involve your own attorney.
- Administration of the fund is handled by the parent organization.
- A charitable deduction can be taken as soon as the donation to the fund is made, even if the fund's distributions take place over several years. Thus making a single gift to a donor-advised fund can provide a well-timed charitable tax deduction without rushing major gift decisions.
- Currently, no capital gains tax is imposed on long-term appreciated securities donated to these funds.
- Costs to manage the funds are low; annual fees total approximately 1 to 7 percent of each fund's principal, which includes investment fees as well as the fee for basic administration of grants. Many community foundations have grantmaking staff who can also be contracted for special or expanded research, due diligence, or evaluation.
- The fund balance grows from both additional gifts and investment earnings and growth.

- Because an institution is managing the fund, it can carry on donors' charitable values beyond their lifetimes.

- Financial and programmatic reports are informative and easy to read; some online services and private exchange forums especially for donors provide added value.

- Donor education programs or site visits are sometimes provided for fund holders, especially through community foundations.

When thinking about setting up a donor-advised fund, be aware of the following potential challenges and think about how you would handle them:

- In most philanthropic or donor-advised accounts established in financial-service institutions the funds are typically managed in much the same way as financial accounts, with the emphasis on administration and distribution rather than on donor engagement and education. As a result, the process can sometimes feel transactional rather than transformational. If you want more engaged philanthropy, you'll need to take the lead. Some institutions offer increased levels of service to those willing to pay for more research or higher levels of analysis or participation. If you are setting up a donor-advised fund simply to pass through your gifts to one entity so that record keeping or anonymity can be maintained, then

---

DONOR DIVA

Stay informed. If you decide to be an anonymous donor through a donor-advised fund, you may also want to make a small donation outside of the fund ($100–$500), through your personal checkbook, to your highest-funded projects. That way you can get direct information about the progress of the organizations and leaders you care about. You can also ask your donor-advised staff to share with you information such as annual reports and evaluations of the agencies before you consider repeat funding (reports go to the institution where your donor-advised fund is housed).

these kinds of donor-advised funds are an easy option. But if you want a higher level of learning, ask about your options for donor engagement and complement your donor-advised funding with other active collaborations with public or social change funds, donor and activist circles, or any of the vehicles mentioned here.

• The financial services institution or community foundation managing your fund may not have experience in working with an outside philanthropic advisor or researcher you may wish to hire. Ask if they do and what the fiduciary and management needs will be. Some institutions are able to offer such team efforts only to larger fund holders (such as donors giving away $100,000 or more a year).

• At some financial institutions or community foundations, a single staff person may manage hundreds of donor-advised funds. Before you place your money, learn what level of research and engagement are available for your account or what additional services you may purchase. Be sure the person you collaborate with has program and community experience in your area of interest, not simply philanthropic administrative experience. Find out if staff members work in a team and what the team expertise may be given your interest areas or objectives. And communicate clearly your expectations before signing your contact with the entity on whom you will be dependent for administrative services.

• The staff of the community foundation or financial services institution holding your donor-advised assets may not have expertise in the interest area you choose to give to, or they may not know the current status of a specific group you have heard about or previously given to. You may need to take time to educate them or to ask them to update their knowledge in the area you care about. And you may need to bring a philanthropic advisor or community leader into your team for sound and ongoing advice and networking. Increasingly, donor-advisor funds are creating community and family-based teams to aid in decision making. Sometimes the foundations will help host or administer these meetings (if you are a client paying extra fees for this service), and sometimes all the work is best done by a volunteer or your own administrative or programmatic assistant. If you find you are not getting the quality or service you anticipated, speak with your donor services manager to try to improve the level of care before going elsewhere. Growth in the donor-advised fund areas has made for much competition, so be sure you have what you need for a positive experience. Annual reviews of your process and management are a good idea as well.

- Check to see if the entity managing your funds has a geographic restriction on where the funds can be distributed, such as restrictions against giving nationally or globally.

- There is no legal requirement for the institution to move any percentage of your donor-advised fund into the community each year. Some foundations encourage a 5 percent payout of assets, however. Moreover, the financial-services institution or community foundation that manages your funds often benefits from fees acquired based on assets held. Therefore the burden of responsibility for making sure your money keeps moving into the nonprofit world is on you.

Venture Philanthropy

In the past couple of decades, a new generation of business entrepreneurs has joined the effort to address social issues. These donors, referred to as venture philanthropists, apply the principles and practices of venture capitalism to the nonprofit sector, including long-term partnerships and strategic management assistance to leverage and augment financial investments. Although one researcher noted that the venture philanthropy field is "so diverse and unsettled it resembles the Wild West," several of the existing venture philanthropy models share a number of characteristics:

- Donors refer to themselves as investors and have high investor engagement.

- Investors initiate projects by convening people and resources as well as responding to requests for funding.

- Investment is long term (three to six years) rather than year-to-year.

- Investors act as managing partners rather than checkbook partners.

- Investors require ongoing accountability rather than follow-up evaluation.

- Investors provide cash, expertise, and problem solving, and closely monitor projects.

- Investors plan their exit or transition from the partnership from the beginning.

In practice, venture philanthropy models range widely, from multidonor funds that adhere closely to the practices of venture capitalists to foundations of wealthy individuals that, while new, actually operate much like traditional grantmakers.

Venture philanthropists refer to the nonprofit partners in whom they invest as social entrepreneurs. Social entrepreneurs are typically described as nonprofit professionals creating sustainable profit models for organizations within a business environment.

Venture philanthropists attempt to counter the undercapitalization of infrastructure that leaves many nonprofits in a constant state of struggle. They point out that traditional foundations tie funds directly to the organization's programs, while leaving it to the nonprofit to find the additional funds necessary to support operational effectiveness. As a result, many nonprofits are unable to raise funds to improve their computer systems and data infrastructure or recruit and train qualified staff.

Some of the philanthropists created by Internet success, including those behind the Google Foundation and eBay's Pierre Omidyar, are applying the type of entrepreneurial approaches that created their successful Internet companies to their philanthropic work. Omidyar Network specifically seeks to invest in social good, with investments going to both nonprofits and for-profits seeking to make the world a better place. At www.omidyar.net, people can connect around issues and even develop projects that may receive small grants of $5,000 to $20,000. The omidyar.net community has also been given funds to distribute, offering the community a new form for figuring out the beneficiaries. In addition to the monetary offerings, and perhaps more important and effective, the community space encourages conversation around shared areas of interest, fostering connections and resource sharing among community members.

Other technologists with wealth, such as eBay entrepreneur Jeff Skoll, have used their personal foundations to contribute to social entrepreneurial projects that blend income generation with improving communities and the environment.

Nonprofit Venture Forums

Nonprofit venture forums represent a new model of showcasing nonprofit groups that you may want to investigate replicating in your community. The most prominent example was organized by Craigslist Foundation, developed by the online community at www.craigslist.org, which connected local nonprofits with philanthropists who wanted to learn more and become involved.

The venture forums generated funding and resources for small, social change organizations and educated donors about a variety of new groups. They have also

SOCIAL VENTURE PARTNERS

Essential to the process of being a venture philanthropist are learning opportunities. One group, Social Venture Partners, was the brainchild of computer software pioneer Paul Brainerd, who enlisted other technology industry leaders as founders. The purpose of Social Venture Partners (SVP) was to build a philanthropic organization on a venture capital model. Since its founding, SVP (www.svpseattle.org) has served as a solid incubator for philanthropic convening and experimentation in the Pacific Northwest and has developed SVPs in other cities across the country that share core principles. Each Social Venture Partner commits to a minimum annual contribution of $5,500 for at least two years.

Social Venture Partners are committed to helping bolster the success of each of the nonprofit groups they are involved with. Such involvement ranges from hands-on work, such as mentoring a child or setting up a Web site, to management support in the areas of finance, strategic planning, fund development, legal work, marketing, and more. Although partners are not required to contribute time and expertise, more than two-thirds do.

Most of the work takes place in small groups of partners, who research social and environmental issues, make investment decisions, and organize volunteer capacity-building efforts to help investees. Since SVP was launched in 1997, they have invested in more than forty nonprofits, granting more than $9 million and providing tens of thousands of hours of volunteer time and expertise.

SVP offers a range of information, workshops, and resources to enhance the personal philanthropy of its partners. Speakers share their expertise on topics such as creating personal giving plans or social entrepreneurship, and on specific social issues, such as children's programs, education, and the environment. They also have exemplary documents and evaluation tools on their Web site as well as an annual conference for all the national and global partner funds to stimulate and share innovation, capacity building ideas, and measurable impact. To manage its growth, SVP sparked the creation of its own incubator, SVPInternational (www.svpi.org), to support and foster a network of SVP organizations worldwide.

held venture fairs in which nonprofits had the opportunity to present their solutions for community issues to more than two hundred diverse members of the giving community. Each evening focused on a different topic—for example, youth-led groups, cultural arts groups, and international programs. The donors came prepared with a packet on each group, including a pledge form with which they could make donations that evening.

Six fairs in one year produced more than $160,000 in cash grants, along with donations of pro bono services and the acquisition of board members and even office space. Another benefit was the consultation the sixty finalists received in presenting their case. Donors, too, benefited by learning about local issues and their possible solutions and being introduced to social change organizations they might never have known about.

COMMUNITY-BASED PHILANTHROPY

Over the course of the twentieth century, what was commonly thought of as philanthropic giving expanded from being the purview of a handful of wealthy industrialists and business owners seeking to balance their amassed wealth with public charity to incorporate more broad-based involvement. The United Way, begun in the 1920s, was the first large organization to pool donors' funds and distribute them to community projects. The creation of traditional community foundations followed, building permanent philanthropic assets in particular geographic areas. As community foundations attracted unrestricted donations, they could distribute those funds to established health, human services, arts, and education institutions.

Beginning in the 1960s and 1970s, an even more democratic form of organized philanthropy emerged. Women, people of color, and others whose issues and organizations were not being supported by traditional foundations and the United Way forged new ground by creating community-based public foundations whose missions were to support grassroots organizations working specifically for societal change. In the late 1970s the Funding Exchange (www.fex.org) gathered many of the alternative funds that were committed to providing support to grassroots organizing locally, nationally, and internationally under one umbrella and sought to strengthen their services and capacities. There are now some sixteen funds affiliated with the Funding Exchange and many with other networks.

These public foundations differ from other funders in their distinctive practices of giving and to whom. Democratic governance structures ensure that decision-making bodies are representative of the communities served by the foundations' programs. Often, donors and activists make decisions together, allocating grants according to the combined wisdom of a diverse group of people. They support organizations whose work addresses the root causes of social, economic, and environmental problems. For example, while a traditional charity might fund a homeless shelter, a community-based foundation might fund community groups working on policy issues related to affordable housing, services for the mentally ill, and living wage standards. In this way, community-based philanthropy is working to address the underlying issues that lead to homelessness as a social problem.

In the late 1990s, a national, publicly supported foundation called Changemakers was founded to help promote community-based philanthropy efforts. Providing guidance for the field of community-based philanthropy, Changemakers has compiled the following set of values derived from and defining the work of community-based philanthropic organizations:

- *Accountable:* Practicing honesty and transparency and answering to a wider community

- *Compassionate:* Being motivated to uplift all beings

- *Inclusive:* Valuing all people equally and treating people with respect without regard to race, culture, religion, language, immigration history, age, class, sexual orientation, gender, or (dis)abilities

- *Democratic:* Involving a broad range of constituencies in decision-making processes

- *Strategic:* Addressing root causes of social, economic, and environmental problems, often with innovative and creative approaches

- *Collaborative:* Working in partnership with like-minded organizations and building bridges between donors and grantees

Changemakers says, "Community-based social change philanthropy is about trusting that people in a community can develop the best solutions to the social and economic challenges they face." Its publication, *Legacy & Innovation, A Guidebook for Families on Social Change Philanthropy,* describes groundbreaking new models for ways that families and individuals can partner with communities to share common goals of better philanthropy.[3]

Because community-based philanthropy helps to build local movements for social change, these foundations are closely tied to the communities they serve and are often the first place to which new, small, or cutting-edge organizations turn for financial support. By the early 2000s, the family of community-based public foundations had grown to more than two hundred organizations encompassing broad social justice funds; women's funds; funds serving lesbian, gay, bisexual, and transgendered populations; and funds in communities of color.

These are community institutions in the broadest sense. Not only do they make grants, they often act as a nexus for networking and community organizing. They also offer opportunities for donors to engage in meaningful ways with people of different classes, races, religions, and cultures. Most major cities and more than twenty countries now have at least one such organization that would welcome you as a donor or volunteer.

chapter NINE

Organizational Giving: Family Foundations and Corporate Giving

*The most effective philanthropy helps people
help themselves and preserves their self-respect.*

—Eugene C. Dorsey

Chapter Eight provided a survey of the vehicles available for making philanthropic gifts. This chapter goes into more depth on two such vehicles: family foundations and corporate giving.

Of approximately 71,000 foundations in the United States, more than 36,700 are family foundations.[1] The Council on Foundations defines a family foundation as one in which the donor or the donor's relatives play a significant governing role. The fact that the number of family foundations doubled in the past twenty years[2] reflects not only tax changes that encouraged the formation of foundations (as well as donor-advised funds) but also families' strong desires to use the form of a foundation as a tool to bring families closer together.

What begins for many heads of family as a wish to shelter family-held or earned resources from taxes can evolve into a creative way for families to get to know each other better and work together for the public good. "I think it's one of the nicest investments allowed in the tax world," said Reed Hundt, the former chairman of the Federal Communications Commission. "We didn't know all the things we would want to contribute to over the next five to ten years. So we said, 'Let's put the money aside while we make up our minds.'"

To support families and legacy initiators in making those decisions on grantmaking and grantmaking processes, advisors and consultants to family foundations have become a new industry. Organizations such as the National Center on Family Philanthropy (www.ncfp.org), the Council on Foundations' Family Foundation program (www.cof.org), or the Association of Small Foundations (www.smallfoundations.org), and those that can be found through Inspired Legacies (www.inspiredlegacies.org) provide advice, facilitation of family retreats and meetings, coaching, referrals, publications, and conferences. Wealth advisors, philanthropic consultants, and community foundation staff are skilled at helping families find the best resources to create healthy family dialogue and decision-making processes. They can help family members sort out their values and interest areas and come to some guiding principles and processes that can make family and community interactions valuable and respectful to all. Many families are seeing the wisdom expressed by such legacy initiators as David and Lucile Packard, who placed on the board of their family foundation not only their children as they came of age but also community advisors and leaders to support exponential analysis and broader thinking.

Starting a family foundation is not the only way for your family to give together or with others. Many donors at all levels of wealth are bypassing the family foundation option and establishing donor-advised funds in their family's name in order to take advantage of the administrative and programmatic wisdom and services of established donor-advised fund managers. Having a foundation permits greater choice and flexibility, but it also requires more attention and time to manage, including hiring support. (See Chapter Eight for more on donor-advised funds.)

If you have at least $1 million (some say $5 million is a better starting point), then starting a family foundation is one option for directing your charitable giving. In doing so, there are important considerations about your management preferences and needs, your realistic and available time, and the reality of whether your family members (spouse or significant other, children) have the time or desire to acquire the skills to run a family foundation.

If you decide to start a family foundation, you can begin by determining whether your accountant or lawyer is qualified to set it up, or by researching other options for assistance through the Council on Foundations or other information sources.

Family foundations must give away at least 5 percent of the fund's asset value annually. That 5 percent can include the foundation's expenses for investments and administration, resulting in less giving going directly to nonprofits. Although it is legal for foundations to count these expenses in their 5 percent of giving, it has also meant that their assets are growing substantially while grantees may not be benefiting from this growth to the degree that could make substantive change. A growing number of foundations are giving at least 5 percent, and some substantially more when their returns on investment are greater, regardless of their expenses. They reason that these funds would have been heavily taxed and therefore available for public benefit through government spending. They take seriously the privilege of being able to steward and move these funds into public benefit in ways that they determine, and see the importance of moving as much money as possible into that public benefit stream, rather than simply building up assets under management.

Because the giving threshold in America relative to the wealth of its wealthiest donors is very low, family foundations make an important contribution in helping to balance giving inequities. If you have a family foundation or are considering establishing one, think carefully about your giving level each year. The amount you give matters to the health of your grantees and the opportunities for your family to make an impact, while remaining in alignment with your decision on the life cycle and health of your foundation.

Donors to family foundations can deduct cash gifts of up to 30 percent of their adjusted gross income annually. If you contribute stock, you can write off the total value of the stock, even greatly appreciated stock. To reduce federal estate taxes at your death, all assets given to a foundation (private or public or to any charity) are fully tax deductible.

If you are considering starting a family foundation, keep in mind that just a few hours and a few thousand dollars of an established and experienced consultant's time early in the process can save your family months of difficult decision making. Even better is to work with a philanthropic consultant over several years to help improve the confidence and relationships within your family, disentangle old habits of interacting, and create new and creative ways of making your family foundation a positive experience. (For more on working closely with philanthropic advisors, see Chapter Eleven.) One of the best resources for starting a family foundation is the publication *Splendid Legacy: The Guide to Creating Your*

Family Foundation, from the National Center for Family Philanthropy (see Appendix I, "Resources," on the CD-ROM).

SHARING VALUES AND GOALS

To begin, families can use the sample values and interests lists from Exercise 2.3 in Chapter Two to share their personal (and then collective) values and goals. Families that have begun to discuss giving and volunteering together are often surprised by all they learn. For example, a man learned that the sister he thought he had nothing in common with was a donor to one of the organizations he most cherished. So often we are filled with assumptions from childhood about our siblings and parents. Meanwhile, some of them have become skilled or insightful people! Increasing communication through dialogues and e-mail exchanges, family foundations or family giving funds can provide new ways of relating and can even help heal past differences.

The Loh Family, as Told by Daughter Jessica

Our parents wanted us to help them give away some money so we could work as a family together. My three siblings and I knew we had different values and ideas, so when we found ourselves at our parents' kitchen table, we thought, how will we ever figure out how to collaborate? I would never have guessed that over the next two years I would find myself loving the ideas and involvement of each of my family members.

We began with our values, then wrote up a statement of the world we wanted (I can't believe we had so much in common!) and then spent a long time on the mission and strategies we might approach. We each talked about three favorite nonprofits that we had been funding or volunteering for personally just to get more familiar with our personal choices and passions. At the end of two years, we not only had helped our aging parents get money out the door, we had also learned to listen to each other and respect that we could take the same mission and investments and have varied ways of getting the same results.

It helped to have the advice of our parents' financial and philanthropic advisors. Knowing what we want to fund is one thing, but finding the matches for our mission took dedication, time, and the expertise of professionals and community leaders and activists, who became our guides and partners. Now I can't wait to work with my siblings and their kids more. I can see how the exercise my parents gave us was as much for our bonding and learning as for the extension of my parents' generosity to the community. I felt very grateful for this amazing opportunity.

SHARING DECISION MAKING

If you determine that you and your family will have your own family foundation, two things to consider are the role of community representatives and the participation of the younger generation. Outside or community representatives on your board or decision-making bodies not only can add balance and sometimes peacemaking to family differences, they also can be sources of outside wisdom or mentoring for family members.

DONOR DIVA

Should next-generation donors always defer to the interests of the older, sometimes the founding, generation of the foundation? What if the older members of the family are losing their mental and physical capacities but will not resign or retire? While the founder can be honored with gifts to some of his or her favorite charities, the older generation in return can spark the next generation's creativity in giving by entrusting them with decision-making power over a meaningful amount of the money to be given away or by stepping aside or coaching the next generation as they lead. For example, one-half could be designated to go to the long-time interests of the founder(s) while another quarter is allocated to the next generation to fund their own interests and one-fourth is earmarked for innovative projects or for core operating support of tried-and-true nonprofits the family might want to fund jointly.

NEW IDEAS IN SHARING FOR
FAMILY FOUNDATIONS: DIVIDING THE PIE

Here are two options for how decision making about allocations of family foundation grants could be made that give next-generation or community members meaningful participation.

Option 1:

Foundation founders: 50 percent of grants budget

Next-generation members: 25 percent of grants budget

Joint projects or decisions: 25 percent of grants budget

Option 2:

Foundation founders: 25 percent of grants budget

Next-generation members: 25 percent of grants budget

Joint projects or decisions: 50 percent (These may be made either with community members joining the decision making or by giving the funds to community-based public foundations or workplace federations for their activist-led decision-making processes. For more about involving community activists, see the Changemakers resource, *Legacy & Innovation: A Guidebook for Families and Social Change Philanthropy.*)

Members of the next generation are aware that answers for many of the world's problems will be best sought by engaging decision makers from grassroots communities or turning over family assets and grants to them. *Classified: How to Stop Hiding Your Privilege and Use It for Social Change,* by Karen Pittleman, and *Creating Change Through Family Philanthropy: The Next Generation,* by Alison Goldberg, Karen Pittleman, and Resource Generation, an organization that engages next-generation givers in their twenties and thirties, are full of examples and stories on how different families have used various partnership methods in transforming family-made money to community-informed decision making (see Appendix I on the CD-ROM, "Resources"). This is an exciting expansion of a trend begun in the early 1970s by the previous generation of inheritors who built the community-based foundations that make up the Funding Exchange and the women's foundations. The new generation of inheritors is even more enthusiastic about how better informed our decisions can be with added community support.

There are many choices in decision making:

- Deciding alone
- Deciding with a family member or significant other
- Deciding with a team of family members or friends
- Giving to one's family foundation and letting other family members decide
- Partnering with community members, family, or both
- Partnering in a funding or giving circle with other donors
- Partnering in a funding or giving circle with donors and advisors
- Turning the decision making over friends, family members, or colleagues
- Turning the decision making over to community advisors or respected advisors
- Giving to the United Way, workplace federations, Jewish Federation, religious community pool, community-based or activist-led foundations, or community foundations that have demonstrated community-based needs assessments and community-based decision-making processes that may or may not include other donor activists
- Giving to religious or spiritually based congregations to decide together

Each of these choices deserves consideration. Each has its own learning component, which is what makes philanthropy so interesting! Giving with others is an entirely different way of considering the future and what might make or leverage important change. Many donors give in more than one of these methods. Some have or are part of a family foundation, participate in a giving circle, give at their workplace, have a donor-advised fund, and give out of their checkbooks or with their spouse at home. That's a lot of detail and process to manage. Consider, after trying varied models of partnering with others, if you have a preference or if there is a simpler way for you and your family. You may wish to hire or expand your own administrative or program staff if you are fully engaged in your giving. Community foundations, women's funds, and organizations like The Philanthropic Initiative, Rockefeller Advisors, Foundation Source, DonorsTrust, Tides Foundation, the Funding Exchange, Treskels Foundation, Rudolf Steiner Foundation, or New

World Foundation all have services for family foundations and donors with collaboration, advice, networking, and in some cases, grants management as well.

To engage the younger generation, establishing committees that provide for intergenerational leadership and mentoring can provide a wonderful learning opportunity for both generations. The next generation can offer their ideas and concerns about everything from the grants process to the investment policies.

It's also useful to give the next generation time to meet separately and the means to have their own support, perhaps from a consultant they choose to work with or from contemporaries of another, more experienced family foundation. Expanding the next generation's expertise, leadership, and voices are key steps to making the current intergenerational transfer of wealth successful. Resource Generation (www.resourcegeneration.org) and the organization called YES! (www.yesworld.org) and its program for young inheritors worldwide, called Leveraging Privilege for Social Change, are valuable organizational resources for the younger generation. (See Chapter Twelve for more keys to success in working intergenerationally.)

Before you put your adult children in charge of your foundation, it's best to have a conscious process to manage the transition. The power dynamics between parents and their children at any age are complex, and the requirements of reporting and in areas such as conflict of interest can bring added stress to your family. Careful teamwork, supported by a team of advisors for an extended period until matters get institutionalized or policies and procedures are set, will help smooth the way. In general, if you will be giving away more than $100,000 in a year and have multiple family members voting in varied geographies, independent staff can greatly facilitate the long-term health and well-being of your family and the foundation.

DONOR DIVA

Many high-end donors have numerous giving vehicles to keep track of. Hiring a personal assistant or part-time administrator for your giving or philanthropy can leverage your own capacity and help keep you better organized.

OTHER CONSIDERATIONS

Three final areas regarding family foundations are staffing, site visits, and opportunities for learning.

According to the Foundation Center, roughly one in eight of the larger family foundations (those with $1 million and above) have paid professional staff.[3] The rest are run by family members or volunteers. Although staffing your own foundation is a lot of work, it can be extremely rewarding. As you have read in this chapter, there are many models available that can greatly ease the process and are worth pursuing (see "Family Philanthropy" in Appendix I, "Resources"). But if you want to make your family funding truly transformative, having administrative staff or support beyond family members is usually the saner route. Hiring adequate staffing or outsourcing most of the work saves enormous time and ultimately resources. Being a professional administrator for your family has its risks and rewards, but it also presents demands that few young families can balance. One new mother who was given the honor of setting up a new foundation office for her father, mother, and sister described it this way: "I had no idea how detailed the work would be. I had training as a teacher, but did not realize how many decisions would be required and how hard it would be to get my family to agree to my leadership as the new director of the foundation. Initially, I thought it was my inexperience. Before long, I realized some of it was their unconscious envy that I was being paid for my work. My husband became tired of our constant family difficulties, and I had much less time for our five-year-old son. As with so many part-time jobs, there was not enough help, so I worked overtime. Within two and a half years, I resigned, we closed the office, and we asked another organization to take over the administration. I did not see it as a failure. I learned to set up the office and our grantmaking systems, and we set many policies and procedures that we still use. But having people who are not family members as the administrators has been a much better decision for us all. Finally my father understands that I was just trying to follow the laws to be sure we were doing proper research and not just doubting his opinion!"

The National Center for Family Philanthropy (www.ncfp.org) and the National Network of Consultants to Grantmakers (www.nncg.org) both offer referrals to consultants as well as performance and ethical standards for those considering this important investment in the capacity of your family foundation.

Site visits to projects you are interested in are also invaluable. Only a very small percentage of foundations make site visits to nonprofits they fund or are considering funding. This is not only one of the most rewarding parts of foundation and funding work, it is also the heart of due diligence and understanding communities. A great deal of education and community-building occurs in these visits. See Worksheet 10.2 in Chapter 10 for how to prepare for a site visit. Be sure to maximize your family experience by having materials from the organizations in advance and by a review of their Web sites. Decide ahead of the visit who will introduce your family, who will share the questions, and who will thank the group and provide some closure and evaluation of the visit.

Finally, take advantage of the many opportunities for learning and expanding your foundation's perspective. Such opportunities can include hiring representatives to inform you about current issues in foundation giving, or sending family members to national, regional, or local issue-specific or industry-related trainings, site visits, or conferences, such as the Council on Foundation's Family Foundation Conference, held each spring in a different location around the country (see www.cof.org), or the Association of Small Foundations' conferences (www.small foundations.org), or Resource Generation's conferences for the Next Generation of Family Foundations (www.resourcegeneration.org). Here you will find hundreds of peer family members and advisors seeking to make family foundations an effective source for all involved and an annual agenda packed with new management, grantmaking, and investment standards. Attending one of these conferences every few years keeps families aware of the professionals and leading families in the field and gives you a chance to see the annual reports and good works of hundreds of others from around the country (be sure to bring your own annual report as well).

DEVELOPING A "STATEMENT OF DONOR LEGACY"

A statement that sets forth the legacy that founding donors wish to leave can be an invaluable tool for a family foundation, as it provides important background information about the foundation's mission for present and future trustees (see the sample statement).

The journal *Living the Legacy: The Values of a Family's Philanthropy Across Generations,* from the National Center for Family Philanthropy, suggests some things that might appear in or contribute to a donor legacy statement (see Appendix I on the CD-ROM, "Resources"):

- The donor's life and accomplishments
- The causes the donor is interested in (generally or with reference to specific organizations) that grow out of that background
- The values, traditions, and perspectives that animate the donor's life and giving history
- The resulting specific intent of the donor for the foundation
- The way the donor wishes succeeding generations of trustees to perpetuate this legacy over time

In an article in the same journal issue, "Donor Legacy: What Is It That History Teaches?" Ronald Austin Wells writes,

> Legacy . . . is an organic, living entity. . . . [Legacy] encompasses not only the donor's original statement of intent, but also all of the subsequent work and accomplishments of the foundation and its grantees. Like all living things, legacy constantly changes, thriving under favorable conditions and waning under those that are less so. And as with all living things, legacy can be nurtured or starved. As time passes, the legacy may become anachronistic, something that has petrified into a fossil fit only for a museum; or it may, treated with sympathy, compassion and intelligence, evolve into a perpetual monument to the human spirit. It is the clarity of the donor's instructions, infused with a trust in the wisdom and good will of succeeding generations, that will decide what the donor's legacy will become.
>
> Indeed, is it not the ethical responsibility of all who are involved in the foundation's work—trustees, family members, staff, and grantees—to vigorously nurture the foundation's legacy through their work over the decades?[4]

Inevitably, family foundations move from being solely directed by the original donor to having decisions made by a board with multiple generations of the original donor's family and sometimes the involvement of nonfamily members. A donor legacy statement can ease any doubts or anxieties family members might have about giving away the donor's wealth or assuming responsibility for more of the foundation's grantmaking—or even about continuing the foundation after the life of the founding donor or donors. Such a statement describes the donor's vision and intent in setting up the foundation and touches on the history of the foundation's giving to date. In doing so, it effectively takes some areas of decision making off the table, reducing opportunities for family discord or contention. A donor legacy statement is also an important guide to the donor's wishes for when they will no longer be available for consultation.

Founding donors and board members are involved in creating this document. In it, the donors clarify the values they want to continue in the decision making of future generations and how much latitude future generations will have in making decisions that might substantially transform the nature of the foundation's giving. Where a board already exists, board members should think about questions that might arise about future giving of the foundation and their individual preferences about its operation.

As a statement of donor legacy made by the family foundation, the document should be formally approved by the board. If a family is creating a donor intent statement when the original donors can no longer be consulted, the process must rely more on detective work and recalled anecdotal information. Some families choose to enlist the help of an outside philanthropic consulting firm, professional writer, or videographer for their expertise and objectivity in conceiving this document. You can record your family's history through the help of someone you know or with a professional, or you can learn to do it yourself through organizations such as www.storycorps.net.

SAMPLE STATEMENT OF DONOR LEGACY

The following statement was created with the help of the consulting firm Grants Management Associates (see Appendix I on the CD-ROM, "Resources") and adopted by the foundation board in 1997, one year before Sidney Stoneman, who, along with his wife, was the original donor, passed away.

In 1957 we established this foundation in memory and honor of Sidney's parents. Over the years, it has served as a vehicle for our charitable giving.

When the foundation was established, its legal instrument made no specifications about the geographic reach of the foundation's giving, the composition of its board, or the focus for its charitable contributions. For many years, the foundation operated informally, with funding decisions initiated primarily by Sidney and with little public visibility.

In 1990 we decided to involve our extended family in the foundation, and formalized the decision by hiring Grants Management Associates to assist with the development of guidelines and the establishment of grant-making processes. We developed an eight-person board, including three nonfamily members, and published guidelines that describe a grantmaking process for the foundation and a geographic scope.

As the foundation moves into the future, at some point it will do so without our involvement. When we pass on, the foundation will become larger and will represent a greater responsibility as well as a greater opportunity. We have every confidence that our wonderful family will provide the thoughtful guidance required along the way.

As the foundation's donors, we would like to think that the foundation will always be rooted in the values and traditions of our family. The purpose of this document is to convey this wish to current and future members of the board of directors.

Part of the Stoneman family's identity and interests have been in the Jewish community. Our participation in this community has been an acknowledgement of our roots and has never promoted sectarianism. Rather, it has supported the achievement of excellence among Jewish people and the fostering of a spirit of brotherhood and inclusiveness with all peoples. We would like our family foundation to acknowledge and continue this participation in the Jewish community. While we have been significant contributors to specific Jewish organizations, we do not want to specify the recipients of future foundation support in this area. Nor do we wish to suggest that a certain amount or portion of available grant funds be directed to these organizations. We ask simply that some funds be directed to Jewish organizations, in recognition of the family's history and values that have been part of the Jewish community in this country and beyond.

Second, the Stoneman family has its roots in Boston. Generations of the family made their homes here, starting with Sidney's father, who emigrated from Russia. We would like the Stoneman Family Foundation to continue to have a Boston presence, with a preference but not a requirement that the foundation annually allocate a significant portion of its grants funds to organizations in the Boston area. At the same time, we understand and expect that the balance of the grant funds will be used to support organizations in the geographic area of interest to family members who are serving as foundation directors.

In relation to contributions in the Boston area, there are a few with which we have had a deep involvement over the years. These include Beth Israel Hospital, the Boston Symphony Orchestra, and Combined Jewish Philanthropies. These organizations have been beneficiaries of significant financial contributions made by both the foundation and us personally. For the future, we request that the foundation directors continue to consider requests from these organizations and judge them in the light of their relevance to the needs of society and their responsiveness to the purposes of the foundation.

The Stoneman Family Foundation always has been a family affair. We would like this to continue into the future. We feel the best way to ensure continued family involvement is by board membership. It is our hope that Stoneman family members will constitute a majority of the board in perpetuity. Failing that, we would request liquidation of the foundation. This being said, we make no further presumptions about representation of different branches and generations of the family, except to say that we expect that the foundation directors will establish policies relating to board membership that are inclusive and equitable.

CORPORATE GIVING AND CORPORATE FOUNDATIONS

The Foundation Center defines corporate philanthropy as "activities that companies voluntarily undertake to have a positive impact on society, including cash contributions, contributions of products and services, volunteerism, and other business transactions to advance a cause, issue or nonprofit organization."

Although large and small businesses are often very generous with contributions of goods or services, business and corporate philanthropy represents only a small portion of donated funds (see Figure 1.1 from *Giving USA* in Chapter One)—4.2 percent of all the funds contributed to the nonprofit sector in 2006. While corporate profits have risen dramatically, corporate giving has declined since its 1986 peak of 2 percent of pretax profits; in 2006, corporate giving represented just 1 percent of pretax profits. The forty-year average for corporate giving is a dismal 1.2 percent of profits.

The picture may be changing, however. The number of corporate foundations has doubled since the 1980s, and a new generation of corporate leaders is bringing new attention to corporate citizenry. If you are a business or corporate owner, consider the various philanthropic ways of joining your communities in addition to cash support: lending executives to nonprofit causes, giving teams time to volunteer together (for instance, building a Habitat for Humanity house, creating a team for a walkathon, or matching tickets to local arts events), encouraging individual employee volunteering through time-off programs, and donating equipment or services. Some companies give incentives for employees who align with certain values. For example, British Petroleum gives free parking spaces to employees who drive high-fuel-efficiency cars or cars that run on alternative fuels. Some workplaces are building volunteer time into the agendas of annual meetings and conferences and calculating and offsetting their carbon footprints.

The Committee to Encourage Corporate Philanthropy (www.corporatephilanthropy.org), of which Paul Newman is a founder, is working to increase corporate giving by advancing the case for philanthropy and inspiring other business leaders to "make a lasting commitment to community giving."

Consumers notice and appreciate corporations that support worthy causes. The *1999 Cone/Roper Cause Related Trends Report* found that 76 percent of consumers would switch brands or retailers to one associated with a good cause when price and quality are equal, and that 87 percent of employees at companies with cause-related programs feel a stronger sense of loyalty to their employer.

If you are part of a corporation—either as a staff member or as a shareholder in a family business—and you want to encourage the corporation to address social objectives in an inspired and planned way, the following are some tips and references for more information and examples of how corporations can practice inspired philanthropy.

Starting a Corporate Foundation

As with developing a personal giving plan, being involved in starting a corporate foundation begins with defining priority interest areas and ways to get involved in these areas. These activities, sometimes called "corporate engagement," form part of an ongoing corporate strategy for community involvement that may also have a goal of enhanced business performance. Such activities offer the potential to have a positive impact on local communities as well as to have direct or indirect benefit to the corporation. Corporate engagement can include both philanthropic activities and activities that tap into the corporation's core competencies and operations, such as its power to purchase, develop products, invest, market, hire and train, and innovate.

In many cases, the most challenging aspect of corporate philanthropy is persuading others in the company that it is a worthwhile undertaking. Corporate board members, shareholders, and even employees can perceive philanthropy as a drain on scarce resources or a distraction from the "business of business." A Ford Foundation–sponsored research report written in November of 2000 by John Weiser and Simon Zadek, *Conversations with Disbelievers: Persuading Companies to Address Social Challenges,* brings together much of the available quantitative evidence of the financial benefits that companies can gain by effectively addressing social challenges as a core element of their business strategy.[5] It summarizes three broad sets of drivers that have moved corporate managers to address social objectives:

- *Values:* represents an expression of core company values

- *Strategy:* supports or enhances a key long-term business strategy

- *Pressure:* responds to a short-term external pressure, such as regulation or advocacy group activities

Values, strategy, and consideration of community needs match key components of the Inspired Philanthropy model of creating a giving plan.

One step to starting a corporate foundation or giving program is to convene or survey a representative cross section of company stakeholders (key executives, employees, board members, and community members) to answer the following questions:

- What is our motivation for creating a philanthropic initiative? Are we interested in doing good or merely looking good?

- What are the values of this corporation? How can our values best be expressed to the world?

- Who are we most interested in benefiting—our employees, our community, our industry, our country, the world?

- How can we best leverage the full range of our resources to provide a win–win outcome for our stakeholders and community?

- Do we have enough philanthropic expertise on our team or do we need outside help?

STRENGTHENING CORPORATE GIVING

If you are a company with a giving record, here are some steps to strengthen your corporate giving:

1. Review your company's true commitment to giving and service. Get the numbers and consider ways to increase your company's generosity and position in the community.

2. Set goals to increase your company's direct and indirect giving (employee lending and material donations).

3. Create a culture of giving all year long.

4. Reward outstanding employees (not just management) with matching their donations. Increase your matches for arts and other community engagement opportunities.

5. Increase giving and volunteerism as part of your employee and management perks and training.

6. Spend less on corporate training and take your teams to work with Habitat for Humanity or other team-building volunteer efforts.

7. Establish, if you don't yet have one, a corporate giving office, with a staff person.

8. Survey your employees, including employees' special-interest groups, and shareholders on priority areas of funding or get the advice of the United Way, the local Community Foundation, or local philanthropic advisors for ways to have key impact in your community in alignment with corporate goals.

9. Require all management to have giving plans and make their service and giving known to employees and the community.

10. Sponsor a giving fair at least once a year, inviting the ten to twenty key organizations that your employees give to, and pour on the dollars and the recognition to key community partners.

11. Have your own giving plan at home. Engage your family as a giving mentor and leader.

12. Be a civic leader and encourage your management to do the same. Create awards, incentives, and merit pools of grantmaking for those who excel as generous and exemplary volunteers and donors.

CORPORATE PHILANTHROPY IN ACTION

The Washington Regional Association of Grantmakers (www.washing tongrantmakers.org)—an excellent resource on corporate and other giving—gives the following examples of how small and mid-sized companies have matched their business activities and needs with their corporate giving programs:

- A furniture manufacturer with a strong interest in conserving timber resources funds community projects dedicated to protecting the environment and providing environmental education.

- A grocery store provides funding to area day care centers based on a brief survey of customers that shows day care to be one of their key community concerns.

- A children's footwear company's corporate foundation supports local programs involving children.

- A beer manufacturer forms an alliance with the local chapter of an anti-drunk-driving organization, helping it conduct a poster contest in high schools to publicize the organization's message.

- A small Internet start-up company creates a Web page to post volunteer opportunities in its local community.

And here are some examples from larger corporations:

- Starbucks paid the salary of an executive with ten years' experience with the corporation to work for a year with the antipoverty group CARE to develop a marketing campaign, mentor senior executives, and develop a project management system.

- LensCrafters, Inc., and LensCrafters Foundation send company associates, doctors, and executives on optical missions to rural America and overseas through their "Give the Gift of Sight" program. According to one associate, "The sense of common purpose is so strong that you return with an indelible understanding of what collaboration and teamwork in practice mean. This translates directly into the workplace and leads to much more productive work relationships all around."

Other areas to consider are determining how much to give (either a percentage of pretax net income or a budget line item based on past experience) and deciding how to give (either through direct cash grants based on proposals received or matching employee gifts, or through in-kind contributions of products and supplies or loaned talent).

For more information on the field of corporate philanthropy, check out the following organizations through their Web sites:

- The Center for Corporate Citizenship at Boston College—www.bcccc.net/
- Council on Foundations—www.cof.org
- Wise Giving—www.wisegiving.org
- The Chronicle of Philanthropy—www.philanthropy.com
- The Conference Board—www.conference-board.org
- The United Way—www.unitedway.org
- Choice in Giving—www.choiceingiving.org
- Our Giving Community—www.ourgivingcommunity.org

PART TWO

Strategic and Creative Ways to Leverage Your Giving

Engagement with Groups You Support

*No problem can be solved from the same level
of consciousness that created it.*

—Albert Einstein

The most fulfilling and exciting part of philanthropy—along with seeing the outcomes of your funding—is in the people you meet, the networks of people you find with shared values, and the leaders and activists on the front lines who inspire you.

Although you may fund ten, twenty, or more organizations each year, you are likely to be actively engaged in only a few directly. You may volunteer for one or two—on a board, for instance, or a committee. Or you may be part of an online network or blog that an organization sponsors and thus feel close to the organization, even though your connection to it is mostly virtual. You may feel you know an organization because a friend, child, or other relative is active with it. You may even be funding an organization because it's the favorite of someone you love or respect.

This is how much of giving has always been done. Unless we devote much of our time to our giving, it's unlikely that we will have first-hand knowledge of more than half of our giving list.

Donors have many options in how they want to relate to the groups they support. Choices range from being completely anonymous and sometimes uninvolved with a group (except for their donation) to volunteering in an organization's programs, assuming a leadership role as a board member, or even joining the organization as a founding donor or initial staff person.

Some donors decide to limit their giving so that they can be a more significant or major donor to just one or two groups. That way, they have the chance to have a more substantive role and closer relationships with those organizations. People choose to work more closely with an organization for many reasons, including wanting to work in partnership to create or leverage change, take advantage of leadership opportunities, explore new careers, or create a balance with a job or family. Figure 10.1 shows the likely options for involvement.

Use Exercise 10.1 to determine your current and potential levels of engagement with the groups you give to.

As you get to know a group better, you may discover that you do not want to continue funding them or to continue at your current level of funding or other engagement. Don't be surprised if your volunteering sometimes decreases your level of giving to a group. More often, we fall in love, over and over again, as we wade deeper into getting to know the leaders and the hard work of these groups we fund or those with whom we volunteer.

For groups that remain important to you and with which you wish to have closer relationships, it's very important how you shape those relationships and the effectiveness of the communication between you and the groups. This chapter

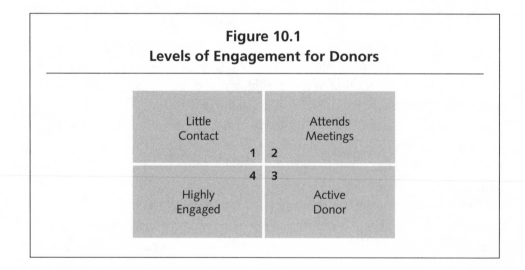

Figure 10.1
Levels of Engagement for Donors

Little Contact	Attends Meetings
1	2
4	3
Highly Engaged	Active Donor

Exercise 10.1
Level of Engagement

List the groups in your giving plan from Worksheet 7.1 in Chapter Seven and indicate the level and nature of your engagement in each, based on the levels of engagement shown in Figure 10.1. For instance, you may be a donor, on the board, a volunteer, or a simple fan.

If there are groups you are engaged with that are not on your giving list, include them as well. Now star (*) or check (✓) the organization(s) with which you might like to engage or participate more. Put a minus sign (–) by groups that you may want to step back from or with which you may be changing your engagement. Some of these may be groups or leaders you have supported for a long time, and you may be ready to seek new partnerships now.

Organization	Level of Engagement (1,2,3,4)	Nature of Engagement	Notes: Next Steps (If Any) and by When

Now, in the final column, note what action steps you will take for each of the groups you want to make a change with, based on your new considerations: state a goal, your next step, and the date by which you will take a step for greater or different engagement.

suggests ways to relate to groups you do or might fund and explores levels of engagement that can help you to see where you are or perhaps to move you from donor to inspired leader.

Finally, it looks at some special circumstances that require sensitive communication, including the questions of giving anonymously, loaning money to nonprofits, and responding to requests from groups outside your sphere of funding.

EFFECTIVE DONOR COMMUNICATION

When you invest in the work of a nonprofit, you are not only expressing your interest in helping to address an issue of concern, but also casting a vote of confidence for the organization's senior staff, board, and advisors. Especially as a major donor, you are likely to want to know just what the organization is doing. However, your enthusiasm and desire for closer contact may outstrip the ability of the organization to respond. Many organizations are funded at a bare-bones level, and each of the senior staff members may already be doing the work of two.

Generally, executive directors recommend that the most productive ways for donors to stay abreast of the organization's work are to attend events, participate in telephone or Web-based donor briefings, and read the group's newsletters, e-messages, Web site postings, annual reports, and other publications. If you are one of many small donors to an organization—providing less than $500 a year—and these standard forms of communication from the organization will not meet your needs, you should discuss your questions and interest with the executive director before making your contribution.

Whereas twenty-five years ago a small nonprofit with two or three staff people may have subsisted on a budget of $100,000 or $200,000, higher costs of living and particularly the high cost of staff salaries, office technology, travel and health care, and retirement benefits (long missing from the nonprofit world) have pushed many nonprofit budgets to three times what they once were. Now we have a nonprofit sector that has begun to offer more reasonable salaries and some benefits. It is important to honor the fact that good people need to sustain themselves, which will require increased fundraising or revenues. This means that to generate sufficient support, organizations may have five hundred to five thousand other donors who join you annually in making a gift. As a result, executive directors and development directors (for the lucky, small percentage of nonprofits who have development staff) typically will have time to interact one-on-one with only one hundred to two hundred of these donors annually by phone or in person (as well as responsibilities to foundation and corporate funders). Other contacts may be made by other volunteers, such as board members or other donors on the development committee.

If you are a major donor, giving more than $500 to $5000, depending on the size of the organization and its staffing, you will most likely be offered the opportunity to interact with senior staff at some point in the year—either in a one-on-one meeting or at an event. These dialogues and events offer important opportunities to meet key staff, learn about the most interesting challenges and solutions emerging from the organization's work, and ask questions. For the few organizations or causes you care most about, attending these events provides your best chance to become a more informed and therefore more effective donor.

DONOR DIVA

Be respectful. Although it is important that you understand the issues the organization is addressing and how it is making the most of your donation, the last thing you want is to dissipate the time of the staff through ad hoc or random requests for information.

Development staff in particular are most likely interested and curious to meet major donors. They are working on cultivating support for the organization or project, and you are sharing your enthusiasm for the organization's work. Most fundraisers are excited, albeit sometimes a little nervous, to make personal connections with donors. For both of you the goal of communication is to be better acquainted so that the relationship and the organization are strengthened. The outcome you should both be seeking is for you to become a better and increasingly generous donor to the organization and a knowledgeable advocate for the group and its cause.

Organizations risk losing key donors by poor or inadequate communication and assuming they know a donor's preferences. As a donor, be sure you and the organization work closely together to maintain trust. If you are hosting an event, make sure you have the chance to sign off on the wording of the invitation and the directions and to maintain the level of privacy that's important to you. If you want to be listed as an anonymous donor, make sure that staff knows that you do not want your name showing up in a year-end givers' list. (More advice for anonymous donors follows in this chapter.)

Staff turnover in small nonprofits makes it essential to put your wishes in writing in a letter that will remain in your donor file. See Appendix E on the CD-ROM for a sample letter you might send or modify to clarify your desires and preferences around your anonymity.

DONOR DIVA

Explain your preferences and then listen. If you have personal preferences in how you want to be contacted and by whom, or you have strong feelings or criticism about the group's communication with you, be very clear about your opinion and let the leadership know your suggestions. Healthy and open communication between key staff and donors can literally make or break an organization.

COMMUNICATING YOUR SUPPORT FOR AN ORGANIZATION

Although it is true that as a donor you will be valued for your financial contributions, your knowledge, contacts, feedback, and insights are valuable as well. Your clarity and recommendations should be duly noted by the nonprofit. If you want to be sure that your voice is heard, e-mail or write the executive director or the board chair of the organization. Written communications can be shared more broadly and remain part of your history and donor file with the organization. When thinking about how you can add value to your support, consider the following questions about what you might ask executive directors, development directors, and key program staff when you have the opportunity to meet with them. You can also add two or three questions of your own:

- In what areas can I, as a donor, be of greater service to the organization? For example, would a challenge grant from me allow you to leverage my contribution to the organization by prompting others to act?

- What are the key issues the organization is focusing on this year? If I know someone with expertise in these areas may I put them in touch with the staff or a board member?

- Are there ways I might contribute my expertise to the organization? (Skills that most nonprofits need include Web expertise, marketing, accounting, networking, fundraising, legal or accounting consultation, and program or community knowledge.)

- What are some of the directions or new strategies or programs you are actively pursuing based on your strategic planning or leadership discussions?

- If you could have exactly what you needed in order to have greater impact, what would that be now? (I am not saying I can give you this but I would like to hear your vision.)

If you are a major donor, it also makes sense for you to initiate communication with the executive director or other development staff to see how you can augment your involvement. If you and the staff person agree on it, it can be especially productive for you to invite a small group of your friends who might be interested in supporting the organization to a meeting with key staff, board members, or both. At a small networking meeting of this nature the director can speak of cutting-edge issues and you can be an advocate on behalf of the work you support. Just as valuable, your extension and outreach expand the social reach of the nonprofit you may care to serve as your mission partner.

COMMUNICATING DONOR INTENT

If you intend to give an organization $500 or more a year, tell them in advance of your gift and when they can expect it. This information will help development staff with their planning. Likewise, if you're certain that you will no longer be supporting a particular organization, a short note, e-mail, or phone call early in the year

---

ADVICE FROM A DEVELOPMENT DIRECTOR

Here is some advice to donors from Dana Gillette, former development director at the Peace Development Fund and now the managing director at Class Action.

- Find some good groups that you want to support and stick with them. If you are just getting to know a group, you may want to start out with a smaller gift and see how it is received. Increase your support over time. A steady donor is an incredible asset.

- If someone contacts you about meeting or about supporting a cause, respond. Whether you say yes or "I'm interested, but not available right now" or "I'm interested in your cause, but not in meeting" or "No, I'm not interested," your clarity helps.

- Let organizations know what you need. If you only want to receive written materials, say so. Being respectful is a two-way street. As a donor, you deserve to be respected. So do the staff or volunteers who are moving valuable work forward. Understand your power as a donor and use it wisely.

- Use your perspective to provide feedback to staff and board members. If you see something encouraging that they are doing, let them know. It is wonderfully uplifting for staff to receive an occasional e-mail saying, "Keep up the good work" or "What a great newsletter." If you are withdrawing support, tell them why. Hard-working staff want to know where they are letting their supporters down as well as when there is praise to receive.

will save it from spending the resources to gain or regain your support (see a sample notification of withdrawal of support in Appendix E).

Healthy transitions when a donor leaves an organization are as important as they are in any relationship. Have a transition plan and communicate, communicate, communicate. Especially if you have been a founder or a key board member or donor, it often helps to hire a consultant during such an important transition in order to create a plan so that the nonprofit you have helped to grow can keep growing and being productive. A word of advice to founders: "founder syndrome" is when founders and those around them lose the capacity due to power and longevity to tell the truth to each other. When that happens, it can be helpful to hire a consultant so that you can have a positive transition out of the group.

Even more important than letting a group know that you won't be continuing your gift is to say why, especially if you've become discontented with the organization or don't agree with its direction. Honest feedback is as useful as it is rare. Staff are usually eager to hear how their work is perceived. They want the chance to review decisions that community members, including donors, don't agree with and to clarify misunderstandings.

Healthy and conscious transitions enable organizations to maintain and expand their work. Poor transitions or leaders who stay too long without a clear mandate from their board and staff can waste money, time, and opportunities for progress. Annual reviews of board and staff, or visits with donors to get feedback, help nonprofits to be accountable.

Further, if you plan to stop giving a major gift to an organization, you may want to work with it to help fill the gap. Consider reviewing the following questions with the development or executive director:

- How can I help you make a healthy transition away from the support I have been providing?

- Could I allocate a percentage of my final donation to the organization to be used for additional fundraising so that you can identify a donor(s) to replace me?

- Are there any introductions I can make to help you when I am no longer contributing to the organization?

- Are there ways I might contribute my expertise to the organization (for example, accounting, networking, marketing)?

DONOR ENGAGEMENT

Peter Frumkin, a professor of public affairs at the Lyndon B. Johnson School of Public Affairs, director of the RGK Center on Philanthropy and Community Service at the University of Texas at Austin, and author of *Strategic Giving: The Art and Science of Philanthropy,* has much wisdom on the nature of philanthropic engagement. "Engagement," he says, "is a critical part of the style defined by a donor. It has implications not only for the overall fit and alignment of the giving strategy, but it also has very clear implications for the nonprofit organizations that are on the other side of the table."

He continues:

> Finding a level of engagement that both satisfies the donor and that adds value to the recipient organization is not always easy. Sometimes there will be a misalignment between a donor that wants a lot of publicity and a cause or organization that simply cannot mobilize the attention that is sought. Other times, donors will want a relatively low level of engagement, but end up funding an organization that continuously seeks to draw the donor into the organization's governance. . . .
>
> Engagement is something that must neither be declared by donor fiat, nor postulated by a recipient. Instead, engagement needs to emerge from communication between the two parties and should aim toward finding a level of fit and alignment that will satisfy both sides of the philanthropic exchange.[1]

Frumkin describes four main types of philanthropic relationships (see Figure 10.2) that produce greater or lesser congruence between donor and recipient organization and greater or lesser engagement of donor with recipient organization:

- *Contractual relationships,* in which donors and recipients simply give and get under narrowly circumscribed terms and then go their own way

- *Delegating relationships,* in which donors delegate responsibility freely to those doing the work

- *Auditing relationships,* in which trust is low and oversight is extensive so as to monitor the precise use of grant funds

- *Collaborative relationships,* in which the two sides work together closely to achieve a set of mutually agreed upon goals

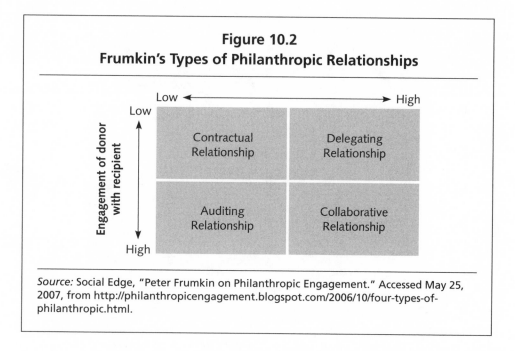

Figure 10.2
Frumkin's Types of Philanthropic Relationships

	Low ←——————————→ High	
Low	Contractual Relationship	Delegating Relationship
High	Auditing Relationship	Collaborative Relationship

(Vertical axis: Engagement of donor with recipient)

Source: Social Edge, "Peter Frumkin on Philanthropic Engagement." Accessed May 25, 2007, from http://philanthropicengagement.blogspot.com/2006/10/four-types-of-philanthropic.html.

"High levels of donor engagement," he notes, "may mean access to resources and talents of great value to the nonprofit. It may also entail a tremendous amount of extra work, as donors need to be handled and satisfied. For this reason, some nonprofits prefer to receive general operating support with as few strings attached as possible. Over time, however, almost all nonprofits learn to work with the different engagement approaches of their donors and understand that considerable variation is to be expected."

Another way to look at the path from less to more inspired and increasingly involved donor is presented in Figure 10.3. This continuum was developed by Changemakers, a national foundation to enhance donor leadership and the community-based funding sector, as part of their curriculum for donors, "The Donor Partner Training." The spectrum shows the steps to becoming a stronger and more active participant in the nonprofit sector, as one moves from being a socially concerned person with resources to becoming a strategic donor, a donor activist or donor partner, a leader or donor organizer, and an inspired philanthropist. Proceeding all the way to the final level could be a full-time endeavor!

Figure 10.3
Leadership Engagement for Donors

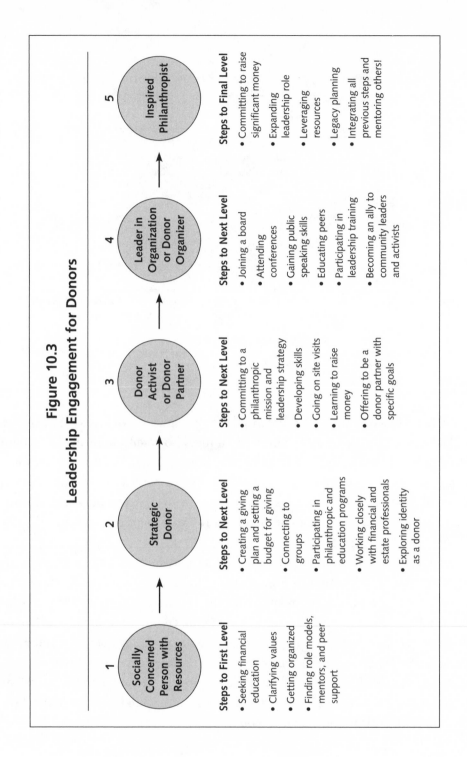

1

Socially Concerned Person with Resources

Steps to First Level

- Seeking financial education
- Clarifying values
- Getting organized
- Finding role models, mentors, and peer support

2

Strategic Donor

Steps to Next Level

- Creating a giving plan and setting a budget for giving
- Connecting to groups
- Participating in philanthropic and education programs
- Working closely with financial and estate professionals
- Exploring identity as a donor

3

Donor Activist or Donor Partner

Steps to Next Level

- Committing to a philanthropic mission and leadership strategy
- Developing skills
- Going on site visits
- Learning to raise money
- Offering to be a donor partner with specific goals

4

Leader in Organization or Donor Organizer

Steps to Next Level

- Joining a board
- Attending conferences
- Gaining public speaking skills
- Educating peers
- Participating in leadership training
- Becoming an ally to community leaders and activists

5

Inspired Philanthropist

Steps to Final Level

- Committing to raise significant money
- Expanding leadership role
- Leveraging resources
- Legacy planning
- Integrating all previous steps and mentoring others!

Even if you don't want your philanthropy to become your full-time job, if you want to commit more of your time or be more strategic with what you are doing now, learning to leverage what you do or give and being engaged in a healthy way with groups you care about is a learning process with great rewards. Consider finding a mentor or coach or attending trainings to continually increase your skills as a donor. What follows is more about each of the more advanced levels of donor engagement and some of the learning tools for moving along the spectrum.

Strategic Donor

A strategic donor identifies himself or herself as dedicating time to make positive change in the world. Strategic donors seek analysis of the root causes of problems and listen deeply to communities for their wisdom and direct experiences to help create a funding and advocacy strategy.

Key Learning Tools for Strategic Donors

- Grounding in identity-based donor group or donor networks (for example, the Women Donors Network, Philanthropy Roundtable, or Jewish Funders Network)

- Participating in site visits to current and prospective grantee groups

---

DONOR DIVA

When offering our skills, expertise, or advice, we need to be clear that organizations have their own boards and their own processes. We cannot expect them to turn on a dime, even when offers of abundance are being made. Nor can we buy our way into organizations and fix them. Becoming a partner with nonprofits requires deep listening and regard for their management, history, culture, and style. It may not seem like your way, but once you are part of the culture of the organization and invited to be at the table of decision makers or helping hands, your rewards and the gains by your community can be worth every step.

- Becoming involved with local or national community-based philanthropic organizations (for example, a local women's fund, or a public foundation affiliated with the Funding Exchange social justice federation)

- Developing collaborations or partnerships among donors and community activists

- Seeking a deepening of analysis through study groups and attending local and national issue-focused or strategy conferences (such as the Philanthropy Roundtable, the National Network of Grantmakers, Environmental Grantmakers Association, or Grantmakers Without Borders)

- Researching and finding your own position on key issues related to economic equity for which you may want to advocate, such as considering the pros and cons of the estate tax (Responsible Wealth [www.responsiblewealth.org] and United for a Fair Economy [wwww.faireconomy.org] are two excellent sources)

- Building skills such as fundraising, public speaking, mentoring, proposal or letter writing, and workshop presentations

Donor Activist or Donor Partner

A donor activist or donor partner uses his or her skills and contacts to work on behalf of a nonprofit organization as a supplement to giving financial support. Donor partners engage in an explicit agreement with a nonprofit organization about how to best serve the organization and be supported to succeed in an agreed-upon role. Donor partners step into positions of leadership on boards, as advocates, or as members of grant and fundraising committees, while simultaneously being an ally to staff and community members.

Keys to a successful donor partner relationship include mutual accountability and a formal or informal contract between the donor partner and the organization, prioritizing the evaluation component of the work, and deeply listening and creating a continual feedback loop.

Skills to Develop and Experiences for Donor Partners

- Mentoring or partnership across class, race, age, and other differences

- Understanding the field of philanthropy and social change

- Fundraising

- Advocacy or public speaking

Donor Organizer

A donor organizer is a donor activist who reaches out to other donors on behalf of positive societal change not only for one organization but for the sake of regional, national, or global movements for social and economic justice and environmental sustainability. Donor organizers see their role as mentoring and inspiring others to join movements for societal change and global sustainability. Donor organizers see part of their advocacy work as engaging other donors and activists in partnerships (study, research, advocacy, funding, direct action, and other collaborations or change strategies).

Skills, Talents, and Commitments of Donor Organizers

Mentoring others on issues related to a field of shared interest or philanthropy in general

Sharing perspective about the leaders and the variety of issues, problems, and solutions in a given field or issue area

Engaging other donors to join in larger, systems-based thinking and collaborative work

Training others in several organizations in a field of interest or geography about fundraising techniques

Giving and raising money for the capacity-building agencies and leaders who help build a field of interest or the capacities of donors

Willingness to participate as a donor educator

Willingness to engage other funders in funding partnerships or initiatives and to serve as lead donors

Advocating for policies, procedures, and structures that will improve the system or field of practice or will increase the number of donors

Helping donors, advisors, and nonprofit leaders use this book

Inspired Philanthropist

An inspired philanthropist has been inspired by others to make a better world and consistently listens and seeks better ways both of making change and preserving what he or she feels is working. An inspired philanthropist allows grantees and other donors to move him or her to action and to expanded contribution of time,

SOME EXAMPLES OF HOW TO BE A DONOR PARTNER

- Make a significant financial donation to the organization representing the level of your care and respect

- Keep up to date with the activities and accomplishments of the organization so that you can be a stronger advocate for its work

- Make clear to the organization that you want to be a partner, and work with the leadership to define what that would mean, ensuring some form of accountability and feedback as part of an agreement

- Offer to stretch to do something you're less comfortable doing, while getting support along the way

- Ask your friends and colleagues to support the organization

- Host an event, invite your contacts, or write letters with notes to friends and contacts

- Accompany the executive director, development director, or board chair on a fundraising visit

- Help the organization get specific feedback from donors and others in the community

- Ask the organization's leaders: What would be a dream come true? Then help to make it happen

talent, and treasure. An inspired philanthropist is one who will leverage others for powerful impact and faster fulfillment of fundraising.

Use Worksheet 10.1 to explore which of the characteristics of inspired philanthropists apply to you and which you aspire to.

WORKING CLOSELY WITH ORGANIZATIONS

When you consider becoming a serious donor partner with an organization, there are several ways to evaluate whether making a large gift will be a good investment of your money. Philanthropist Peter Kent told the magazine *More Than Money,*

> When I made my first $100,000 gift to a nonprofit organization, it was a big stretch for me. I wanted to help the organization build its capacity

Worksheet 10.1
Inspired Philanthropist's Checklist

Action	Applies to Me	I Aspire to
Know my values and what or who inspires my giving		
Create a giving plan and budget and give throughout the year		
Have a vision of the effect I want to have		
Do my homework and meet leaders and groups		
Coordinate my financial plan, my giving plan, and my estate plan for consideration of my legacy goals		
Align my giving, investing, and volunteering with my values		
Evaluate agencies and leaders I intend to invest in		
Increase my giving annually as inflation adds to the cost of nonprofits' work		
Look for models and solutions beyond and within my local community		
Stay committed as a donor for more than three years		
Never leave home without my address book		
Mentor other donors		
Work for lasting change by seeking the root causes of poverty and other social ills		
Seek transformative, system-shifting solutions		
Be an early donor to a funding campaign and give gain at the end to help the campaign meet its goals		

(*continued on next page*)

to operate at a vastly different level than it had been. These six questions helped guide me to risk such a major gift:

- Do I judge this area of work as critical?

- Is it timely for the work of this organization to grow?

- Will I be excited to build a relationship with this group for the next five or more years?

- Do I trust and respect the leadership, including the staff and board?

- Do I judge the organization's finances as solid?

- Has the group gone thorough strategic planning?[2]

To answer questions such as these requires learning a great deal about an organization. Two steps to move you in that direction are examining the organization's budget and making a site visit where you can see them in action and ask some questions about how they operate.

Reviewing an Organization's Budget

One way to get some detailed knowledge about a group's financial situation is to review its budget and balance sheet. Some organizations conduct financial audits if their budget exceeds $250,000, especially if they have received a grant that the funder requires an audit for. The results of these audits are available to the public on request. Organizations with budgets between $100,000 and $249,000 more often have their financial accounts reviewed by their accountant; you could request a copy of that review if one exists. The public annual summary that all nonprofits are required to file on Form 990 is also good to examine (available for most nonprofits at www.guidestar.org).

Here are some elements to look for in reviewing an organization's budget, adapted from the book *Robin Hood Was Right*, by Chuck Collins, Pam Rogers, and Joan Garner:[3]

- A variety of income sources or a plan to diversify funding to include individuals, foundations, and grassroots strategies.

- Evidence of local community support in the form of member contributions or income from grassroots fundraising.

- A realistic relationship between program and budget. For example, has a statewide organization budgeted for statewide work by including travel expenses? If a group works in a low-income community, does its budget show that it is truly accessible to the community—for example, through adequate child care and transportation expenses?

- A willingness to spend money to raise money, especially for fundraising strategies that also have programmatic benefit, such as direct mail and special events, which raise visibility and educate the public.

- A reasonable expense line for salaries in terms of paying staff living wages with benefits. Look for salary differentials that indicate serious inequality among different staff positions. If a budget is all salaries, it can be a warning that the work is entirely staff-driven and that community involvement is lacking.

- Deficits. Look for big changes in income and expenses from one year to the next. Both these indicators can show instability.

- Sources of funding: Is there a great deal of government or corporate funding and, if so, does it place a constraint on the type of organizing the group performs?

- Accountability structures: Are there mechanisms in the organization for fiscal oversight? Who sets the direction for the organization, and what input do they have into financial decisions? Are the people who write checks the same as those who receive the checks?

Making a Site Visit

Another way to learn more deeply about how an organization functions is to see some of its work in action. If you have made or are planning a major gift, request a site visit. To make the best use of your time and that of the organization, use Worksheet 10.2 to come prepared to focus on what you want to learn.

SETTING YOUR GIVING BOUNDARIES

Anonymity

There are reasons not to give anonymously, including wanting acknowledgment for your ideas, contributions, or work on behalf of an organization or wanting to challenge other donors to put their voices and know-how where their money is. Sometimes you want people to know who you are so you can share information and leverage projects. At other times giving anonymously can simplify life and be a practice in humility. Or you may be trying to avoid more solicitations than you feel comfortable receiving. Regardless of the size of a gift, you may not want to be recognized as a donor among people you know or work with. Whether you choose to give anonymously is about your own style and preference.

One situation that can arise is being a major donor while working within an organization as a staff or board member. If you don't want your role as a worker to be affected by your status as a major donor, you have a couple of options. The first is to tell the development director or executive director that you would like to keep your donations private. Explain why it's important to you and ask that your anonymity be respected and noted in your donor record.

A second option is to have the gift be truly anonymous: it can be made with a cashier's check or come from an unidentified donor-advised fund you have set up at a foundation or financial services company. Shielded by the institution, you're

Worksheet 10.2
Preparing for Site Visits

Step 1. Preparation

Define the goal of your site visit, such as to learn about the organization and its work or to determine the appropriateness of a future or further gift.

If the organization has sent you a funding proposal or background information, read it.

Review the organization's Web site and e-newsletters if available.

Step 2. Questions to Ask

Consider the questions you want to ask from among the following subject areas and possibilities.

I. **Program and Leadership**
   A. What is the organization's mission or primary purpose?
   B. What are you trying to accomplish?
   C. What are the organization's primary programs or activities and its immediate and long-range purposes?
   D. What is the organization's primary strategy to achieve those goals?
   E. What is the most exciting thing the group is doing now?
   F. How does your community perceive the organization's work?

II. **History**
   A. How long has the organization been doing what it does? Why was it formed? Has its mission or purpose changed during the past three to five years?
   B. What is the organization's vision for its work over the next year? Over the next three years? Do you have a written and board-approved strategic plan? If so, may I have a copy? How and why do you see the work changing? What impact do you think your project has had on the issue the organization is addressing?
   C. Who does your organization serve? Who are your constituencies?
   D. Who is your leadership body? What kind of people and talent have been involved? How do you support your staff and board to develop their skills and awareness?

III. **Organizational Functioning**
   A. How many people work with and for the organization, in what capacities? Do board members, senior staff, and volunteers reflect your clients and other constituents?
   B. Who decides what? Are constituents involved in staff, board, and volunteer leadership?
   C. How does your organization define success? How do you decide when to alter strategy or direction?
   D. Is there anything else you'd like me to know?

(continued on next page)

Worksheet 10.2
Preparing for Site Visits, Cont'd

IV. Fundraising

A. What is your budget?

B. How much of your income is earned, how much is contributed?

C. How would you describe your business model?

D. What are the organization's sources of earned and contributed income?

E. What are your fundraising goals? Do you have a fundraising plan? Who is involved in fundraising? How many board members and how many staff members are trained to ask for money from donors or funders?

F. Does the organization have a cash reserve? How big is it as a proportion of the budget? How much of a cash reserve do you think is essential in order to preserve your work through hard times?

G. Does the organization have an endowment? How large is it? What is its purpose?

H. If I am unable to fund this project, or I can fund only a percentage of your request, how will this affect its going forward?

I. What is the most useful gift a donor or foundation could give you now?

J. What other fundraising support do you need now?

V. Impact

A. What results are you seeking in your work?

B. How will you know when you have been successful?

C. How do you evaluate your work, your staff, and your board's effectiveness?

D. How do those you serve help you measure your impact?

E. Do you quantify your impact or demonstrate results for funders?

F. If I am a donor or funder giving $_____, will I receive your annual report or other reports of your success?

G. What has been a failure or a challenge in the past two years?

H. What have you learned from that challenge and how are you addressing it?

I. What can you realistically achieve with the budget you currently have?

J. How do you allocate your resources?

K. When you are not successful in a strategy, what do you do?

L. On a scale of 1 to 10, with 10 being excellent, rate your agency on its achievement of results and tell me why you chose that rating.

M. Do you hire an outside evaluator, do you do your own evaluations, or do you use some combination?

N. Do you share your audited financial statements and most recent 990s with donors upon their request?

O. If we give to you, what opportunities for engagement or donor education might there be? Do you have a formal program for donors or a way to steward our leadership?

free to ask for reports or request that the foundation conduct an evaluation of your grant or gift (see "Donor-Advised Funds" in Chapter Eight).

An anonymous gift can have greater impact if it comes with a message. Instead of giving instructions that your gift simply be listed as anonymous to the public, consider substituting descriptions such as "from a young change agent," "from a dedicated environmentalist," or "from a faith-filled senior supporter."

One person who was volunteering for an organization to which he was also a major donor said that volunteering gave him insights into the work of the group that no proposal could ever communicate. The one person on staff who knew about his giving respected his privacy, so he could check out the work quietly, help a project he cared deeply about, and know how well the money was being used.

If you choose anonymity for some or all of your donations, make clear to the organization how you prefer your anonymity to be maintained and what you would like in the way of communication from the organization. To be sure your anonymity is maintained when staff changes, it's useful to have a letter in your donor file, such as the sample in Appendix E, that clarifies your intent and specifies how you wish to be acknowledged or thanked. If you have a spouse or partner who is listed on your checks (if you give by check) indicate what your preference is in terms of them being listed and how. When a new staff person, executive, or development director joins the organization, reiterate that your letter is in the file. Your few minutes on this matter may help ensure your own privacy and the nonprofit's respect of your preferences.

Loans

Occasionally an organization faces a time-limited cash-flow bind, and a short-term loan could help them get back to financial self-sufficiency. This is often true of start-up organizations or projects, or when priorities of major funders change and an organization is left without an expected source of income. Enormous swings in the economy, such as those that occurred in the early 2000s, left some organizations with cash reserves depleted. Some money to tide them over while they gear up other fundraising activities may be crucial.

If you've been a steady and major donor to an organization, the time might come when the organization approaches you for a loan. If you've had a close relationship with the organization, their financial situation should not come as a surprise to you. If you're particularly close to the group, however, your emotional connection might make it more difficult to assess the practicality of their request.

If you are considering loaning money to an organization, get financial and legal advice and have a formal loan agreement with a reasonable repayment schedule signed and dated. Add a clause for mediation or arbitration should the loan need to be renegotiated. During the course of the loan, send loan payment reminders with preaddressed payment envelopes sixty and thirty days before each payment is due.

Appendix G on the CD-ROM addresses issues that arise concerning loaning money to an organization or to friends.

Requests from Groups Outside Your Giving Sphere

Many of us receive a variety of fundraising appeals—often more than we know what to do with—and they come in a variety of ways—everything from direct mail, door-to-door solicitation, and phone calls to lunches for donors and other events. Depending on the group, we may see these requests as incursions into our privacy or wonderful opportunities.

The key is to choose to engage with the kind of fundraising that best informs and inspires you and set limits on the rest. Having a giving plan helps you be clearer with solicitations outside of its framework. Here are some suggested responses that may help you establish your boundaries with requests for donations you do not wish to make.

When Someone Comes to Your Door

"I'm sorry. I respect that you're trying to make a living and care about XYZ group. But I don't make gifts in this manner. If you want to leave me material, with your name on the envelope as the solicitor, I will be happy to consider it, and will call the group to check it out. If I send a contribution, I will use your envelope. Thank you."

or

"I don't make gifts in this way. It's nothing personal. Good luck."

When Someone Calls from a Group You Don't Know or Care About

"I'm sorry, but I don't give money over the phone. Good luck."

or

"What you're doing is wonderful work, I'm sure, but I don't give in this manner. Send me some information by mail and I'll consider it."

Other possible responses:

"I've already allocated my budget for this year."

"I have a giving plan and your issues and mission are not a match for me."

"I'm giving to groups that are particularly important to me."

"I'm concentrating my available funds on other issues this year."

"I am sorry, but our funds are already designated. But because I care about your work, I will try to send or bring someone to your next event."

When Groups Send You Mail You Don't Want

Here's one donor's approach:

> I put all requests that I don't care about in one box, and ones I do care about in another. Every few months, I write to all the ones I don't care about and ask them to remove me from their mailing list. This way I feel I have done my part to try to reduce my mail and save them expenses too.

We can be respectful of those who raise money for causes they admire or are being paid to do so, while being clear on our own priorities. At the very least, we can be kind. Having a giving plan or legacy plan can make us better communicators!

chapter ELEVEN

Creating Greater Plans for Your Family, Heirs, and Humanity

This we know: All things are connected like the blood
which unites one family. All things are connected.
Whatever befalls the earth befalls the sons of the earth.
Man did not weave the web of life. He is merely a strand
on it. Whatever he does to the web he does to himself.

—Attributed to Chief Seattle

This chapter is written for donors, but it will also be useful for professional advisors and development professionals. We hope that this chapter and the supplemental materials for advisors and nonprofits found in Appendix B will inspire and equip others to form their own legacy planning teams. We are indebted to Phil Cubeta, wealth advisor and member of Inspired Legacy partners' advisory team, for his significant contributions.

It takes an effort to surmount the substantial denial about death in our culture, despite its very real presence. Without being able to face the fact of our inevitable end, we are unable to plan for what will happen to our assets—and our intentions for the world—toward the end of life and after we are gone. Consider this: although some 90 percent of Americans make charitable gifts during their lifetimes—and 61 percent give every year—fewer than 11 percent of Americans mention *any* charities in their wills. Among the most wealthy—those with the top 2 percent of assets—only 15 percent arrange for charitable giving from their estate to nonprofits.[1] Even among attorneys, who should be encouraging their clients to plan carefully for their giving after death, it is estimated that nearly 75 percent never get to complete or have not updated their own paperwork and plans.[2] This is an activity on which each of us must become personally engaged.

All it usually takes to move us from denial to action is the loss of a close friend or relative who has yet to pass on their values or their wishes or who leaves a messy or puzzling patchwork of unresolved relationships and difficulties. It is a shame to leave those we love without direction or security, when a few hours of careful planning and execution can make a world of difference.

The great thing about legacy planning is that it can also wake us up to many lifetime possibilities:

- Long-term visioning and planning with family and loved ones
- Fulfilling dreams
- Facing realities
- Setting new goals
- Releasing fear
- Deepening intimacy or clarity with our friends or loved ones
- Propelling long-term efforts by some of the nonprofits or the leaders we count on
- Giving and investing with new objectives and spirit
- Working at a new level of teamwork with trusted advisors
- Considering gifts in our lifetime and beyond to nonprofits and people we love.
- In short, what seemed initially something to avoid can become an expression of our values and one of the most creative activities we do! Legacy planning is part of actualizing a lifetime of love, commitments, and ideas.

As this book has repeatedly underscored, creating family philanthropy and links and partnerships with community are ways of fostering the future. In particular, we must take time to work intergenerationally. Legacy planning is a gift for all generations; done well, it can transform each person and organization involved and become the avenue of greater generosity and a better world.

No matter where you are on the income or asset scale, being intentional with how you use your social and financial capital during your lifetime and after it are part of your story and your personal mythology. For the sake of your heirs, for your own dreams, and for humanity at large, you want to have as great an impact as you can. That is why your approach to your giving is as important as your civic responsibilities of birthright, voting, and achieving all you hope to with your family and community.

BEGIN WITH THE END IN SIGHT

Even if you have current and updated wills or trusts, this chapter will help you prioritize your intentions, get to work on what is still unresolved or incomplete, and communicate about your legacy. If you have yet to engage this part of life, consider starting now, even if you are in your twenties or thirties, to begin "with the end in sight." We have a lifetime to learn and grow and accomplish our vision for a better life and a better world.

Many people feel they are too young to be doing legacy planning. If you're one of them, here's an assignment that might stimulate your thinking: consider what you would say to your real or imaginary family of younger relatives and community members at your ninetieth birthday. What would your shared wisdom be? What values would you want to encourage in others? What will have been your achievements, lessons learned, and wisdom for the next generation? If you're really brave, you might even consider what you would like your obituary to say about what you accomplished or left behind for the world.

In fact, it is a privilege to consider our legacies for the world and our families. But without careful planning, we cannot be assured that any of our intentions will be fulfilled. Let it therefore be our moral responsibility to do all we can to be intentional and to focus steadily on turning our plans into decisions and documents for others to implement. It is a way for us to share in solving the challenges of our times.

Chapter Seven stressed the importance of an integrated approach to your financial planning, philanthropic planning, and estate planning. If you have been working through the exercises in the chapters so far, you have now established and prioritized your three top values, issues areas, or populations or social problems that you want to address. You may have your giving plan in working order, and you may have decided to align some of your investments and your volunteer time, fundraising, or policy influencing with your goals. Now is the time to consider communicating your wishes, vision, and plans so that your effectiveness extends beyond your life.

Legacy planning, as you can see in Figure 11.1, encompasses all your previous planning, including finances, giving, and your estate. It prepares for the intentional passing on of your social, financial, and wisdom capital for the benefit of your beloveds and future generations. For planning to become inspired, we must consider the whole of our lives, including our spiritual beliefs; our financial obligations; and our family, community, and global needs as well.

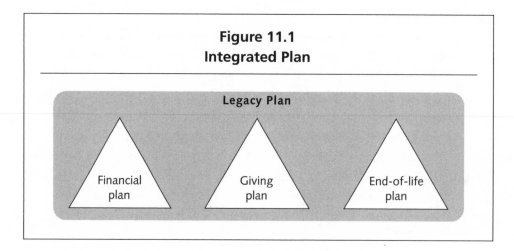

Figure 11.1
Integrated Plan

Legacy Plan

Financial plan

Giving plan

End-of-life plan

PRUDENT PLANNING

Much of what we learn from our family money mentors and financial advisors is about planning conservatively with care, or "prudent legacy planning." In this chapter we explore what we call "inspired legacy planning"—planning that goes beyond mere prudence to be responsive to what is highest and best in us. An inspired legacy plan includes a prudent plan but moves to higher ground, taking into account our family values, virtues, and vision and what we want to do for others. An inspired plan makes sure our family is well taken care of but also supports you in creating a lasting positive impact on your community and the causes you care about.

Even if you have no heirs, legacy planning is best done with some family members or friends. For those without remaining family of origin, consider your chosen family or friends in this process. Best practices in philanthropy have taught that in order to be fully "inspired" and have lasting influence, inspired giving decisions—and inspired legacy decisions—should be informed and ideally shared by some representatives of the constituencies we aim to serve. If you truly want dynamic impact, begin by having the beneficiaries in mind and by bringing them into your planning process. Imagine what excitement there can be if you engage as codesigners those who you hope will fulfill your dreams.

There are several benefits to planning your legacy. First, you will have the satisfaction and security of knowing that you have a prudent plan that will provide enough income for you, your spouse or partner, and your heirs. Your needs and wants will be met. Second, you will also have an "Inspired Plan," one that goes beyond "enough for us" to abundance in the life you live in community with others. Third, as you develop a process that is true to your ideals, your experience in planning with your advisors should be positive, uplifting, meaningful, and effective—not a cold, dry process only but one that is joyous, creative, and fulfilling.

Before you begin inspired legacy planning, then, you want to have a prudent plan in place. A prudent plan makes sure that there is "enough," whatever enough means to you, for you, your spouse or partner, and your heirs or children, whether you live to a very old age, die prematurely, become ill or disabled, or retire.

A prudent plan generally has the following elements:

- *Cash flow and budgeting:* makes sure you have enough for current expenses and that you are saving for the future

- *Retirement:* provides enough for you and dependents if you live to normal life expectancy and work until retirement

- *Education funding:* provides for education of your children, if applicable
- *Disability:* insures that bills can be paid even if you are disabled
- *Life insurance:* provides enough to care for those left behind
- *Investments:* provides a balanced portfolio adjusted for your risk tolerance
- *Income tax:* minimizes income taxes or has you pay what you may deem fair
- *Property and casualty:* protects against property and casualty losses
- *Liability coverage:* protects against lawsuits and claims of creditors
- *Estate plan:* includes a will that has been updated or reviewed in the past three years and leaves the right assets to the right recipients in the right way:

    Includes powers of attorney and health directives

    Includes something personal from you as a final note or testament conveying thoughts and feelings for those you love

    Provides details of your end-of-life wishes

SHAPING AN INSPIRED LEGACY PLAN

- An inspired plan nestles a giving plan inside the standard or generic prudent financial and estate plan. When your inspired plan is complete, it will provide for you, your heirs, and for society. Which of these elements of an inspired plan are included or up to date in your planning? Which need work?
- A clearly articulated vision, with goals and priorities
- An advisory team that cares about and respects your legacy vision, values, and the articulation of your hopes for your family and community.
- Enough income to preserve family lifestyle
- Risk management to handle death, disability, sickness, or incapacity
- Business succession planning, if appropriate
- Investment planning
- Income tax considerations
- Estate and gift planning, including lifetime gifts and bequests, and through successive generations
- Family governance of family-owned or family-controlled entities

- Education and mentoring for heirs in the roles they will play in the family trusts, the family business, and in other family entities, such as a foundation

- Education, mentoring, and role-modeling for heirs in the roles they will play in the community, not only as holders of jobs and possessors of wealth but also as active citizens and community leaders

- Opportunities for discussion with advisors, family, and nonprofits or heirs on your giving and legacy intentions

- Detailed end-of-life preferences and a plan for your executor and heirs to ask questions about your needs

- Monitoring of the plan and its results for self, partner, spouse, family, and society

As wealth advisor Phil Cubeta says, "A better world is not sold in stores. Money alone cannot create or conserve it. Your giving and your leadership may inspire others to step forward. Your giving plan will be all the stronger to the extent it can mobilize the voluntary efforts of others and serve as a rallying point, or tipping point, among those who are served by your gift and uplifted by your personal example and leadership."

CHARITABLE ESTATE PLANNING

The portion of an estate plan that includes charitable gifts can take many forms and offers many creative alternatives benefiting both donors and recipients. For example, charitable estate planning vehicles such as charitable remainder trusts

DONOR DIVA

Even the most preoccupied among us most likely have a deep and abiding dream, an ideal, that if encouraged will flame up and drive our planning process. Too often these dreams do not make it into our plans. Give your greatest gift ever: a conscious transition that considers those you love and what you can do intentionally to live and leave an inspired legacy.

can allow you to transfer highly appreciated assets to a charity and still receive an income stream from those assets while you're alive. When you do this, you bypass capital gains taxes and take a partial income-tax deduction. With the vehicle of a charitable lead trust, for another example, you can designate a nonprofit as the "current income beneficiary" of some assets and your children as the "remainder beneficiaries," so they will receive the assets following a specific period of time. The key personal benefit is estate tax savings. For the nonprofit, the trust provides money for current projects. For donors with multiple millions, charitable lead trusts are a widely underused vehicle that could be a win-win for your interests and passions.

Charitable estate planning is a complex, creative, and highly technical field that a competent estate lawyer, financial advisor, and certified public accountant can help you with. Many people, especially those with sizable assets, find that lawyers and tax accountants do not take the initiative to suggest charitable estate planning options. They will not know your heart, your passion, or your vision of a better world unless you tell them. You don't need to become an expert yourself in the tools and techniques of planning, but you do need to convey your goals and priorities to

---

DONOR DIVA

If you decide that you want to leave money or a valuable gift to a nonprofit organization, consider letting the organization know that it has been named as a beneficiary in your will or trust. This is important information for an organization to have so that it can understand your intentions as a legacy donor. Except in situations in which you have made written pledges, it is best not to mention the figure or percentage you may have left them, as this may change over time. However, if you fear that knowing of a legacy gift will encourage the organization to ask you for more money during your lifetime or to treat you differently than they might now, communicate your preferences regarding such things when telling them about the bequest.

your advisors so that they can create a plan that reflects your ideals as well as your prudent concerns. Learning to speak a little of the advisor's language also helps you achieve an optimal outcome. Your local university, hospital, public or community foundation, or any other large nonprofit institution cultivating donors probably offers charitable estate planning workshops, with no obligation that your estate plans include them.

It is very important that your will be as specific as possible (whether in a letter or more formal document or in audio form) so that those executing your estate understand your charitable intent. Giving specific designations or examples of what kinds of projects or geographic limitations you have in mind for your charitable bequests is an important part of your estate planning.

One avenue to ensuring that your bequests are handled as you would wish is to designate one or more people to be charitable advisors after your death. These may be family members, friends, philanthropic or community leaders, or financial or legal professionals who have known you or your interests well. These advisors interpret your wishes with a nonprofit you may have named in a bequest or with a foundation or trust that you may have contributed to or set up upon your death. Convene this group of advisors or representatives during your lifetime, if only for one meeting, to let them know your dreams and charitable intent. Be sure the meeting has a note taker and is recorded and transcribed for future use as needed. Signing and dating the transcript once you have edited it or made adjustments has added impact for your heirs and advisors.

Many community foundations and increasing numbers of financial and fundraising organizations offer educational programs on the legal, financial, and tax aspects of philanthropic estate planning. Thanks to the branding all over the country by Leave a Legacy (a program of the National Committee on Planned Giving), some outstanding legacy education programs and advertising have increased public awareness of the advantages of giving more at death and through planned gifts. After all, as Paul Schervish, director of Boston College's Center on Wealth and Philanthropy, has noted, we are amidst the largest intergenerational transfer of wealth that has ever occurred.[3] Giving more is a natural part of the benefit of being wealthy or having accumulated wealth.

There is a great deal to consider depending on the marketplace and the specifics of your personal situation. Attending at least two such programs can help you learn the language of planning and participate with your advisors meaningfully as a partner in the planning process. Inspired Legacies (www.inspiredlegacies.org) also offers programs for donors, advisors, and nonprofits on the integration of legacy and philanthropic planning. Wherever you live, there are many people trained and poised to ask you truly interesting and useful questions to discern what is most important to you. Almost no other process in life can bring forth so many joyful possibilities and the resolution of so many potential concerns.

WORKING WITH ADVISORS FOR INSPIRED OUTCOMES

Your giving is likely to be more successful if you work with a financial professional to know and understand your spending, your cash flow, and the creative and wise timing and uses of your assets. An industry of wealth advisors, investment advisors,

ESTATE PLANNING AND CHARITABLE GIVING

Estate planning means planning for the orderly handling, disposition, and administration of your goods and money when you die. Charitable estate planning is a vehicle that can help you give after you die in ways and amounts that often you could not give during your lifetime. There is a misconception that only those with a lot of money or other assets need to undertake thoughtful estate planning, including writing a will. That's not true. If you have any money in a bank or retirement account, own a home or other real estate, or own anything of any value—a car, a work of art, jewelry—you have the chance to decide what will happen to these possessions after your death. If you don't decide, the government will decide for you. For those with larger estates, to die without an up-to-date will can cost a significant fraction of your wealth at death in unnecessary taxes. Estate planning, in short, lets you provide for loved ones, make gifts to causes you care about, and save your heirs income and estate taxes.

Bequests to the nonprofits you love and trusts for your family or heirs can save your estate and heirs substantially while continuing your legacy of charitable gifting. Your estate plan is more than dry legal documentation. Your estate plan is a testament to who you are and what you love. Make sure your estate plan reflects what is most important in your life so that your plan truly becomes your lasting legacy.

financial and estate planners, accountants, lawyers, and philanthropic advisors offers advice about establishing giving programs (see Appendix I, "Resources," on the CD-ROM). Working with good advisors will help you to assess your material and leadership assets so that you are aware of your capacities and limitations.

Choosing an advisor who is knowledgeable and has a great reputation is essential, but you might also look for advisors who share at least some of your values, communicate effectively, and honor and add value to your work as a donor. Giving takes time and care; it also requires clear, realistic goals and patience.

Following are some questions an advisor should ask. However, many advisors are so focused on the technical side of planning that they may neglect to ask the big-picture questions. By preparing your answers in advance, you may enable your advisors to serve you better.

- What do you want your legacy to be? What would you like your giving to say about who you are and what you believe?

- Have you considered ways to spark giving during your lifetime with your children or other family members?

- How much time do you want to devote to philanthropy? Do you know the services that we provide and what they cost? What role do you want an advisor to play in supporting your philanthropy?

- How much do you want to leave to the next generation and how do you want it distributed?

Here are some specific questions that you may want to ask an advisor. It is important to realize that these questions are not the stock in trade of estate planning. Many of them fall under the category of financial planning—that is, planning for what happens while you are alive. By raising these questions in an estate planning interview you signal quite properly that for you a legacy is to be lived as well as left. You are not all about death. You want to make an impact while alive. These questions help provide the right framework for the discussion with your advisor. If you are asking these questions of an estate tax attorney, she or he may refer you to an overall financial advisor to get certain of your questions answered. Planning is generally a team effort.

- Can I afford to be more generous now? Can I afford to be more generous later? What about at death? How are you calculating that?

- What amount of money can I afford to give annually and at the time of my death that would best minimize taxes, help my favorite causes, and still get the right amount of money to my heirs?

- Can you provide estimates early in the year as well as a year-end figure for the maximum dollar amount I will be able to give to nonprofits before I have given so much that I can no longer get a current income tax deduction?

- I am considering a donor-advised fund, a supporting foundation, or a private foundation for my giving. What are the pros and cons of giving through different vehicles? Which ones might work best for me given my income, goals, and asset structure?

- Can you help me establish charitable legacy or estate gifts that will benefit my community, my family, and my friends? Are you reasonably expert in this area, or is someone in your firm a specialist?

- Would it work better for my tax picture if I gave appreciated stock instead of writing a check?

- Are there legacy strategies such as buying insurance to cover multiyear pledges or other trusts or funding vehicles that I should consider now?

- I'd like to help pay for my grandchildren's education. What's the best way to do that?

- Do you have experience working with a team of advisors who can help integrate financial, tax, estate, and philanthropic planning? How do you and others on the team get clear about my philanthropic aspirations? Are you comfortable talking about my ideals and how to actualize them? If not, can you refer me to a potential member of the team who is passionate and informed in this area?

- How do you feel about socially responsible or green investments? Can you or someone on the team support my interest in this area of investing?

- I want my ideals to drive the planning process. I am also determined to have real impact on the causes I support. Are you willing and able to help me with the due diligence that will be needed to monitor my mission-based investments? If not, can you recommend someone else to add to this planning team?

The wonderful thing about having a trusted financial advisor or team is that, if they are the right fit for you, they are likely to provide you with guidance and resources on how to manifest many of your dreams. Communication is key. We all know from our personal and business lives that good communication is a two-way street. Good communication takes an effort on both sides. Husband and wife, partners and friends, clients and advisors, and advisors with other advisors on the team need to work at eliciting and fulfilling your goals, objectives, and aspirations in a spirit of mutual respect and common purpose.

Some people feel that their advisors aren't interested in helping them move to a more inspired level of planning. Philanthropically engaged donors often say things such as the following:

- My advisors just want to sell me something or run up the billable hours.

- I feel foggy about my money, and I have no idea what my advisor is saying when he starts talking about taxes. I'm afraid to ask stupid questions.

- My advisors don't hear me when I say I care about something more than money. I am more idealistic than my advisors give me credit for being.

- The planning process is so dry, so expensive; I hate it.
- My documents are out of date because I just can't bring myself to go through this all again.

Advisors, too, are often frustrated by incomplete communication and say things such as the following:

- Clients come into my office without a clear idea of what they want. I wish they could provide dates, numbers, and names—who gets what, when, and how much?
- Clients bluff me. They pretend everything is under control, that their plans are great. But when I begin to get the facts, lots of data are missing and much work remains to be done.
- Every family has issues, but I am not a marriage or family therapist. I can't reconcile spouses' goals or tell parents how to raise their kids.
- I don't think people generally are generous.
- Success for all concerned will only be achieved when client and advisors meet as a team to articulate and achieve all the client's goals—both those of prudence and the more inspired, visionary goals.

Don't play the blame game or fall silent in frustration. Philanthropic planning at its core is far removed from the languages of tax and law. Advisors are lucky to have clients like you. As a truly engaged giver, you are the exception to the rule. So to get the outcomes you need and deserve, you are the one who must come forward to guide the conversation toward the language of love and social benefit. Once you do, and advisors hear you, the whole tenor of the engagement changes and you work with advisors as partners in a noble effort. You lead on ideals. The advisors will follow with the tools and techniques. An inspired legacy team starts with an inspired legacy lead partner—that will be you. You speak up for what is good and right.

Appendix A on the CD-ROM collects a number of documents that can be helpful in working with advisors to create an inspired legacy plan. These documents include a series of memos to your advisors detailing who is on your advisory team, the kinds of communication that are most beneficial for you, and samples of a memo you might want to provide your advisors outlining your vision for your planning process and the legacy you wish to leave. After you have been working

> ## DONOR DIVA
>
> Advisors want to do the right thing. They want you as a satisfied client who speaks well of them. They will meet you on higher ground, putting their skills to work on behalf of your highest purposes, if you provide clarity, good data, and leadership. There are some things that you truly cannot delegate. If you want the best results and an inspired legacy, then your focus for several key hours is essential. This is important work to prioritize for those you love.

with your advisors in this way, you can use the following checklist to evaluate how an advisor responds to your desires to help you determine if this person is the kind of member you want on your team.

Appendix B contains resources for advisors and nonprofits who may be working with donors to help achieve an inspired legacy planning process. Use Exercise 11.1 to assess your advisor's compatibility with your needs.

Remember that as with surgeons, bedside manner is important but is not the whole job. You are hiring advisors to be technically competent. As long as you have at least one advisor on your team with whom you can communicate at a deep level, others can be hired for their technical skills, as long as you or your most trusted advisor succeeds in building a good, strong working team on your behalf.

BECOMING A LEGACY MENTOR

Once you have worked with your attorney or advisors to create a prudent plan, you are ready to take your planning to a level of greater impact. To achieve the results you want for society, you must step forward as a legacy partner. A legacy mentor is someone who leads and convenes her or his family, heirs, and advisors around their ideals so that the planning not only serves material purposes but also produces a resoundingly positive impact on the lives of those around us. Exercise 11.2 lays out the suggested steps to becoming a legacy mentor and helps you identify which areas you need to address now.

Exercise 11.1
Checklist for Assessing an Advisor

10 minutes

Rate your advisor's responses to your communications on a scale of 1 to 5 (with 5 being the highest), then look at the overall picture of how comfortable you are working with this person.

Advisor Response	My Comfort Level
Does the advisor reflect back your vision, goals, hopes, and dreams in such a way that you can recognize yourself in that "mirror"?	5 4 3 2 1
Does the advisor see what makes you unique?	5 4 3 2 1
Is the advisor compassionate and empathetic?	5 4 3 2 1
Does the advisor respond tactfully to sensitive personal information?	5 4 3 2 1
Do you feel a connection and a bond?	5 4 3 2 1
Is this someone in whom you feel comfortable confiding?	5 4 3 2 1
Does the advisor use plain English and help you understand the issues?	5 4 3 2 1
Does this person give you credit for your ideals, as well as your success?	5 4 3 2 1
Does this person get excited about the thought of helping you create plans that will express and pass on your values as well as money?	5 4 3 2 1
Does the advisor seem like a team player?	5 4 3 2 1
Does he or she listen as well as talk?	5 4 3 2 1
Does the advisor pick up on subtle cues from you and your partner or spouse? Or do you have to insist on important points over and over to get the point through?	5 4 3 2 1
Would you enjoy working with this person as a cocreator of your life and legacy plan?	5 4 3 2 1
Do you trust and respect this advisor?	5 4 3 2 1

Exercise 11.2
Becoming a Legacy Mentor

15 minutes

Rate yourself on a scale of 1 to 5 (with 5 being highest) on how well you are completing the following legacy tasks. Underline those on which you know you need to take further action, then place a star next to the four or five that you will work on during the next few months.

1. Wealth Planning

Rate Yourself

A. My essential paperwork is in order (and user friendly).					
I. I have a completed financial plan.	5	4	3	2	1
II. I have a completed legacy plan including trusts, insurance and medical power of attorney.	5	4	3	2	1
III. I have explained the location of key paperwork to my executor, partner, or medical power of attorney.	5	4	3	2	1
B. I recently met with my financial and estate planning team.	5	4	3	2	1
C. I have a transition plan in place for my business or real estate interests.	5	4	3	2	1
D. I have at least one key advisor I trust.	5	4	3	2	1
E. My taxes have been minimized or I am paying my fair share.	5	4	3	2	1
F. I am active in my planning—financially and philanthropically. I feel confident the structure of my plans meets my needs, serves my values, helps my family, and offers the best gifts for my community or my favorite causes.	5	4	3	2	1

2. Self

Rate Yourself

A. I know what is most important to me, and I am diligent in making sure that my values are integrated into my philanthropic, financial, and legacy planning and daily consumer choices.	5	4	3	2	1
B. I am intentionally creating my mark on the world.	5	4	3	2	1
C. I seek out more information on giving and legacies regularly.	5	4	3	2	1
D. I use my time, energy, and talents intentionally.	5	4	3	2	1
E. I recognize I am leading others by example.	5	4	3	2	1
F. I am tending to my personal health and well-being.	5	4	3	2	1

(continued on next page)

Exercise 11.2
Becoming a Legacy Mentor, Cont'd

3. Loved Ones
                                                              Rate Yourself

A. I have discussed—at length—my values of family   5 4 3 2 1
   and community service with my partner, kids, parents,
   siblings, and close friends.

B. I have arranged for estate and lifetime planned gifts.   5 4 3 2 1

C. I have designated key personal items or art to family   5 4 3 2 1
   members or friends.

D. I am actively engaging the next generation in planning   5 4 3 2 1
   for my legacy and for theirs.

E. I feel confident that my executor and spouse or   5 4 3 2 1
   partner understand my end-of-life wishes and have
   them detailed in writing or on audio.

F. I have made peace with those I need to.   5 4 3 2 1

4. Community
                                                              Rate Yourself

A. I have an annual giving plan for my donations to   5 4 3 2 1
   nonprofits.

B. I am actively engaged with other legacy leaders,   5 4 3 2 1
   mentors, or peers to consider how to leverage my
   influence to help advance what is important to me
   and my community.

C. Through my work, I leverage resources and use   5 4 3 2 1
   my influence to create a positive impact for the
   community.

D. I have identified the very best way to use my talents   5 4 3 2 1
   as a nonprofit volunteer, and I volunteer my services
   on a regular basis.

E. I am doing my fair share for my family and my   5 4 3 2 1
   community.

F. I realize that active sharing of my best practices   5 4 3 2 1
   may help others, so I offer to help others as much
   as I can to set priorities about living and leaving their
   legacies.

PLANNING FOR YOUR HEIRS

A key element in developing a prudent and inspired legacy plan is to consider who you are most concerned about in your family and which organizations and leaders you want to designate to continue your work and memorialize your life. Sometimes this step comes near the end of life. One terminally ill donor worked with her family to personally pass on her legacy. She or her family members wrote to each person she wanted to say something to or the family members she wanted to leave a remembrance for upon her death. They also reviewed her charitable bequests and made calls if there was any need for clarification. Having done this gave her and her family enormous freedom and peace during her final days. The greatest of all gifts are love, your personal touch, and attentive time. Use Exercises 11.3 and 11.4 to make notes on these elements of the plan you will establish now, before the end is so near that planning becomes burdensome. You will be considering your family, friends, and nonprofit heirs. Then take a few minutes to decide whether you wish to engage a philanthropic advisor to help you pull the pieces together so that you leave the legacy of love that inspires you. This is, after all, your legacy, and these choices are yours to decide. Sometimes talking with someone about your intentions and fleshing out the details that will appear in your will or estate plan can lead to greater impact. Many a technically competent estate or financial planning team would be even better if it included a passionate advocate to spearhead your highest priorities, beyond money and taxes.

REVIEW

Now would be a good time to review where you are in your planning process. First, use Exercise 11.4 to help you review your legal situation with regard to your will and other documents. Then use Exercise 11.5 to see if you are using your advisors to your best advantage.

LEAVING BEQUESTS OR TRUSTS TO THE NEXT GENERATION

Leaving money to heirs is a wonderful legacy, but it can also raise important questions. Money left outright or in trust can leave heirs with questions about what the money "means" and what you meant by leaving it to them in the form you did. You would be surprised, even shocked, at how often heirs misunderstand and read unpleasant intentions into an inheritance or trust document. When money is left

Exercise 11.3
Who Are You Planning For?

15 minutes

1. On the following worksheet, list family, friends, and charitable organizations you want to include in your legacy planning. Your next step may simply be writing a note or talking with the person or group to acknowledge their good works or importance in your life, or you may want to note how you want to reach out to them during your remaining lifetime.

Name of Person or Organization	What I Plan to Leave Them (% of estate or $ amount)	To Do	Next Step (talk with them or with advisors)

2. Next to each name in the preceding list, using a scale of 1–5—with 5 meaning that you are in sufficient contact with them now, 1 meaning that you need to see them or talk soon—note in the margin where you are with each person.

3. Everyone usually has one person they are most concerned about. It's good to get those concerns out in the open, where they can be dealt with. Is there anyone on this list that you are concerned about especially? If so, list them and what you are concerned about. Then consider how to address that concern.

Name: _____

Your thoughts or concerns and actions you will take:

_____

_____

(continued on next page)

to a child by a parent who has died when that child is too young to remember much, leaving letters, videos, and a record of your values, hopes, and dreams is especially healing. Even if your children are grown, it is wise to leave them a loving record of what you meant. It can take the coldness out of the probate process and reassure them that your choices are motivated by your bond with them. Of course, nothing is better than your living voice, face to face. Since no one can be certain of the circumstances of his or her own death, you may want to be diligent about dialogue now and making your wishes or expectations clear. It can be so helpful to free heirs of their guessing by transparent conversations about your wishes, especially with adult children or your spouse. If there are contingencies to your leaving money (for example, when a child receives money from a trust only if she or he

Exercise 11.4
Current Wills, Legal Documents, and Titling of Assets

10 minutes

I am not a legal expert, but basically, my wills and other legal document do the following:

___ I have no will.

___ My will leaves everything to my spouse or partner, then to the kids or other relatives, friends, or organizations.

___ My spouse or significant other and I have wills that minimize taxes by passing what we can to heirs tax-free.

___ My will and that of my spouse or partner have been gone over recently with a tax attorney to minimize taxes through fairly complex planning.

___ We last talked to an attorney about our wills in (approximate year) _____.

___ My highest personal priority is to make progress on my legacy planning by:

_____

_____

I will do this with the help of (who) _____,

(by when) _____.

_____

has completed a certain level of schooling or earned his or her own income for a certain period of time), make them known as well. Get a shared understanding, even an agreement. Don't let the last will and testament come as a big surprise, shrouded in mystery and legal language.

Many people want to be sure that children or spouses have "enough" from their estates. Then the important question becomes "How much is enough?" This is a question that, while good to discuss with one's spouse or partner and one's advisor, should also be considered for a family meeting or a meeting with your heirs. You might start such a conversation by asking heirs to guess how big your estate will be. You may be surprised at how wrong they are. Most surviving spouses and

Exercise 11.5
How Advisors Can Help

10 minutes

In the following to-do list, check which of the tasks your advisors have carried out, and make notes on any that are incomplete or for which you have questions.

Advisor Tasks	Notes
____ Review current legal documents and provide summary	
____ Assess gaps in current planning	
____ Assess the feasibility of a philanthropic project, now or later	
____ Help reduce estate and income taxes	
____ Help develop a program to transfer my business to heirs	
____ Help with an exit strategy for my business	
____ Review existing insurance for adequacy	
____ Coordinate my planning team to get the job done	
____ Suggest referrals to allied professionals	
____ Other:_____	

partners say they "had no idea how much money and property there was." They are often surprised at how many varied assets there are and how complex the financial matters are. You may have debts or loans that need instruction for managing or forgiving, and you may have some stock or property that you really don't want sold. These are instructions best discussed with your advisors and then presented while you are still competent to talk about them with your family. You may also want to hear your children's wishes or discuss with them how you will be distributing their inheritance (for example, if you are thinking of leaving one child more because he or she has been working in the nonprofit or social service field or has been able to save less for retirement).

This kind of inquiry is simply a direct way to gather the thoughts and feelings of your family as you are reviewing your plans. Listen carefully and take notes. You may be surprised, and your family members are bound to be, by your inquiry and consideration. Even if things change, your family or heirs will remember that you were considerate enough to engage them or try to. Even if the conversation seems tense or difficult, just imagine how much more difficult it would be for the family to sort out after you are gone and can no longer guide them through a process to shared understandings and, if need be, reconciliation.

One way to communicate your plans and your commitment to family is to stage a family retreat with one of the many family advisors who facilitates family weekends. Organizations such as The National Center for Family Philanthropy, The Council on Foundations, Inspired Legacies, or the Heritage Institute have trained professional wealth counselors and coaches to support you and your family through this process.

NEXT STEPS

Once your inspired legacy plan has been drafted by your advisors, you may want to present it formally to your family, perhaps even before you finally sign off on all the documents. Some people call this a "dress rehearsal" for reading the will.

While you are alive, you act as the steward of your resources. After you are gone, someone else may have to play that role. If you are planning to establish trusts for children and grandchildren to protect and distribute family assets, carefully choose trustees or those who will manage your affairs, communications, or oversight. Again, as with planning, some trustees excel in technical capacity, whereas others may excel in human understanding and empathy or even wisdom. Increasingly, people are leaving room for two trustees, one a family advisor or family member, another a corporate trustee to make sure that both wisdom and competence are well represented. Articles on the Inspired Legacies Web site (www.inspiredlegacies.org) and at www.heirs.org discuss creating trusts and choosing trustees so that beneficiaries are well served. If your child is under age eighteen, the opinion and work of your trustee is particularly important to the well-being of your family. The choice of a beneficiary may affect beneficiaries for decades to come, so having at least one of the trustees be a family member or friend who is a good communicator and knows your children or spouse is a good idea. Many family members or friends are willing to serve for only a modest fee or no fee.

DONOR DIVA

Leaving each of your children or siblings exactly the same percentage or amount of your estate or gifting (except when there is mental or physical disability or other special circumstances) avoids the permanent consequences of estates divided or tied up because of a lack of trust or past difficulties. Consider leaving your money and your love equally. At the same time, also weigh the question, "When is fair not equal, and equal not fair?" Circumstances often do differ. One child may have lots of money; another may have gone into a career that required personal sacrifice. In the case of a family business, one child may work in the business, and another may not. Is it fair to divide the business equally, when one child is doing all the work? These dilemmas are precisely why a good advisory team is important. The team can help you weigh your options, decide what is right, and communicate clearly.

A well-chosen trustee can be more than an administrator of the terms of the trust. He or she can also be a mentor, someone to whom the heirs can look—as they might have looked to you—as a role model. In some trusts the beneficiaries can take over some responsibility for the trust at a certain age. Having a trustee who as mentor can prepare heirs for that role then becomes key to a successful handoff of responsibility.

Leaving a legacy to your spouse, friend, or children is often a life-changing event. The most loving thing you can do is to prepare yourself, your advisors, and your family for what is inevitably ahead. Death is a hard word, but death does not end all. We live on in the memory of others. We live on in the good works we have done. And we live on in the legacy of love and the traditions and values we pass on. Nothing of the best in us will die, but we must take the time and make the commitment to build and pass on our own inspired legacy. Great joy comes from such a legacy. You can begin by living that legacy now in your current giving and in all you do for others.

Growing and Partnering with the Next Generation of Givers

Surplus wealth is a sacred trust which its possessor is bound to administer in his lifetime for the good of the community.

—Andrew Carnegie

In 1999 I attended a conference called the "State of the World," at which I was one of two presenters asked to discuss the future of philanthropy in the twenty-first century. My copresenter, who spoke first, worked for a dynamic family foundation well known for its innovations in education and community building. I was shocked to hear his basic message: that the twenty-first century would be filled with the same self-interested, unimaginative giving that the vast majority of current wealth holders and family foundations now demonstrate. He concluded, "I think little will change without a serious cultural change."

I was disappointed that he did not touch on the enormous growth and development of family foundations and that he did not seem to want to inspire the participants from around the world to get involved in greater giving, to lend their business acumen, and to invest a great share of their wealth in philanthropy. Nor did he share examples of cutting-edge philanthropy that participants could invest in or encourage those present to mentor and support the next generation of givers and decision makers.

At the time, I felt that my colleague had lost an opportunity for engaging a set of new donors, and I tried to compensate with cheerful examples of how the World Wide Web has enabled us to see problems around the world as interrelated and has made philanthropy more available to all. In hindsight, however, I think his message probably had the more lasting impact, and that he was right: established philanthropy needs a serious cultural change. Too many people still regard philanthropy as a bastion of self-interest of the wealthy. As givers we must reach beyond our class- and race-based self-interest in order for this picture—and the reality it mirrors—to change. My colleague was right.

But there is good news as well: the next generation of givers, particularly from families of wealth, is much more savvy than the last. They have developed their own expertise and resources that are enabling their full participation in giving whether or not their aging parents and grandparents make a place for them at their family funding tables. They are generally more directly engaged with nonprofits and their communities, and many factors—more integrated schools, a wider representation of nationalities among their peers, easy access to a wide range of information through the Internet—indicate that the next generation of leaders and givers has more of a global and multicultural perspective in their giving and living choices.

Only a few years ago there were few resources to help parents and children think about giving and service. Now, thanks to the proliferation of resources on the World Wide Web, there are many opportunities for youth worldwide to share their passionate concerns and interests. Organizations such as Resource Generation, YES!, and Emerging Practitioners in Philanthropy, among others, are helping donors from fifteen to forty years old define their values and find their place in philanthropy. We have every reason to feel more hopeful. As service learning has become a standard aspect of much elementary school education in the United States, many kids today are beginning to learn about the nonprofit world and to experience the vast possibilities for social engagement that already make giving a natural part of their lives. This chapter discusses some of those resources and gives some inspiring examples of children and youth reaching out to make their communities better places.

LEARNING EARLY ABOUT GIVING

To inspire the values you want your children to develop, start early to tell them stories about giving and service. You may also want to begin a home library of books that inform and inspire you and your kids about giving (see Appendix I, "Resources," on the CD-ROM). In particular, children need to understand that sharing, giving, and volunteering create community and help develop some of the most powerful skills one needs in life: team building, listening, and empathy. Not only is empathy an antidote for narcissism, it's the way we will create a more compassionate and caring world. The Council of Michigan Foundations and the Women's Fund of the Milwaukee Foundation have developed some terrific programs for kids related to giving and service. The Women's Fund of the Milwaukee Foundation has produced a book on giving, *The Giving Book, A Young Person's Guide to Giving and Volunteering,* which is a great primer for young people ages five to eight. The Council of Michigan Foundations' K–12 curriculums for teachers and parents are now being used in many schools nationwide and globally (www.learningtogive.org).

A wonderful book of stories and guidance for parents for youth ages six through fourteen is *The Giving Family: Teaching Our Children to Help Others,* by Susan Price (published by the Council on Foundations; www.thegivingfamily.org).

One inspiring program is R U MAD (Are You Making a Difference), developed by the Education Foundation in Australia and being launched in schools all over that country (www.rumad.org/au). High school classrooms choose an issue they want to change and design a way to make that difference. One classroom's focus, for example, was "R U MAD about the overuse of paper bags in stores and the waste of trees they cause?" The classroom project for the year was to figure out how to make, market, and distribute canvas bags to local grocery stores as alternatives to paper, as well as to do public education. Many of the schools have adopted the projects schoolwide.

Programs to develop financially literate youth (FLY) are cropping up to provide parents and children with workshops, curricula, and tools to advance the learning of future generations. One such is The Falconer Group in Traverse City, Michigan, which provides materials, programs, and clubs that support the philosophy that instilling responsible fiscal behavior comes through a combination of character development, financial savvy, and strong decision-making skills (http://falconer group.com). Another FLY program can be found under the auspices of the National Heritage Foundation (www.financialliteracy.us).

Those who start family foundations can engage their kids and young adults from an early age. Young people can be volunteers, interns, researchers, grant-making partners, donors, marketing and outreach leaders, advocates, and great resources to inspire every generation. (For more on family foundations, see Chapter Nine.)

One easy way to stimulate youthful giving is through Youth Give (www.youth give.org). This Web-based giving vehicle offers youth gift-giving cards that are replacing material gifts from grandparents and parents and even from kids to each other. With the money in their YouthGive accounts, young people can choose to direct their donations among a wide range of issue areas and organizations—from local to global.

What these resources share is the outlook that young people's interests matter and that their engagement happens best when accompanied by mentors, parents, teachers, and friends who encourage their generosity and participation.

Some parents or grandparents are giving their kids youth-giving cards and challenging them to come up with reports on how they would solve problems or how they would spend $1,000 or $100,000 if they were head of their own foundation (which some of them will be!). When kids contribute themselves, their parents sometimes match their gifts or give some incentive for putting in extra volunteer hours.

Another innovation comes from The Triskeles Foundation (www.triskeles.org), whose youth-mentoring project places kids in internships with outstanding leaders.

The following two stories show how young people are being taught by family members to be givers.

Sarah Silber: Growing Up Giving

From the time I was born, I received small gifts of money on my birthday and at holidays. When I was nine, my parents opened a special "gift" account for me and began teaching me the meaning of the account's interest and balance figures. When I was sixteen, my grandmother encouraged me to begin contributing some of my savings (then $3,200) and my time to projects that interested me. My grandmother made a deal with me: for every hour I volunteered and for every dollar I gave of my own money, my grandmother would contribute a dollar to my "Giving Fund" for future use.

I began keeping newspaper and magazine articles, brochures, and flyers about issues and groups that interested me. After a while I noticed that most of the information I had collected was about dolphins and abused children. I realized that one way I could help in these areas was to give money. To help me understand how groups would use my donations, I made a list of groups I had read about and looked them up on the Internet. I also learned about the Environmental Support Center in Washington, D.C., and looked up their information. Then I began making some donations.

Now twenty-three, I get a sense of the groups I support or might begin supporting through reading their mailings or Web sites or visiting the projects themselves. My list has gone beyond dolphins and abused children. I keep files alphabetically by organization, with a contact sheet for each to remind me of past ideas and actions with the groups. I sometimes make donations to organizations in honor of friends or other family members. Since I turned eighteen, I have been giving away $300 a year.

I have developed my own funding cycle, writing checks twice a year: around the time of my birthday and the year-end holidays. Since I collect and file information all year, I spend only about twenty minutes at the end of each year creating my plan. The plan helps me stay focused and keep my priorities clear, and it makes it easier to turn down requests for donations outside of my giving categories and funding times.

Wendy Stewart: Holiday Giving

One of my giving strategies is to teach my nieces and nephews about philanthropy. Starting when they are around age nine, I call them at Christmas and explain that I'm giving them a certain number of dollars to give away this year. (Their parents and I decide the amount together.) I talk with each child about their interests and concerns about the world. With young kids, I think it's important not to get too heavy about this; I don't want them to give out of guilt or to feel they must begin carrying the weight of the world. But I want to find something that will be meaningful to them.

This has been a great project for a number of reasons. First, by hearing what my nieces and nephews care about, I get to know them better. Second, it's our project, something they do with Aunt Wendy. Third, when they're older, I expect to begin to talk with them about how they do their philanthropy—for example, how often and how much they want to give. I hope to spark conversations about impact and strategic giving.

Use Exercise 12.1 to take a moment to think about your own experiences of learning about giving.

TEENAGERS AND GIVING

Many groups, including the Girl Scouts, United Way, women's funds, and community foundations, have jumped in to counter all the consumer messaging that kids get with new messages of caring. Youth Advisory Councils, classroom programs in schools, or school projects teaching kids to make a difference take place daily across the world. Inspired Legacies has a new curriculum for Youth Giving Circles on its Web site, and many churches, synagogues, and mosques focus their energies on bringing youth on board to improve the world.

With new youth giving cards emerging online (see YouthGive.org), youth giving power is about to be unleashed. But tending to and mentoring our kids at home makes the greatest impact, including taking our kids to our nonprofit work and activities to get them engaged and learn the power of giving to others.

Teenagers can be particularly avid activists, as many are deeply concerned about the state of the world. Here are some inspired examples based on teens following their values and passions that may spark ideas for you or a teenager in your life.

Graciella Villa Franca grew up in a small town near Tucson, Arizona. When she was thirteen, she realized that, although her Latina relatives provided food and information about the community to many immigrants to their town, new immigrants needed more care than her relatives and the local government agencies were providing. She came up with the idea for a center where new immigrants and refugees could get help in starting their new lives.

Graciella talked to her friends and family members about her idea, and several of them met with the town council. An architect produced a drawing for a building that incorporated her ideas: apartments for temporary housing for seven families and a place of meetings and an information center. Over the next five years, Graciella and her cousin helped put on more than thirty-five community fundraising events for the project.

Today, thanks to the persistence and vision of one teenager and a lot of help and effort by others, the center has been built. Twenty-four teens from the area play a key role in providing welcoming and referral services.

In 2006, Palmer McInnis, a seventeen-year-old in the Houston area, raised a prize-winning goat; painted it pink in honor of breast-cancer awareness and in memory of his stepmother, who had died of the disease; and sold it at the Pasadena Livestock Show and Rodeo for a whopping $115,000, which he donated entirely to a local breast care diagnostic center. The previous year, Palmer had donated $10,000 from the sale of a prize-winning heifer to the same organization.

Inspired Legacies invited Palmer to participate in a week-long summer youth-giving camp for kids aged eleven through seventeen, put on in partnership with local Houston schools. The camp taught kids about youth-giving circles and giving cards and took them on site visits to learn more about service and the nonprofits in their communities.

Lin Chao had seen a program on her local public TV station about hip hop and decided her community needed a space where a group of young people could read or recite and move to their poetry and hip hop songs. At a local library, she got permission to hold a Friday night poetry slam in an upstairs room. At first twenty kids came to the slam; eventually more than fifty kids came. Local bookstores helped Lin and her friends publicize the weekly event and in exchange sold books and hip hop CDs at the slams. A local stereo and audio store donated a microphone for the kids to use in exchange for publicity at the event. From that spark, and with no funds of their own necessary, one town's teens have a fun place to express themselves.

YOUTH AS GRANTMAKERS

Some philanthropic institutions are bringing young people into philanthropy to help with youth-related funding. Local community foundations have pioneered youth advisory committees (YACs) as a new model of youth-directed philanthropy. A YAC assesses local youth needs in order to recommend grants from a designated youth fund. Foundations tend to recruit young people to such committees from varied racial, socioeconomic, and academic backgrounds—including those who aren't already school leaders—in hopes of making their groups representative of the community. The young people research potential recipients of funding and make giving recommendations. Sometimes the youth advisors are also involved in raising money for the fund.

YACs provide community foundations with a peer perspective on youth programs and youth-related needs in the community and allow young people a direct say in deciding where charitable money should go. YACs also give foundations an opportunity to teach teenagers about philanthropy, with the hope that they will be more likely to be involved in giving, as they get older.

TEN WAYS FAMILIES CAN ENCOURAGE KIDS' SPIRIT OF GENEROSITY

1. Model abundance or sufficiency, not fear, secrecy, and inadequacy.

2. Talk about giving, volunteering, and service and demonstrate each.

3. Be a mentor with your children about money and giving, or find someone who can mentor them in this area.

4. Set giving, volunteering, and work ethic standards early on.

5. Teach responsible budgeting and planning about money. As kids get older, teach them about responsible checkbook and credit card management.

6. Set up a giving account for contributions (through your bank or at www.youthgive.org or your own special account at your family foundation, if you have one) and seed it with money, and give ongoing age-appropriate guidance. (For instance, review together a few nonprofits online and in person.)

7. Provide motivation for anonymous gifts and generosity.

8. Balance needs and wants with global understanding and consideration. Know where your family is on the economic spectrum, and help your kids to understand what that means (see Chapter Five).

9. Create a family giving plan and include your kids' values and priority issues and concerns.

10. Increase your community service hours as a family and as a mentor for your family. More volunteering and less TV or computer time might open the hearts and minds of your whole family.

In Rochester, New York, for example, six teenagers and two adult advisors work within the Rochester Area Community Foundation to hand out $10,000 a year in grants of up to $750 each to fund programs run by youth peers. "In the history of charitable organizations, young people who came to us were often viewed as problems needing to be addressed, as kids-at-risk," says Jennifer Leonard, who heads the foundation. "In the last ten years, there's been a large mind-shift, that looks at young people as potential sources of great strength for themselves, their families, and communities."

In another example, the Silicon Valley Community Foundation (California) recruited high school students from the communities of East Palo Alto and East San Jose, less prosperous communities bordering some of the country's most affluent neighborhoods, to their Youth In Philanthropy committee. The committee gave away about $20,000—nearly 15 percent of which they raised themselves—to youth-initiated projects.

"The whole concept of philanthropy is pretty new to most of them," says adviser Julie Dean. "They're tough grantmakers. By the time they get to the end, they're asking really good questions about groups' motivations and grilling them on their budgets. They learn a lot of critical thinking skills."

Many high school students are now raising money and giving it away through a similar model within their schools. If you are a young person, you may want to think about forming or looking into possibilities of joining this kind of group; if you are an adult, you may want to help fund a YAC. For more information about youth advisory councils, see www.ysa.org.

If you belong to a nonprofit that has yet to form a young person's committee, or doesn't have youth interns or youth on its board, contact Youth on Board (www.youthonboard.org) or Resource Generation (www.resourcegeneration.org) for some great resources. Inspired Legacies (www.inspiredlegacies.org) also has resources on youth giving circles and how to encourage giving in the next generation.

YOUNG PEOPLE ASK ABOUT GIVING

Like adults, young people can have limited time, conflicts of interest, and questions about how best to use their resources. Here are some questions young people have about how to make choices that reflect the world they care about, along with some suggested answers.

Q: I want to volunteer my time for issues that interest me, but I'm not really sure I can take the time away from homework and everything else I'm doing at school. I'd also like to earn some money.

A: Having a balanced life is important. Getting involved with things you care about is exciting and will inspire the rest of your life. You may need to make choices about your extracurricular priorities in order to do everything. Also, for most people, the busier you are the more efficient you are with your time and getting things done. Volunteer work with an organization or project gives you some experience, knowledge about the work, and contacts that could lead to some paid hours.

Q: When I volunteer, I always seem to get the busywork. How can I get other experiences?

A: A lot of volunteering is doing basic tasks, but there can also be variety. Watch others and the volunteer jobs they have, then ask your supervisor for more and varied experiences. You can also call a local volunteer center or talk with a teacher at school about wanting other experience. The key is to know and be able to articulate both your skills and what you'd like to learn more about.

Q: My parents tell me to save my money for college, but I want to help out some of my friends or donate to help change the world. What can I do?

A: Keep a record of how much you earn or get for allowance and how much you spend. Then consider how you might shift things around so that you can allocate your time or dollars to fulfill both your own dreams and those your parents may have for you. Ask your parents if they feel comfortable with you donating a portion of your allowance or using it for gifts. And think about what seems like a good giving level: how about 5 percent for friends and gifting, 5 percent for non-profit organizations that are trying to change the world? Parents and grandparents have the right to share their opinions and wisdom, but money you earn for allowance is up to you to allocate to the things that matter to you.

Q: I know I am spending money on CDs and supplies or extra clothes for school that I really don't need. How can I stop overspending or wasting?

A: When you get your allowance or get pay for work, divide the money right away and put it into envelopes. The envelopes might be labeled "money to save," "money to give," "money to spend," and "money to invest or lend." Even the spending money could be divided into "money to spend on essentials" and "money to spend on extra stuff." It's good to realize that, like others, you sometimes waste. The key is to know you can change and to try to do so. Also try giving to others or donating some of the extra stuff you have accumulated. There are many organizations that collect clothing, toys, and the like and redistribute them to needy children. You can also make cash donations to these groups. Or hold a garage sale with some of your friends and donate the money you earn that day to a cause you care about.

Q: I want to help women and children who are refugees or immigrants. How can I do that?

A: There are many Web sites that can help you find international resources. Start by thinking about how you want to help: Do you want to help people who need basic food, shelter, or medical support? Or do you want to learn more about changing some of the policies that cause people to migrate from their countries or become refugees? Here are a few resources you can start with:

- www.youthgive.org
- www.globalfundforwomen.org
- www.iearn.org
- www.gwob.org
- www.globalgiving.org
- www.justgive.org

YOUNG INHERITORS GIVING AND LIVING

Listening in on a discussion among younger people from the next generation of donors reminds us of younger people's idealism and the hope it brings to the future.

Beth: My parents have spent the majority of their time maintaining multiple houses and material goods and then complaining about the stress of managing so many people to help take care of their "possessions." Why not be happier and live more simply?

Justin: We have more than we need. The only time I truly see my parents happy is when they are engaged in helping others. It's a no-brainer for me. Why get some job and push myself to make six figures and lose all sense of what's important, when I could have a simpler life and extend what I already have to others?

Armando: Creating stronger communities is what matters. I worry that with this great gap between the rich and poor, giving and service will not compensate for all the advantages still given to those at the top. I want to give a chance to those who are just entering our country or system. My family and I want to be sure that we open doors and help people through those doors to a better way of life. We want to change the culture, not be part of the privileged few who only seem to gain more.

Toper: The real problem is income and inequality of opportunity. I am trying to think and act on how we can not just open doors but share power or even reduce our own influence or dominating class positions. I think the world revolving around the rich is not only not good for us, I think history has shown in the dissolution of other cultures that it will be our demise.

Kim: While my family has worked hard and achieved, we have been centered on our own success while the world teeters at the edge of disaster. Wars, natural disasters, religious fundamentalism, and terrorism thwart human security. As I began to volunteer after the earthquakes and the disasters of the early 2000s I thought, this is what has meaning. Helping others. The tutoring and mentoring and advocating I do for improving not just the lives of the kids I work with but for the whole system of education has given me what I did not have before—joy, purpose, community, and renewed hope. I think through investing in kids and giving teens a chance to voice their dreams and opinions, we can find many of the leaders and answers we will need for the great shifts ahead.

Anthony: I don't see happiness in the families who spend time accumulating. My people spent all this time gaining civil rights and I am grateful. But rights are being lost every day when we have leaders who vote for profits and not people. My path will be to invest in leaders who will shake things up. I want to find the leaders who are doing groundbreaking research and organizing and policy making. My parents taught me to put one-quarter of all I had in the "giving jar" as I grew up. I've heard that most people in the U.S. give only 2 percent of their incomes annually. If you have much more than you need, why not give or invest 50 percent or more in others? Why can't we live more simply and then work to change conditions for others? I want to find community with other donors who are ready to create a different society. I don't see us having the skills and know-how to get us a world of real sustainability and justice. Research shows that the effects of our energy policies now will have the polar caps melted in a few years and increased flooding and natural disasters. Do you want to be drowning in money as the world drowns? Not me. We have to get fully engaged together to figure out the solutions to these problems. Sitting around thinking about what to do with my life is not an option. We have a world to save now. My people are dying from neglect. So too are the world's poor. I won't sit back and watch TV and invest in mutual funds of companies that do not care.

Here are some suggestions from this group of young donors for new younger donors who have $25,000 or more to give.

- Face your privilege and wealth and use your wealth and influence wisely.

- You can raise more money than you can likely give. Get skilled at leveraging and promoting the strategy and groups and leaders you love!

- Know where you are in the socioeconomic spectrum. Tell your advisors what you plan to do with your giving and get input but don't give up your principles, just your principal.

- Get into a community of mentors, donors, and activists who are working to make change and to improve their philanthropy.

- Read about how others have dealt with giving their wealth.

- Invest time and money in your own capacity and learning: go to at least one donor conference a year (www.donorleaders.org), go to one issue-oriented conference, and get a philanthropic coach (www.inspiredlegacies.org) or mentor or experienced community leader to help guide your way. If you are going to have more than $50,000 a year to give away, consider having a donor-advised fund or hiring a philanthropic advisor and an assistant to keep you organized.

- Know your values and the dreams you have for society as the heart of your giving. Then meet people and ask questions. Create a unified vision that is informed by community.

- Dedicate yourself to planning and strategies and finding nonprofit leaders and organizations that match your strategies.

RESOURCES FOR THE NEW GENERATION OF GIVERS

Resource Generation (www.resourcegeneration.org) is a national organization that works with young people, mostly in their twenties and thirties, who have financial wealth and engages them with each other in learning about how to use their wealth for social good. Programs include national workshops and conferences, local meet-ups at dinners, and Donor Organizing Institutes where young people can expand their leadership and fundraising skills. Resource Generation also publishes books, guides, and worksheets for young people and parents. *Creating Change Through Family Philanthropy: The Next Generation,* by Alison Goldberg, Karen Pittleman, and Resource Generation, and *Classified,* by Karen Pittleman and members of Resource Generation, are excellent tools for young people who want to engage their peer community of other inheritors and to work for societal change.

The nonprofit worldwide youth activist education organization YES! (www.yesworld.org) holds a conference each year called "Leveraging Privilege for Social Change," at which future and current leaders under age thirty-five from around the United States who consider themselves privileged come together to identify their passions and to support their concerns for making positive change in the world.

Over a five-day period participants address such questions as these:

- What's happening in the world?

- What are we seeing, and what do we want to shift?

- What does it take to create real and lasting change?

- How can we deepen our understanding of the realities of our times, and develop, build, and implement effective models of transformation?

Adult allies also join for part of the dialogue. The collaborations forged by many of these next-generation groups are truly inspiring. If you want to feel hopeful, check out what the next generation is doing to advance our collective future.

- Get involved with nonprofits and their leaders. Become a donor and a donor partner over time.

- Learn to ask good questions and to listen well.

- Go on site visits and make your giving process real. Ask what's needed. Then help groups get what they need, both by lending your voice and by putting leaders in front with donors and funders so they can pitch for themselves.

- Consider how to support an organization or its leaders to collaborate with others and to achieve their highest intent.

- Accept that figuring out how much of your life will be spent using philanthropy as a strategy will take time! Getting overwhelmed is natural. Coming and going from the pressure to do it well—both internal and external pressures—is part of figuring it all out.

chapter THIRTEEN

For Donors Who Have Much More to Give

We should give as we would receive, cheerfully,
quickly, and without hesitation; for there is
no grace in a benefit that sticks to the fingers.

—Seneca

People with high net worth or more wealth than they really need have even greater reach in sharing their abundance with the nonprofit sector. Many wealthy people have found meaning in their lives by including philanthropy as part of their public or private identities. It is enormously satisfying to help shape a project or mobilize others to volunteer and donate to programs and organizations that reflect your deepest wishes for the world. As with any giving described in this book, donating large amounts of money each year will be more effective and more satisfying if it is done thoughtfully based on your interests and values in balance with what is needed in your community and your chosen areas of funding.

When making decisions about how much you can and want to give, consulting with financial advisors and funding peers can be invaluable for developing systematic ways of thinking about your giving and for getting emotional and practical support. Advisors have a great deal of knowledge about changes in tax law and what may be possible for creatively financing some of your philanthropic wishes. (See Chapter Eleven for more on working with financial advisors.)

This chapter presents a number of resources that may be helpful in thinking about giving more and in partnering with groups you give to.

FACING AND SHARING OUR GOOD FORTUNE

How can those of us who have so much make a truly valuable impact?

It was a historic development in philanthropy when Warren Buffet, one of the world's wealthiest men, decided to transfer three-quarters of his assets—more than $31 billion—to the philanthropic source he most admired, the Bill and Melinda Gates Foundation. Buffet not only honored the Gates family and institution for their excellence with his action, he did what few do: having arrived at the top of his asset class, he decided to give it away during his lifetime. Undoubtedly, part of his motivation was to inspire other wealth holders to mirror his important actions and reap the enjoyment of directing their assets to solve problems that will benefit the greater society during one's life.

Although the wealthiest among us contribute the greatest amount of the funds that go to charity in the United States, we know that most of us could probably give more and give with greater results. Consider this finding from the New Tithing Group's paper *Wealth and Generosity by State* (available at www.newtithing.org): "Charitable giving would jump by $27.5 billion a year if every wealthy American donated at the same rate as the most affluent people in the nation's five most generous states (Georgia, Minnesota, Nebraska, Oklahoma, and Utah). That amounts to a 15 percent gain in the amounts individuals contribute annually. The seven states with the greatest wealth—those where the total assets held by residents were the highest—did not rank in the top 25 percent of most-generous states. Those states were California, Connecticut, Florida, Illinois, Massachusetts, New Jersey, and New York."

When considering how much to give, the real question is not how much do we give now, but what will it take for us to solve some of the problems that are facing us, such as global warming; worldwide poverty; and the pressures on global leadership, public education, and public health systems? And how can we all work better together across race and class and difference to solve some of these problems? Is it possible that, through better engagement and being better philanthropic leaders, we can inspire better donor education that could lead to more strategic giving and more effective policymaking?

GIVING FROM NET WORTH

Donors with high net worth often consider whether or not to give from principal. In the past, donors were invariably advised to "conserve principal." This is no longer the only wise choice.

Claude Rosenberg is an investment manager, founder of the group New Tithing, and the author of *Wealthy and Wise: How You and America Can Get the Most Out of Your Giving.* He and New Tithing's executive director, Tim Stone, have created a Web site for donors and investment advisors that presents a method for calculating what he calls "affordable charitable giving levels" (www.newtithing.org). Rosenberg makes a compelling case, backed by state-by-state statistics, that most of those holding the top 2 percent of American assets can afford to more than double their giving without significantly impairing their wealth.

The One Percent Club, headquartered in Minneapolis, is proving his point. The club is a voluntary association of individuals, most of high net worth, who have committed to give annually to nonprofit organizations of their choice the greater of at least 1 percent of their net worth or 5 percent of their income. The underlying idea is that giving should be based on net worth, not just annual income. Members state that having a 1 percent minimum standard has brought discipline to their giving. Founded in 1997 by Tom Lowe and Joe Selvaggio, the club now has more than one thousand members and is supporting chapters throughout the United States. After its first year, the One Percent Club found that its members had given $7 million more to charities than the previous year. Members are now giving more than $100 million per year to charities of their individual choosing.

Donor education initiatives like this have spread. The Two Percent Club in Denver asks corporate leaders to increase their giving to two percent of pretax profits and also encourages executive giving.

The One Percent Club makes an interesting point about the real cost of giving in this piece from their Web site (onepercentclub.org) by *Twin Cities Business Magazine*:

A Small Price to Pay

While there are great personal rewards for giving back, most members are surprised that they can make a significant difference without sacrificing their lifestyle—especially when the tax advantages of charitable contributions and capital gain avoidance are factored into the equation. Compare the ten-year growth rate of $5 million in net worth to the same net worth after deducting a 1 percent contribution.

Assuming a conservative after-tax earning rate of 7 percent, the untouched $5 million in net worth nearly doubles in ten years, growing to $9.8 million. The same net worth minus the annual 1 percent gift reaches the same value of $9.8 million in the very next, eleventh year. It truly is a small price to pay.

Organizations such as Inspired Legacies (www.inspiredlegacies.org) and the 50 Percent League (www.50percentleague.org) help donors who are considering giving more than 1 or 2 percent think about the social and financial implications of doing so. The 50 Percent League's Exploring Member program provides support to people who want to figure out what their full giving potential might be. The League encourages people to think systematically about their present and future financial needs, determine "how much is enough," and engage whatever surplus they have to make a better world. Their Web site includes brief vignettes from dozens of their members, many of whom are giving a full 50 percent of their income. Here are two examples:

John Hunting

Why should a fortune be something you leave only after you die? When I got a $130,000,000 windfall in 1998, I decided to give it away quickly. If you're an environmentalist like me, given the state of the world, you can't afford to wait.

When I was six years old, my father gave me stock in a small company he cofounded, Metal Office Furniture Company, which made fireproof safes and steel wastebaskets. Eventually it became the world's largest manufacturer of office equipment, Steelcase. In 1998, the company went public, and my stock surged.

I had started a foundation, the Beldon Fund, so when my stock rose in value, it seemed natural to pass $100,000,000 of my new wealth to the foundation. The Beldon Fund was set up to run for ten years and will spend out by 2009. I've also decided to give away the rest of my inheritance by 2010.

The wonderful thing about giving away more than half of my income is that it frees me up to make more political contributions. I believe in giving as much as possible to political candidates and causes. Environmental issues are strengthened or destroyed by what Congress and the president do. I give the maximum tax-deductible amount, 50 percent of income, to foundations and charities, and then give the rest to partisan groups (such as 501(c) 4s, PACs, and 527s).

I believe that it is immoral to hoard money when global warming is on the verge of destroying the ecosystems we depend on. The time to give is now.

Becky Liebman

I was happily working as a reference librarian for many years when serious money came to me. This threw me for a loop. Suddenly I was faced with questions like, "What is real work?" and "Could I be more proactive in the things I say I care about?" and "What's the best thing I can do with my dumb luck?" I decided to wade into the world of social change philanthropy and become a, gulp, philanthropist.

What motivated me? Certainly my family: growing up, we had serious dinner conversations on topics like the maldistribution of wealth. We never expected to be wealthy ourselves. (My parents said they simply "overshot the mark" while manufacturing tiny inductors, and ended up passing millions to each of their children.) I was strongly affected by the year my husband, kids, and I spent in Mississippi, forming deep friendships with people in stressed communities. Later, donor education groups like More Than Money and the Social Justice Fund helped me grow as a giver. For all those reasons and more, five years ago I left my comfortable library work and started volunteering full time with organizations like the Algebra Project and Quality Education as a Civil Right, and now, three days a week, in a minority-majority elementary school.

My husband and I committed to contributing 75 percent of our assets to social justice issues. I've had fun moments in my philanthropist identity, but I've also had to face the discomfort of being close to people and organizations that are struggling financially when I am not. I've had to accept that once you start writing large checks, you are seen as someone who writes large checks, and that this attribute looms larger than qualities more personally meaningful. Ah well. The challenge is to take the opportunity—but not myself—seriously.

To help you think more specifically about how much to give, Exercise 13.1 uses the same concept as Exercise 5.2, "How Much Should You Give?" in Chapter Five, but from the perspective of giving from net worth, allowing you the chance to include equity in calculating your philanthropic budget.

Exercise 13.1
Giving from Assets

10 minutes

In thinking about what percentage of your net worth you want to give, you might start by looking at the chart below. Find an approximation of your net worth, then look across the row until you see the amount you would like to give away. Look at the top of the table to see what percentage that is. Do the amount and the percentage feel right to you? If not, where is the disparity? If you have given in the past, what percentage of your net worth does your past giving represent? How does it compare with the amount or percentage in the table?

If your net worth is	and you want to give					
	1%	3%	5%	10%	15%	20%
$250,000	2,500	7,500	12,500	25000	37500	50,000
$500,000	5,000	15,000	25,000	50,000	75,000	100,000
$750,000	7,500	22,500	37,500	75,000	112,500	150,000
$1,000,000	10,000	30,000	50,000	100,000	150,000	200,000
$2,000,000	20,000	60,000	100,000	200,000	300,000	400,000
$4,000,000	40,000	120,000	200,000	400,000	600,000	800,000
$5,000,000	50,000	150,000	250,000	500,000	750,000	1,000,000
$10,000,000	100,000	300,000	500,000	1,000,000	1,500,000	2,000,000
$20,000,000	200,000	600,000	1,000,000	2,000,000	3,000,000	4,000,000

This year I want to give $_____, which represents _____ percent of my net worth.

Next year I want to give $_____, which represents _____ percent of my net worth.

Women Moving Millions: Women Making History

In early 2005 a remarkable event occurred. In planning her estate, philanthropist Swanee Hunt, director of the Women and Policy Program at Harvard's Kennedy School of Government and former U.S. ambassador to Austria, decided to give her sister, Helen, $6 million to honor Helen's work with nonprofit groups and women's foundations. "Why wait til I'm dead!" she found herself thinking. "It would be so much fun to watch her and her young daughters and sons distribute the money to worthy women's foundations for their important community-based nonprofits."

In turn, Helen decided she would give an equivalent amount along with her time to launch an initiative for those who wanted to propel more million-dollar gifts. This important campaign, partnered with the Women's Funding Network, became Women Moving Millions: Women's Funds Making History. It has been amazing to see how many women have been moved by this campaign to their greatest acts of generosity. In a few short months more than fifty new million-dollar donors have joined the Hunts and forty other trailblazing women before them in making gifts of $1 million or more to one of the 125 women's funds nationally and globally.

Can you imagine giving (or raising) $1 million for a project you love? Remember to sketch your plan in Exercise 3.6.

EXPERIMENTS IN GIVING

Other intuitive ways to think about how much to give are offered by Anne and Christopher Ellinger in the following section, adapted with permission from "How Much to Give," in the magazine *More Than Money*.[1]

> Many donors have asked us to suggest quick-and-easy ways to experiment with giving levels. Although we prefer that people figure out how much to give by systematically considering their current and future financial needs, we know that sometimes it's impossible to make the time for a thorough process.
>
> Here, then, we share some of the quick-and-easy giving guidelines that ambitious givers have used. We illustrate each option through a fictional character: Julia Harlow, single, age twenty-nine, an inheritor and freelance software consultant.
>
> ### Income-Based Options
>
> **1.** *Give a percentage of income.* Julia's grandfather taught her the value of tithing 10 percent of her income to give away, saving 10 percent, and spending the rest. After she received an inheritance that took care of her future retirement needs, Julia started giving 20 percent away (her original 10 percent plus the 10 percent she had been stashing away).

2. *Add realized capital gains to your income.* This year, Julia's portfolio saw $50,000 in realized capital gains (because her investment managers advised selling some stock which had gained in value). Even though those gains were reinvested, Julia counts them as income when she donates 10 percent of income.

3. *Give all investment income.* As a consultant, Julia earns about $55,000 a year after taxes. Because this more than covers her current living expenses ($45,000/year), and because she enjoys the feeling of supporting herself through earnings, she contributes to charity all her investment income.

4. *Give all earned income.* Over several years, Julia's $1.4 million inheritance, which she invested in a balanced fund, has netted her $50,000 a year in income. Given that her earned income has fluctuated over the last few years, she decides to live on the more dependable investment income and donate all her earned income.

5. *Give "windfall" income.* In addition to other giving, Julia has a special giving account into which she puts unexpected financial windfalls. Last year this included $11,000 from her grandmother, $2,000 finally returned from a loan she had written off, $50 from being let off the hook for a speeding ticket, and $12,000 gained from changes in the tax law.

6. *Add your anticipated tax deduction to your gift.* Julia plans to donate $20,000 this year to charity. Her anticipated tax savings from charitable deductions would be $5,000, so she adds this amount to her gift, enabling her to increase her donation without additional out-of-pocket costs. This option (plus giving a small percentage of assets) is promoted in detail at www.NewTithing.org.

Asset-Based Options

1. *Give appreciation.* This past year, Julia's portfolio gained $60,000 in value. Judging her current assets as already ample, she adds this amount to her giving budget, first subtracting 3 percent for inflation.

2. *Give by forgoing appreciation.* Julia decides to move half of her assets into secure, community development loan funds at 3 percent interest (the rate of inflation). The loan funds enable people in low-income communities to start businesses and buy homes. By receiving 3 percent rather than the 6 percent return on those assets she had been getting over time on average, she is in effect donating $21,000 a year to enable people in those communities to improve their lives.

3. *Give assets you feel comfortable giving.* Julia's portfolio has grown by $400,000 since she inherited it. She decides, as a first step, that she can comfortably give $100,000 into a donor-advised account without sacrificing her future goals of child rearing and retirement.

4. *Give to the point of feeling uncomfortable.* Julia decides she can afford to be more generous but doesn't know exactly how much. She tries out an experiment of giving a little more each year, until she feels just a bit uncomfortable—and then evaluates it the following year. In the first year she gave 1 percent of her assets, in the second 2 percent, in the third year 5 percent; in the fourth she went back down to 3 percent.

5. *Give expected inheritance.* Julia discovers her parents plan to leave her another $3 million. At Julia's encouragement, her parents change their will to direct Julia's portion into a charitable fund that she and her siblings will disburse, incidentally saving estate taxes.

In addition to the giving experiments above, we sometimes encourage people to try giving far less than they habitually do, or to take a deliberate break from giving at all. For people who give compulsively (perhaps out of guilt, or because it gives them an identity, or because they can't say no) it can be fruitful to experiment with giving nothing for a discrete period of time, to see what feelings and insights arise.

The question of how much to give is just one aspect of giving, of course, but a vital one. We hope these options stimulate you to design your own short-term experiments while you map out your long-term plans more systematically.

NETWORKING WITH OTHER MAJOR DONORS

Giving has been for many people a private matter. It can be a spiritual, creative, and centering process, but it can also be a chaotic, unbalancing, and isolated one. Increasingly, donors who want to learn from others are joining networks, attending conferences, and enrolling in courses on giving to connect with other donors and learn more about the art and craft of philanthropy. Tracy Hewat, former director of Resource Generation, points out, "When we exchange ideas, information, and experiences, we also help inspire and create solutions for each other and the world. This collective experience transforms us. Money becomes a tool that can change your life and help others change theirs."

There are informal networks of donors from every population, issue, or affinity group you can imagine: younger donors, conservative donors, donors of color, women donors, environmental funders, donors who fund religious programs, donors concerned about children and education, funders who give internationally, gay donors, donors to the arts, and funders of disability issues. Although most of these networks are for educational value primarily, some engage periodically in collaborative giving initiatives or donor or giving circles. (The Council on Foundation's Web site, www.cof.org, lists some of these "affinity groups" in philanthropy.) There are enormous advantages to belonging to or attending some of these affinity groups or donor or funder networks, including the following:

- Meeting peers with shared interests or geography and generally some shared values

- Engaging with others from a broader geographic area—regional, national, or even international

- Hearing good speakers and gathering resources that are educational

- Exchanging ideas and networking

- Promoting collaboration on philanthropy or on a particular issue

Examples of some organizations through which you can access these forums are the Black Philanthropy Conference, Native Americans in Philanthropy, Hispanics in Philanthropy, Asian Pacific Islanders in Philanthropy, Funders of Gay and Lesbian Projects, the Environmental Grantmakers Association, the Jewish Funders Network, the Council on Foundations, the Philanthropy Roundtable, the National Network of Grantmakers, and the Association for Small Foundations (see Appendix I, Resources on the CD-ROM).

The industry of donor education has expanded tremendously since the 1990s. A wide range of organizations offer informative programs for funders, including community or public foundations and local United Way branches. Donor education programs are also offered by philanthropic support and consulting organizations around the country, such as the Association of Small Foundations, the Philanthropic Initiative, Changemakers, and Resource Generation (see Appendix I, "Resources," on the CD-ROM). Banks and trust companies, wealth advisors, philanthropic advisors, and investment and estate advisors sometimes hold programs for clients and prospective clients. The Institute for Philanthropy in London (now home to the Rockefeller Foundation's Philanthropy Workshop), Hewlett Foundation, and Stanford University's M.B.A. program all offer courses for philanthropists.

One model of a pilot donor network was Marin Independent Donors in California, an informal group of donors giving at least $10,000 a year. Dues of $100 to $1,000, depending on each donor's annual giving, helped defray mailing costs and speaker fees. A volunteer steering committee planned the quarterly programs, which included the following types of topics:

- How to involve your children in your giving

- What nonprofits really want from donors

- Matching your philanthropy to community needs

- Collaborating in your grantmaking

- Anonymity versus disclosure: pros and cons

- Historical role models in philanthropy (such as Madame C. J. Walker and Andrew Carnegie)

- New trends in giving

There are now hundreds of donor groups that meet to discuss giving on a regular basis. New Ventures in Philanthropy, the network for regional educational groups for funders, lists more than thirty-five giving groups and hundreds of giving circles (www.givingforum.org). The Web site www.donorleaders.org lists other established donor networks.

Although most donor networks are national, some are global, such as the Chicago Global Donor Network (www.chicagoglobaldonors.org) and other donor and funder networks develop locally.

Another example is the Women Donors Network. At its founding meeting in 1990, the Women Donors Network had twenty-five members whose combined net worth represented more than a billion dollars. Now the network has more than 150 members nationally and leverages amounts in the multimillions; it also provides support to some of the leading women donors in the United States. Members qualify by giving at least $25,000 toward projects with a social change outcome or result. By the early 2000s, these 150 women were giving an amount equivalent to a year's grantmaking from all the U.S.-based foundations serving women and girls—about $75 million dollars annually. But these networks do more than quantify their members' grantmaking. They are critical to the development of a new generation of philanthropic leaders.

By sharing strategies on e-mail listservs, panels at annual conferences, and at quarterly meetings, members of these donor networks who participate actively not only advance more quickly as more strategic donors but also find partnership in funding, friends, and company, making site visits to nonprofits together.

Beyond grantmaking, donors' influence is also enhanced by exemplary leadership in these networks. One donor, for example, recently responded to her congressperson's request for campaign funding with a counterproposal: travel with her from his district in New England to the New Orleans gulf coast region to see the situation there firsthand. When he accepted this invitation, the donor used her contacts to set up a twenty-four-hour visit that included a tour of some of the hurricane-devastated areas and meetings with key people from community organizations active in the area. She reported to her Women Donors Network partners:

> With plane tickets, my hotel, the overinsured rental car (with absolutely invaluable GPS), dinner at a nice restaurant (which I picked up for the organizational representatives), the whole thing ran me about $900. It seemed like a good use of my money and my access: both my access to my congresspeople and my access to strong community activists in the gulf.

For more information on how to get connected, contact your local regional grantmaking association, community foundation, United Way, or public foundation, or any of the resources listed in Appendix I on the CD-ROM or updated on the Inspired Legacies Web site (www.inspiredlegacies.org).

All the following types of gatherings offer avenues to become more involved in specific nonprofit activities:

- Foundation staff and donors share experiences and ideas or make site visits together to community groups.

- Donors and activist or community groups discuss how a specific problem might be addressed.

- Donors and foundation staff or board members share information on e-mail listservs or Web sites.

- Donors, activists, and foundation staff meet to discuss common problems and solutions.

If you are reluctant to be "exposed" as a donor or vulnerable to increased requests for funding because of participation in such meetings, you can always explain that you are simply interested in the issue or trying to gain more information without revealing your funding, status, or financial position.

Most donors have found joining at least one network or attending one annual funders conference to be life-changing. These are the places to find role models and some great ideas and innovations.

KEEPING TRACK AND BEING RESPONSIVE

High-end donors may be funding twenty to fifty projects a year and be invited to fund hundreds if not thousands of others. If your giving is not being managed through a donor-advised fund or family foundation, you may want support to help keep track of your philanthropic involvements. Many wealthy donors are hiring a part-time personal assistant, secretary, or philanthropic advisor who helps with organizing the paper (and people) that surround philanthropic work. Five to ten hours a week of such help can make a huge difference in keeping your giving plan and giving systems organized. Donors often hold back from adding this expense, but this investment in one's own capacity as a donor can make for greater effectiveness and freedoms. (See www.inspiredlegacies.org for sample job descriptions for personal assistants.)

The power that comes with money makes the role of a donor a privileged one in most communities. Leaders and other donors need your time and perspective as well as your financial contributions. It can feel daunting and sometimes even objectifying given the hundreds of nonprofits who hope you will fairly consider them. It has become common for especially high-end donors not to respond to requests by mail, e-mail, and phone. The message this gives is that you are busy. But it also wastes valuable time and resources for organizations, particularly if you know you will not be funding them.

> ## DONOR DIVA
>
> Give appropriate support to your philanthropy. If the volume of information and requests you are processing takes the joy out of your giving and makes you appear unprofessional as a giver, you will benefit from hiring help. Do what you are best at, and bring in team members to fill in other responsibilities as feasible. Much like hiring a good advisor, this step can increase not only your effectiveness and impact but the joy in your giving as well.

Whether considering funding the requests you receive or not, those who contact you personally should receive the courtesy of a response, even if by e-mail. It helps to have good systems and an assistant—whether periodic or regular. Responding to the nonprofit community within a week of a call or a month of a mailing is considered best practice by those who care to strengthen and not deplete valuable resources. We must do our best to improve our own capacity to engage with the nonprofits that we care about.

The Power of Partnership:
Transformative Philanthropy

*How wonderful it is that nobody need wait a single
moment before starting to improve the world.*

—Anne Frank

The world is at a truly amazing—and frightening—crossroads. Advanced technology, sophisticated scientific discoveries, and superior health care all contribute to a feeling of security and possibility for those of us fortunate enough to have access to them. Yet the effects of climate change, terrorism, the rise of religious intolerance and fundamentalism, worldwide disease, and poverty challenge our comfort and alert us to huge inequities and crises ahead. We need leaders who understand that we are globally interdependent and must share responsibility, opportunity, and resources. Caring about the world and our fellow planet dwellers, we are propelled to act. As philanthropists, we have to discipline ourselves to be more strategic and to give more in a timely way. No one sector alone—government, business, or the nonprofit sector—can make the changes needed. I believe that well-organized nonprofits that know how to leverage business, government resources, and the networks of their own constituents will have a major role in leading the way to necessary change.

Just as all sectors need to cooperate to address these enormous problems, all parts of the nonprofit sector need to come together as well. We cannot afford to have donors in one corner, nonprofit leaders in another, those we are serving in another, and advisors elsewhere. Likewise, the United Way and the community foundations, the social change and workplace federations, venture philanthropy, and giving circles need to be working together with corporate and government funders and advocates. The World Bank and funding agencies that created foreign aid dependency of the past must work anew with private and dynamic sources such as the Gates Foundation, the Google Foundation, or the Global Fund for Women that seek a better way of working with communities. Solutions to problems or models for crucial interventions are as likely to be found thousands of miles away in community programs or in the boldness of front-line activists as in our own larger agencies, around government policy-setting tables or at think tanks.

Collaboration is key to understanding the problems, their solutions, and who's doing what and when. Just as transpartisan politics has emerged through projects such as Reuniting America (www.reunitingamerica.org), so too, transpartisan philanthropy has been born. People of difference are listening to each other anew.

The Internet has given us the tools to see the problems and connect our work, but the hard work of collaboration is more than just posting wants and needs. We have the power and the will to come from our compartmentalized areas of knowledge and skills to diverse circles of inspiring and strategic change. Imagine putting the basis of our unified concerns in the centers of our hearts, communities, families, and collaborations so that we can cross-pollinate and share varied approaches to arrive at a higher level of problem solving. This level of collaboration is our task ahead. The new trend in the twenty-first century is our shared generosity and our interdependence.

It will take visionaries and artists; heady planners and technicians; farmers, social workers, clergy, and financial people; labor and corporate leaders; and activists from the right, left, and center perspectives, all envisioning and cocreating a more humane and sustainable world. The best news is that it's happening! Environmentalist, entrepreneur, and author Paul Hawken and the Natural Capital Institute have applied open-source technology to create an international directory and networking tool that links and empowers what Hawken calls the "largest and fastest growing movement ever on earth—the sustainability movement." The directory is called WiserEarth (World Index of Social and Environmental Responsibility:

www.wiserearth.org). At its launch online in April 2007, WiserEarth compiled the contact information and missions of more than one hundred thousand nonprofits or nongovernmental organizations in 243 countries, territories, and sovereign islands. These civil society groups all over the world are working toward social, economic, and cultural change.

Given the exponential growth of the nonprofit sector in the past twenty years, the future holds great possibilities for collaboration leading to effective action. Leaders and policymakers will be fueled by the far-sightedness and inclusivity of what is emerging as a new shift in the field of philanthropy called transformative philanthropy.

With the Internet and new media available for new forms of dialogue and research, we have tools that enable us to take a more integrated view of the world and engage in conversations about the world we want. At many circles and tables where decisions and plans are made for ourselves and society, we should consider together how transformative philanthropy's lens or vista can address questions such as these:

- What is needed? What can be done? What must be prioritized?

- Who's doing what—and who is doing what most effectively?

- What role does government have now and how does it differ country by country?

- What role should the corporate and religious world play in balancing social and environmental needs?

- Who are great leaders? How can we sustain them and support the next generation of leaders as well?

- What are the models that are proven and working, and how can we accelerate their accessibility and bring them to scale so that more people understand and can replicate these strategies and exemplary methods?

- What are our assets? Who is exemplary at completing the pieces that need to be filled in? What are the gaps in delivery, production, or service?

- How can we educate the public about what needs to be done—including enlisting mainstream media?

- How can we have a coherent vision and strategy that can be addressed across many organizations, companies, governments, and countries?

These are very big questions and offer a new framework beyond giving because our hearts are touched by need. Tools such as the WiserEarth Web site enable networking online, but can we work beyond virtual community toward common purpose? The opportunities for a new level of breakthrough because of the power of the Internet and new technologies give us great hope. But for each of us the personal journey is one that is also learned through experience and by thinking about how to expand our impact.

From my own journey—moving from intuitive funding to building funding infrastructures—comes one example of opening one's heart and mind to new ways of thinking about—and doing—philanthropy.

MOVING FROM CHARITY TO CHANGE

Watching my parents give to many wonderful charities, I realized that the networking they did as they attended events and met with leaders of nonprofits and their boards was essential to their social lives. I began to wonder about the balance between the motivations of the donors at these grand events and their philanthropic impact—was it all about giving parties, buying chic and expensive clothing, and being seen? I wondered if they knew whether the money they gave and the volunteering they did actually made a difference.

When I was fourteen, my mother responded to my questions about effectiveness of giving and my desire to help end poverty by setting up a giving account for me. She also required my brother and me to volunteer, as she was doing, at least five hours a week. In the process, I learned that, although those annual black-tie events and chic nonprofit parties do sometimes cost many thousands of dollars, a great deal of funding does come from them. This funding mainly benefits large, established organizations or the up-and-coming trendsetting favorites of the younger set.

But I also wondered what smaller groups did without the time, money, staffing, volunteers, or contacts to be able to pull off a major event that would get exposure to wealthy donors. It was clear there were issues of class, race, access, and power. I would spend a lifetime trying to understand and change them.

The world I wanted to see would have more opportunity for more people and would not just cater to the wealthy and their needs and interests. This is a worldview that, over time, I found I shared with many other new inheritors, as we learned to invest and give. Our time was different from our parents'—we came of age when established social rules were being questioned, and broken, in many areas of society. Philanthropy became one of them. This is how I began my own journey to consider how to give away some of the million dollars I had inherited.

When I moved from New York to California in the early 1970s, my cousin George Pillsbury brought me on a visit to a new social change foundation. Vanguard Public Foundation in San Francisco was one of the first funds that invited wealthy donors and activists to collaborate to see how we might produce more lasting social change.

By 1976, I had decided to give away at least $50,000 a year (in equal proportion from my salary and from the investments and the principal of my inherited money). Soon I understood that if I lived more simply I could give even more, with more impact. By the time I was twenty-six, I realized that I could expand my impact further if I learned to listen to and work with nonprofit leaders and donors, to be an advocate for needed changes, and to raise money from others. I learned first to raise hundreds, then thousands, and eventually millions of dollars. Because of my privilege, I felt a responsibility to reach as far as I could into the circles of great wealth to ask my peers to join me in helping address community and world problems we shared. I also found that I loved doing this work!

Volunteering with Vanguard Foundation gave me the chance to learn from and work alongside other donors, community leaders, and activists to consider solutions and fund initiatives. I found this a much more enjoyable way to learn and to fund than going to fancy parties. My mentors and guides were knowledgeable about multiple issues and were themselves from varied classes, races, cultures, and ages. Learning with them, I had to rethink the stereotypes and behaviors I had brought from childhood about power and privilege. My new partners taught me to think globally and act locally and to build bridges to global work and the people whom many of my daily choices affected. I learned to give and show up locally, nationally, and globally.

I did not act from guilt. I knew I had simply received lucky cards at birth and had a responsibility to use those cards well. Guilt, which I observed in so many of my peers with inherited money, seemed like wasted energy. The question for all of us is, what are you going to do with the resources and resourcefulness you have? Or as activist Orland Bishop has said, *"How can we transform that which we have been given?"* I decided with others to apply the model of community-based philanthropy to form women's foundations and other funding circles, bringing in donors at all levels of giving. I was simply amazed by the emergence and sincerity of women and girls and more people of color joining these efforts and diversifying philanthropy. Their contributions and ways of giving were anything but traditional, and their stories opened wider my heart and purse.

As I entered my thirties I became increasingly inspired by the possibilities I saw while going on site visits worldwide and throughout the United States. I realized that I not only wanted to contribute all my inherited money (or rather, as I saw it, to "invest" it in great leaders and projects), but also wanted to earn enough to be able to continue giving away at least 40 percent of my income annually.

I realized in my forties that I needed to gain serious skills as a nonprofit entrepreneur and money magnet if I was to catalyze the kinds of changes that I saw the nonprofit and NGO sector needing. I sought out new mentors (younger and older) and community partners, and once again, I was not disappointed. I also began to see new models of philanthropy in public foundations, federations, and giving circles. A real breakthrough in who makes decisions about giving or informs that giving has been achieved as family, private, and corporate foundations have begun to put community members on their boards. Because these community members have firsthand experience in the foundations' funding areas, incorporating their knowledge, contacts, and outlook has produced more informed philanthropy and better outcomes.

Over many years, I have had the honor to participate in expanding the infrastructure of philanthropy, so that a field once thought to be only for wealthy givers is now filled with donors from all walks of life. This democratization of philanthropy is in itself the greatest transformation in the field. In my own activism over the past thirty-four years, I have prioritized a giving strategy that promotes giving collaboratively with other donors, community leaders, and activists, as well as educating donors and activists about community needs from the perspective of those affected by those needs.

Over the years, I have visited more than two thousand nonprofit groups across the country and around the world. I have seen the power of one person or a small group of people to create change through dedication to their dreams for their communities and the world. I learned to discern projects that focused on change from those that offered charity alone. I have learned that the knowledge about community problems and solutions is there. We need to trust local activists and the leaders of our times. And we need to partner with them to help them get even stronger. Work by the global women's funds has been exemplary in this methodology. One place to read about such leaders is at Ashoka (www. ashoka.org), which describes itself as "The global association of the world's leading social entrepreneurs—men and women with system-changing solutions for the world's most urgent social problems." During the past twenty-five years, Ashoka has elected more than eighteen hundred leading "social entrepreneurs"—"individuals with innovative solutions to society's most pressing problems"—as Ashoka Fellows and provided them with living stipends, professional support, and access to a global network of peers in more than sixty countries. "Ashoka Fellows," they write, "inspire others to adopt and spread their innovations—demonstrating to all citizens that they too have the potential to be powerful changemakers and make a positive difference in their communities."

The Inspired Philanthropy Giving Model (in Figure 14.1) shows the significance of incorporating community needs and engaging those who are being served in order to create better outcomes. The model places all philanthropic activity within the context of the cultural and social forces that influence us. Within that changing reality, our giving is based on a combination of being rooted in our own values and passions while being informed by community need, as we determine what we want to change, create, or affect. We move then to assess potential nonprofit partners in alignment with our personal philanthropic mission, taking into account their mission and values and the quality of their leadership and previous efforts. These steps help us create our own giving plan, using it to support those causes and organizations we have come to care most about. It also includes using our leadership and influence on their behalf and creating partnerships with others working toward similar goals.

Figure 14.1
Inspired Philanthropy Giving Model

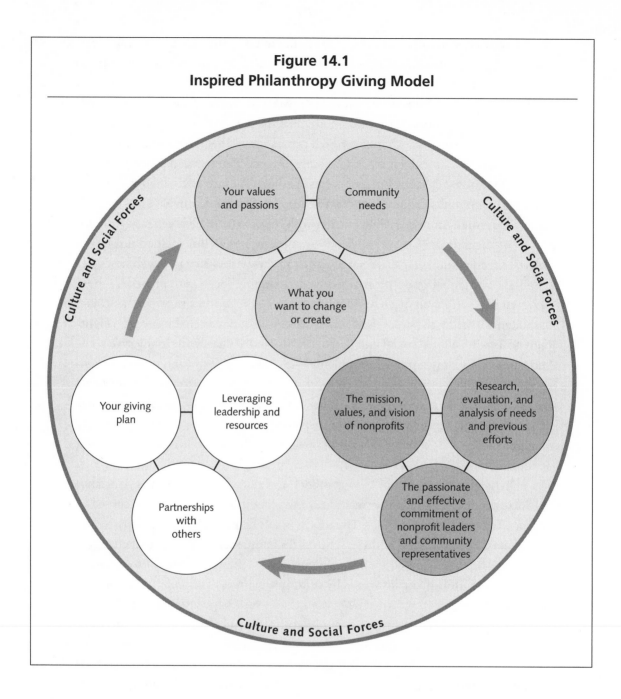

Transformative philanthropy can be seen as the result of moving through the Levels of Philanthropic Intervention presented in Chapter Six and reproduced here in Table 14.1. It is a lifetime of work; perhaps by seeing how this work has progressed for me, you will move through or try out some of these levels or strategies more confidently.

I spent the years of my twenties learning how to address Level One: Needs Philanthropy. It was surely a heartfelt kind of giving, as I derived satisfaction from giving to direct service. In my thirties, I found Level Two: Empowerment Philanthropy. During those years I made donations to empower individuals to take care of themselves and to develop skills they needed. This, too, was a positive experience in the ways it enabled people to build on their assets. In my forties, I began funding at Level Three: Capacity-Building Philanthropy, which moved organizations and communities to build essential alliances, systems, staffing, leadership, and resources. During this period of volunteering, organization building, board work, and giving, I focused on helping hundreds of social change and community-based organizations, along with women's foundations, to become established, grow, and strengthen their infrastructures.

From the early 1980s to the present, this work has included strengthening the infrastructure of philanthropy itself. Colleagues and I have been building donor networks, organizing thousands of donor education conferences, helping initiate donor and activist giving circles, and convening gatherings at which advisors, donors, and activists could work together to learn more about giving and determine strategies. We are also developing Web sites and using social networking sites and e-mail listservs to keep communities communicating between meetings and to document best practices and breakthrough leadership stories. Blogs and the use of new media videos on www.youtube.com and www.karmatube.org and text messaging allow us to communicate day and night in varied forms with potential partners around the world.

New avenues of communication moved philanthropy into a much more dynamic mode and propelled it forward. Over this time, as wealth had accumulated from strong markets and unimaginably successful technology startups, the nonprofit community also expanded to provide many new ways of service to the public—growing from just 220,000 nonprofits in the 1970s to the more than 1.5 million organizations that exist today.

Table 14.1
Levels of Philanthropic Intervention

	Funding Focus	Merits	Limitations or Challenges
Level 1: Needs Philanthropy *Addresses immediate and recurring needs*	Relief efforts (disasters, hunger, wars) Care programs (day care, shelters, refugees) Cultural activities Religious services	Alleviates urgent and critical needs Responds quickly to unforeseen events Takes care of vulnerable populations Draws attention to key social issues Offers simple and accessible ways to relieve donors' urge to "do something" Gives donors opportunities to build civic muscles (generosity, solidarity, and so on)	Focuses on symptoms (tip of iceberg) Relief effects are typically short-lived Often amounts to a drop in the ocean Relief efforts are rarely synergized Can disempower people through dependency and perpetuate the problem Can easily feed donors' propensity to guilt-based and reactive giving
Level 2: Empowerment Philanthropy *Empowers individuals to take care of themselves*	Education and mentoring Job training and skills Personal growth and spirituality Tool acquisition (books, computers) Living infrastructure (building homes, wells)	Builds people's assets to help them become more effective in directing their lives and meeting their own needs Encourages self-responsibility rather than dependency Has more lasting effects	Receptivity to training varies Disempowering effects of training if based on "we know better than you" attitudes rather than partnering with target population to find optimal solutions Limited way of dealing with root causes

Level 3: Capacity-Building Philanthropy *Expands groups' ability to serve the commons*	Leadership and management training Developing systems for IT, fundraising, and so on Strategic planning Capital campaigns Building alliances Creating needed organizations	Empowers organizations and communities Minimizes waste and inefficiencies (doing more with less) Maximizes beneficial impact (doing more of the right things) Improves accountability, building trust with donors Fosters collaboration through networking and coalition-building	Finding organizations ready and willing to learn to be more effective Possible negative side-effects of sustainable funding (endowments can make organizations less responsive) Current bias against allocating philanthropic money to administrative costs
Level 4: Systemic Philanthropy *Develops systemic solutions to collective problems*	Research think tanks Policy or legal reform Shifting consciousness Civic engagement Media reform Collaboration among key stakeholders	Deals with the root causes of problems Targets most effective change strategies (replicability or tipping point effects) Most lasting and comprehensive impact if successful (for example, campaigns to stop smoking; support use of organic food, and so on) Highest leverage of philanthropic dollars	Hard to identify and implement comprehensive solutions Current strategies are often polarizing (conservatives versus progressives) Takes time to create visible impact Harder to mobilize donors Highest risk of failure May be best chance for breakthrough

NEW FORMS OF COLLABORATION

In the past ten years, I have found myself more fully engaged in Level Four: systemic or transformational philanthropy. For me this work has involved considering philanthropy through a larger lens to view the interconnectedness of solutions and how, beyond determining the root causes of problems, we can better collaborate for lasting and comprehensive impact for the greatest good for the most people, not simply addressing one issue or problem. If we are serious about the future, we can no longer indulge in funding less than what is essential to the well-being of the whole of humanity. This is the level at which we must address the very difficult questions of how we will survive and help the planet do so. As Norman Cousins has said, "All things are possible once enough human beings realize that everything is at stake."

It has been projected that by 2040 at least 35 percent of existing species will be extinct.[1] Scientists fear that within an even shorter time all the species of fish now in the sea will have died. These are horrifying and sobering considerations. Imagine our children and grandchildren understanding and facing this reality. But will these scientific projections wake us up to new behaviors or inventions? Collaborating in new ways has become an imperative.

Duane Elgin, one of the foremost social scientists and authors on the future of the planet (www.awakeningearth.org) offers in the report *Transformational Philanthropy* these strategies for funders to consider:[2]

- Funding networks ranging from established foundations with experience and resources to startup venture funds and groups of young entrepreneurs looking for high-leverage investments in support of a sustainable and compassionate future. These include progressive foundations, venture philanthropy organizations, networks of young donors, and innovative philanthropists.

- Trusted people networks that, in turn, can identify projects around the world that have the potential for deep, systemic change in favor of a more sustainable and compassionate future. Trusted advisors bring a trusted human face and network for identifying high-leverage areas of support.

- Internet or computer groups working on new forms of linking that can erase geographic distance and use highly "intelligent" computerized networks to facilitate matchmaking between donors and recipients around the world.

Many within this community would like to dramatically reduce the middleman role of traditional philanthropic institutions and have services and skills flow as directly and efficiently as possible from the Donor (Helper) to the Recipient (Doer). Moreover, some within this community view philanthropy more in nonmonetary terms, emphasizing the contribution of personal talents and networking skills. Key resources in the computer network area include Joe Firmage's ManyOne.net, Tom Munnecke's GivingSpace.org, Nipun Mehta's CharityFocus.org, Peter Copen's iearn.org, and Jim Fournier's various projects undertaken through Planetworks.org.

Elgin concludes:

> By combining innovative funding networks with trusted people networks and global computer networks, there is the potential to create something larger than any one community can accomplish in isolation. If all three work together, a self-reinforcing system can emerge that combines the experienced management of resources with intelligent networks of global reach and the guidance of trusted networks of people. This higher-order system could accomplish together what no two of them could accomplish alone—create a truly transformative network of exchange that can nurture vital seeds of innovation as we move into a time of historic, global transition.

PROPERTIES OF TRANSFORMATIONAL PHILANTHROPY

In the mid-1990s, the National Network of Grantmakers reported that only about 5 percent of American foundation funding was addressing social change. Most funding was still focused on alleviating the symptoms of problems and not the source of the problems themselves. Meanwhile, the major threats to the planet—disease, war, poverty, and environmental degradation—called for greater attention and solution. A new kind of philanthropy was called for—one that worked at a higher level of reflection, analysis, strategy, and funding.

One of the clearest descriptions of transformational philanthropy and how it differs from traditional philanthropy comes from Fran Korten, who was a program officer with the Ford Foundation in Asia for twenty years and is now the executive director of the Positive Futures Network:

Transformational philanthropy is for organizations pursuing a large vision of social change—organizations that see the depth of the ecological and social crisis that is upon us and are working to bring about a deep shift in consciousness in the way we live and in the possibilities we can see for our collective future. Transformational philanthropy is willing to be more daring—to be less specific in its outcomes and more holistic in its frame. As we think about consciousness change, we have to be prepared to pursue long-term goals. Much of traditional philanthropy is aimed much more at the short-term and at more concrete objectives. Communications and convening play a bigger role in transformational philanthropy because of the importance of shifting consciousness and providing support and connections for people pursuing pioneering visions and actions.[3]

Peter Copen, president of the Copen Family Fund and founder of iEarn (an Internet-based initiative technologically linking teachers and students around the world to work together on social and environmental projects) adds:

Transformational philanthropy means having a large vision, one that will create a new paradigm—a paradigm that will exponentially reduce suffering (and enhance the evolution) of people and the planet. It also means asking some big and important questions and having the courage to fund projects that live within those questions, not knowing how they will turn out. Why? Because a new paradigm cannot be adequately described or conceived by the language and concepts of the old one.[4]

The following are nine components from the report on transformative philanthropy that have emerged from wide-ranging conversations in the field that help to shape a now refining universe of transformational initiatives:

- Recognize that we have entered a time of global change and a historic window of opportunity
- Take a whole-systems, integral perspective
- Build strength by actively embracing diversity
- Tell a bigger story about the nature and purpose of life
- Bring a reflective consciousness into the functioning of systems

- Foster self-organization at the grassroots level

- Provide leadership that ignites a belief in transformational change

- Approach change in transformational ways

- Recognize and appreciate multiple ways of knowing

MOVING GIVING AND LEADERSHIP TO THE NEXT GENERATION

Like many public philanthropists who are advisors to funders, in an average year I receive by e-mail or mail thousands of ideas and proposals for good ideas by innovators. It has been my honor to try to get to know some of those leaders or architects of a new society and to endeavor to understand their work and, when possible, to support them, if only by sharing their works or proposals with others. I have also made a commitment to seek out communities of donors, activists, advisors, and leaders working diligently to make systemic change or to experiment with varied strategies and outcomes.

Along the way, I have met extraordinarily talented, committed, and amazing people. Our exchange with each other is a prayer, guised in what some call "the donor dance," but for me it is at its best a form of service. Matching donors and leaders, the dreamers and the dream makers, with each other and connecting them to their highest purpose or to advisors that can support them, is the greatest blessing of all. For it is out of these small steps that great things evolve. And now there is an entire industry or at least a band of angels who accompany many donors and leaders as they do their best. Some are trained at places such as Rockwood Leadership Institute (www.rockwoodleadership.org), some by Social Venture Partners (www.svp.org), Social Venture Network (www.svn.org), The Women Donors Network, the Leveraged Alliance, YES!, or Resource Generation, some through business or family mentorship or within the new field of wealth coaching. All of these forms of guidance and accompaniment for "transformative donors" draw on traditions of deep listening, the direct transmission of wisdom and knowledge from one person to another, and catalyzing each person's own wisdom and insight.

I am often asked to help mentor or accompany young men and women activists and future donors in the shaping of their careers or responsibilities as change agents. It is my happiest work to learn from them, to listen to their hopes and fears, and to share with them some of the people and lessons learned that have been given to me. The Social Venture Partners Web site (www.svp.org) includes a blog that shares advice for new donors and leaders. This kind of sharing is an important trend, as we face the coming retirement of so many leaders, board members, and donors who have been the backbone of the nonprofits that were founded twenty-five to thirty-five years ago. Given the size of the baby boom population—some 79 million people born between 1946 and 1964—and especially the number of women who went into the nonprofit field in the 1970s, we are about to experience a huge wave of retirement as many of those aging boomers move out of executive leadership of nonprofit and foundation boards and staff.

This intergenerational transfer of leadership will create new forms of partnership as organizations bring on the next generation of leaders at the management level. Because these new leaders do not have twenty to forty years' worth of fundraising contacts, we must ensure careful transitions during this important wave of change ahead. There are lessons to learn from arts organizations worldwide, which, because of the devastation of premature death from the AIDS epidemic, have already faced some of these issues. These nonprofit transitions need to be made quite consciously for the nonprofit sector to stay healthy and resilient. We should count on seeing reorganization and some healthy changes ahead. There are many, many new initiatives that require our attention, our knowledge, and the acceleration of knowledge so that we might ensure greater progress and improvements in our society and field.

If you are not mentoring someone from the next generation in your family or workplace on your love for and knowledge about philanthropy, nonprofit management, or leadership, consider doing so. Think, as you move from one meeting to another and one contact to another, what you can do to take someone who does not have your experience, privilege, or access to those meetings as your guest, observer, or participant. You will be helping to develop the next generation of the nonprofit community.

REASONS FOR HOPE

In early 2007, I heard Lester Brown, acclaimed social scientist and author of *Plan B 2.0: Rescuing a Planet Under Stress and a Civilization in Trouble,* speak on the perils we all face. I found myself facing my own fear amid his predictions for the globe, even amidst his optimism of what possibilities are before us. Brown told the story of how President Roosevelt, facing dual enemies in World War II, worked with automotive industry leaders to transform their industry from building cars to building arms. To transform the country to wartime capacity, federal policies banned sales of autos for other than war-related activities in the early 1940s.

Now we are faced with problems that require this same kind of bold action by our leaders and commitment on all our parts. Will we all mobilize? As Brown says, "Saving our civilization is not a spectator sport."

With short-term thinking we are apt to make choices that will not serve us in the long run.

Bernard Lietaer, economist and author of *The Future of Money: Creating New Wealth, Work, and a Wiser World,* reminds us that our current monetary system does not give adequate incentive for us to think or invest for the long term. So too, philanthropy. We tend to fund people—our friends or people we like and their projects—for one to three years. But we must find the strategies, leaders, and organizations that fulfill our missions and those needed for humanity and enable their success for longer stretches.

A MODEL OF TRANSFORMATIVE COLLABORATION

In 2006 I was invited to join an unusual collaboration that has sparked my own hope beyond anything I have ventured into before. Susan Davis, a business entrepreneur who has started more than twenty networks based on a collaborative process she has developed using the KINS method (Key Initiator Network Strategy—read more about it at www.capitalmissions.com), invited twenty innovators and twenty donors from multiple sectors and disciplines to collaborate over an extended time on an initiative called The Tipping Point Network. The Tipping Point Network seeks to catalyze a globally sustainable economy by focusing philanthropists on jumping sustainability's market share from 2 percent to 10 percent—the "tipping point" after which they believe the global economy can be expected to find an accelerated path toward sustainability.

The group includes people involved with sustainable businesses, social scientists, academics, an ordained minister, socially responsible investors, young leaders, donor activists, leaders in sustainable agriculture, entrepreneurs, a foundation representative, grassroots leaders, and several national and local nonprofit leaders. We evolved the following statements of values, vision, and mission:

Values: Generosity, trust, honesty, responsibility, patience, and love, by listening, challenging, and supporting each other.

Vision: "We cocreate a healthy earth and an economy that can sustain all."

Mission: "We partner with others to cocreate and fund breakthrough initiatives for a sustainable world."

After some study together on global and national conditions, each member prepared a two-page proposal for a project for the Network to consider. We compared our ideas to Lester Brown's "Plan B 2.0" outline, including strategies named by Brown such as "building a new economy, eradicating poverty, restoring the earth, feeding seven billion people well, stabilizing the climate, and designing sustainable cities." We added strategies of our own, including shifting the culture, local community building, prayer, philanthropy, and investing.

Thanks to the generosity of Marion Weber, the philanthropist and founder of Flow Funding (www.flowfunding.org), the Network was given $100,000 to allocate to new and established programs that fit our values and our mission. The donor joined in the grantmaking afternoon to observe how new funders and those who had never worked together before would blossom. We were each to allocate $4,000 of her gift to each other's projects and to tell each new "grantee" why we gave them the money. Suddenly our philanthropy became deeply personalized, which was especially potent for some of the established funders whose philanthropy had become a detached process of cutting checks or hiding behind donor-advising gatekeepers. We felt full of the gratitude for each other's work and for each other's support. The tables were turned on who was most grateful. The collective wisdom and support of this group of peers has enabled the birth of a Tipping Point Fund as well as an unleashing of heartfelt hope in all of us.

Although not everyone can participate in such a circle of peers, there are options for involvement online and in person in communities all over the world. This is the dawning of the highest level of collaboration our world has ever been part of. Coupled with the transfer of wealth and the transfer of nonprofit and business leadership to the next generation, these next years are perhaps the most crucial we have faced. We must not forget that we are part of a community, a country, and a global community. There are projects and leaders in every community that deserve your support.

The Inspired Legacies Web site (www.inspiredlegacies.org) reports on projects that we consider to be transformational or worthy of review. (See the sidebar

"Transformational Projects" for some of my current favorites.) You will find updated projects there for your inspiration and engagement as well as links and videos from www.KarmaTube.org, which showcase ordinary heroes and heroines who reach out every day to serve others. This, too, is the future of philanthropy, for the immediacy of seeing others joyfully served is contagious, and it is this and our collective grace that will ignite a new generation to give of their talents and dollars as never before.

TRANSFORMATIONAL PROJECTS

The following list includes some of my favorite projects and movements. Find your own or discuss with others what they think merits funding and giving of your most precious resources: your time and the brilliance of your ideas and capacities. Each of these projects, organizations, and movements deserves pages unto itself. To learn more about and to get in touch with these initiatives and organizations, go to www.inspiredlegacies.org. Engage or partner with or give to them as part of your overall giving and leveraging, and you will unleash your own generosity and enable a better world for all.

Organization	Transformational Method
Ashoka	Systems-changing projects and leadership networking
Bioneers	Meta-level community building
The Bravewell Collaborative	Meta-level giving circle on alternative health and healing
Charity Focus, Network for Good, Charity Navigator, Planetworks, Pledge Bank, Global Giving, Gift Hub	Web portals and blogs for engagement in service and giving.
Changemakers	Links to community-based philanthropy and the democratization of philanthropy
Conversation Café, Choral Earth, InterMission, Rockwood Leadership	Meta-level community building
Co-op-America, the Social Investment Forum, The Interfaith Committee on Corporate Responsibility, the community banking movement	Alternative and sustainable economic alternatives

Organization	Transformational Method
The Faith and Feminism Initiative of the Sister Fund, The Women's Perspective, and the Ministry of Money	Donor education and service to the poor by and for religious and spiritual leadership
The 50% League's Bolder Giving Project	Redistribution of wealth
Flow Funding	Giving social innovators and visionaries funds and empowering them to become philanthropists
The Foundation Incubator, Center on Philanthropy	Meta-level philanthropic research and field support
The Grameen Foundation, Pro Mujer, NamasteDirect	Micro-lending to the world's poor who cannot qualify for traditional loans
Inspired Legacies	Transforming philanthropy and catalyzing innovation and connections in the legacy planning and donor education fields
Link TV, Channel G, KarmaTube	Transformative media
New Ventures in Philanthropy	Innovation of philanthropic infrastructures and tools
Passageworks	Transformative education
Redefining America	Bridge-building across politics and philanthropy for transpartisan agreement and collaboration
Responsible Wealth, United for a Fair Economy, Class Action	Economic and social justice organizing and research
Social Venture Partners, Robin Hood Foundation	High-level donor networks for venture and social entrepreneurial philanthropists
Synergos	Global networking and meta-level systemic change
TEWA: The Nepal Women's Fund	Meta-level local and global community building for transformative change

Organization	Transformational Method
The Threshold Foundation	Established donor network merging spirit, leadership and philanthropy with a community of creative souls
The Tipping Point Network and Fund	Meta-level sustainability innovation and breakthrough projects
Transforming Money Project of The Rudolf Steiner Foundation, The Fund for Complementary Currencies, TimeBanks, Small is Beautiful, Terra	Alternative currencies and reimagining money
The Women Donors Network, The Women's Funding Network, The Global Fund for Women, The Ms. Foundation, The National Center for Research on Women, The Astraea Fund for Justice, and The Women Moving Millions Initiative	Transforming leadership in philanthropy for women and girls
WiserEarth, the Alliance for New Humanity	Mega-level sustainability connectedness
The World We Want	System-changing ideas and a blog to match
YES!, The Leveraged Alliance, Resource Generation	Building leadership capacity, consciousness, and innovation in young donors and activists
YouthGive, Youth Giving Circles, Learning to Give, RU MAD!	Transforming the way that youth give and engage in nonprofits

I have been guided and encouraged to "counterbalance" the news of exponential greed, violence, and injustice with the news of *exponential* love, care, and compassion. Those who are practicing transformational philanthropy are certainly on that joyful path. The groups and stories here—and others that you find—are a portal to a world beyond and in each of us. This world and its interactions, if you surrender to its spirit, will open your heart. It is the future we are building, and the world we want and pray for. We are each called to do our best for the whole of humanity. May you enjoy and be graced by the journey, and may we reach for and connect with one another with exponential faith and love.

Now take your own next steps toward inspired philanthropy. The questions in Worksheet 14.1 will help you get started.

Worksheet 14.1
Take Your Next Steps

The three changes I will make as a result of reading this book are:

1. _____

_____

2. _____

_____

3. _____

_____

The next three steps in my giving or leadership or planning will be:

1. _____

_____

2. _____

_____

3. _____

_____

NOTES

Preface

1. Says Jeff Grossberg of the nonprofit The Bridge in an e-mail message (May 25, 2007): "There are considerable variations in estimated assets currently held in donor-advised funds and family foundations, due primarily to most financial institutions not having to report what part of their assets are held in donor-advised funds prior to 2007. A survey of fifty leaders in the philanthropic services industry and of banking executives with direct responsibility for their high net worth clients' charitable giving conducted by the Bridge in 2006 revealed consistent projections between $500 billion small change and $1.5 trillion is accumulated in such funds at this time, with $1 trillion a commonly used 'working standard.'"

2. Guidestar. "About Us." Accessed May 25, 2007, from www.guidestar.org/about.

3. Reuniting America. Accessed Feb. 15, 2007, from www.reunitingamerica.org.

Introduction

1. L. Durán, "Caring for Each Other: Philanthropy in Communities of Color," *Grassroots Fundraising Journal,* Sept.–Oct. 2001, *20*(5), 4.

Chapter One

1. General Accounting Office, *September 11: More Effective Collaboration Could Enhance Charitable Organizations' Contributions in Disasters.* GAO Highlights, Dec. 2002, GAO-03–259. Accessed Mar. 26, 2007, from www.independent sector.org/pdfs/gao911final.pdf.

2. Network for Good, "Impulse on the Internet: How Crisis Compels Donors to Give Online." Accessed Mar. 26, 2007, from www.groundspring.org/learningcenter/nfg-disaster_giving_study.pdf.

3. Clinton Global Initiative, "Commitments." Accessed Jan. 10, 2007, from www.clintonglobalinitiative.org/netcommunity/Page.aspx?&pid=395&srcid=895.

4. INDEPENDENT SECTOR, *The New Nonprofit Almanac in Brief: Facts and Figures on the Independent Sector 2001.* Accessed Mar. 26, 2007, from www.independentsector.org/PDFs/inbrief.pdf.

5. K. Klein, *Fundraising for Social Change,* 5th ed. San Francisco: Jossey-Bass, 2007, p. 5.

6. Bureau of Labor Statistics, *Volunteering in the United States, 2006.* Accessed Mar. 8, 2007, from www.bls.gov/news.release/volun.nr0.htm.

7. INDEPENDENT SECTOR, *The New Nonprofit Almanac in Brief: Facts and Figures on the Independent Sector 2001.* Accessed Mar. 14, 2007, from www.independentsector.org/PDFs/inbrief.pdf.

8. United for a Fair Economy. "CEO Pay Charts." Accessed May 21, 2007, from www.faireconomy.org/research/CEO_Pay_charts.html.

9. I. Shapiro, "New IRS Data Show Income Inequality Is Again on the Rise." Center on Budget and Policy Priorities, Oct. 17, 2005. Accessed May 21, 2007, from www.cbpp.org/10–17–05inc.htm.

10. C. Gaudiani, *The Greater Good: How Philanthropy Drives the American Economy and Can Save Capitalism.* New York: Henry Holt, 2003, p. 10.

Chapter Five

1. A. Shah, "Poverty Facts and Stats." *Global Issues,* Nov. 24, 2006. Accessed Mar. 15, 2007, from www.globalissues.org/TradeRelated/Facts.asp#fact1.

2. Children's Bureau, Inc. "Child Poverty." Accessed Feb. 15, 2007, from www.childrensbureau.org/pdf_files/advocacy/1.pdf.

3. Ramonet, I. "The Politics of Hunger," *Le Monde Diplomatique,* Nov. 1998. Accessed May 21, 2007 from www.globalissues.org/TradeRelated/Facts.asp#fact2.

4. G. Muirragui, "A Letter to a Colleague," *Double Standards,* Aug. 3, 2004. Accessed Jan. 17, 2007, from www.doublestandards.org/muirragui1.html.

5. INDEPENDENT SECTOR, *Giving and Volunteering in the United States 2001.* Accessed Mar. 26, 2007, from www.independentsector.org/programs/research/GV01main.html.

6. D. Johnson, "Income Gap is Widening, Data Shows," *New York Times,* Section C, page 1, March 29, 2007.

7. *Foundation News,* Mar. 2005.

Chapter Six

1. Guidestar. "About Us." Accessed May 25, 2007, from www.guidestar.org/about.

Chapter Seven

1. Adapted from Resource Generation workshop materials.

Chapter Eight

1. National Committee on Responsive Philanthropy, *Giving at Work 2003.* Washington, D.C.: National Committee on Responsive Philanthropy, 2003.

2. S. Shaw-Hardy, *Creating a Women's Giving Circle.* Rochester, Minn.: Women's Philanthropy Institute, 2000.

3. Changemakers and S. Yang, *Legacy & Innovation: A Guidebook for Families on Social Change Philanthropy.* San Francisco: Changemakers, 2007.

Chapter Nine

1. Foundation Center, *Foundation Growth and Giving Estimates,* 2007 ed. New York: Foundation Center, 2007. Accessed May 21, 2007, from http://foundationcenter.org/gainknowledge/research/pdf/fgge07.pdf.

2. Foundation Center, "Key Facts on Family Foundations, 2005." Accessed May 25, 2007, from www.ncfp.org/publications-main-specialresources.html.

3. Foundation Center. "Key Facts on Family Foundations, 2006." New York: Foundation Center, 2006.

4. R. A. Wells, "Donor Legacy: What Is It That History Teaches?" *Living the Legacy: The Value of a Family's Philanthropy Across Generations,* 2001, *3.*

5. J. Weiser and S. Zadek, *Conversations with Disbelievers: Persuading Companies to Address Social Challenges.* Boston: Center for Corporate Citizenship at Boston College and Institute of Social and Ethical Accountability, 2001.

Chapter Ten

1. P. Frumkin, *The Four Types of Philanthropic Relationships,* Social Edge, Oct. 3, 2006. Accessed Feb. 22, 2007, at http://philanthropicengagement.blog spot.com.

2. P. Kent, "Effective Giving." *More Than Money,* May 2001, *26,* p. 22.

3. C. Collins, P. Rogers, and J. Garner, *Robin Hood Was Right.* New York: Norton, 2001.

Chapter Eleven

1. Gift Hub, "Blogging Philanthropy." Accessed Jan. 24, 2007, from www.gifthub.org.

2. Inspired Legacies, extrapolated from the American Bar Association survey of members, Mar. 2005.

3. J. J. Havens and P. Schervish, *Why the $41 Trillion Wealth Transfer Estimate Is Still Valid.* Boston: Boston College Social Welfare Research Institute, Jan. 2003. Accessed May 22, 2007, from www.bc.edu/research/cwp/meta-elements/pdf/41trillionreview.pdf.

Chapter Thirteen

1. A. Ellinger and C. Ellinger, "How Much to Give?" *More Than Money,* Dec. 1998, *20,* p. 14.

Chapter Fourteen

1. E. O. Wilson, *The Creation: An Appeal to Save Life on Earth.* New York: Norton, 2006.

2. D. Elgin and E. Share, *Transformational Philanthropy: An Exploration,* Awakening Earth, Feb. 2002. Accessed February 22, 2007, at www.awakening earth.org/pdf/transformational_philanthropy.pdf.

3. Elgin and Share, *Transformational Philanthropy.*

4. Elgin and Share, *Transformational Philanthropy.*

INDEX

citizen reactions to, 177; contributions as percent of pretax profits, 176; and corporate engagement activities, 177–178; and creation of foundations/programs to address social needs, 178–181; defined, 176; new attention to corporate citizenship in, 177; resources for, 180, 181; steps to strengthen, 179

Council of Michigan Foundations' K–12 curriculums for teachers and parents, 239

Council on Foundations, and family foundation assistance, 164, 172

Couple giving plan, sample of, 119

Cousins, Norman, 278

Craigslist Foundation, 158

Creating Change Through Family Philanthropy: The Next Generation (Goldberg, Pittleman, and Resource Generation), 168

Crisis-healing philanthropy, 5

Cubeta, Phil, 211, 217

D

Davern, Michael E., 82

De Bary, Patricia Murrill, 73

Dean, Julie, 246

Deciding how much to give: and balance between personal wants/needs and the greater good, 77; and consumption versus giving, 79; and desire to give, 76; and determination of giving potential, 78–81; exercise for, 80–81, 85; experiment for wealthy donors on, 259–261; from family foundations or donor-advised funds, 81–82; lifestyle guides for, 77; and lifetime giving exercise, 85; and major giving practices, 76–77; and personal attitudes toward money, 74; and personal values and

beliefs, 77–78; from principal, 82–84; stewardship and, 77

Democratization of philanthropy: and community-based funds, 139; and creation of new forms for giving, 8

Development staff, major donor meetings with, 189–190

Dickinson, May, 29

Donations to public charities, tax deductibility of, 83

Donor circles, 138; creation of, 153; defined, 139; donor education in, 153; institutional affiliations of, 148; minimum donation to, 138

Donor decision making, new strategies and structures for, 137

Donor education: industry, expansion of, 262–263; for philanthropic estate planning, 219; sources of, 198

Donor engagement with groups, 185–209; and communications with groups, 191–193; continuum of, 195, 196*fig10.3*; and donor anonymity, 190; and donor feedback, 193; effective communication in, 188–190; finding satisfactory level of, 194; and founder syndrome, 193; and interaction with senior staff, 189; levels of, 185–187; of major donors, 189–190, 191–192; and positive transition out of group, 192–193; questions to ask group, 188, 191; and setting boundaries for giving, 204; standard forms of communication in, 188; through written communication, 191

Donor legacy statement: creation and purpose of, 172–173; formal approval of, 174; as guide to donor's wishes, 174; sample, 174–176

Donor motivation, 132

Donor networks: access to, 262; advantages of belonging to, 262; contacts

265; formula for, 255; giving experiments for, 259–260; and giving from net worth, 255–258; and giving as percentage of wealth, 255; giving threshold relative to wealth of, 165; and meaning making through giving, 253; and million–dollar gifts campaign, 258–259; networking with other major donors, 261–265; and new level of consciousness about giving, 108; paid professional advisors and staff of, 170, 253–254, 265; as percentage of net worth, 255; pledges and endowments of, 22–23; rate of giving and ability to give more, 254; and the real cost of giving, 255–256; Web sites for, 145–146

Higher-order system of funding, strategies for creating, 279

Hong, James, 145

Honored obligations, donations for, 88

Hooft, Mila Visser't, giving circle of, 150–151

Household giving: compared by income, 24; and religious notions of giving, 29

Hundt, Reed, 163

Hunt, Swanee, 258–259

Hunting, John, giving plan of, 256–257

I

Identity-based donor groups/networks, donor grounding in, 197

iEarn initiative, 280

"Imagining a better world" exercise, 53–56

Immigrant communities, giving traditions and institutions of, 6

Impacts of giving, 21; tools and worksheets for evaluating, 60, 125–126

Income inequality gap, and social responsibility of more affluent citizens, 25

Income-based options for giving, 259–260

Independent Charities of America, 148

INDEPENDENT SECTOR, 24

Independent sector: budget requirements of, 189; contributions to U.S. economy, 22; critical role and power of, 25–27; current investment practice in, 97; functions and missions of, 21–22; growth of, 275; impact of government budget cuts on, 25; innovation funding in, 26–27; intergenerational transfer of leadership in, 282

Individual giving: and comparative perspectives on income, 74–76; and giving vision, 56; increasing importance of, 25; predominance of, 22, 23; and tangibility of impact, 97. *See also* Personal giving plan

Inspired Legacies (organization), 78; donor assistance of, 256; legacy and philanthropic planning advice of, 220; Web site reports on transformative and worthy projects of, 284–285

Inspired philanthropist: characteristics of, 199–200; checklist for, 201

Inspired philanthropy: beliefs about, 11; model, 273, 274*fig14.1*; paradigm, 2*fig1.1*; in planning, 15

Institute of Southern Studies, 28

Intentions for giving, worksheet for clarifying, 122-123

International giving: advantages of, 100; as emerging opportunity for private philanthropy, 100; and onsite intermediary organizations, 101; as percent of U.S. giving, 100; resources for, 101

Internet and new media, uses of, 275

Internet groups: and donor-recipient matchmaking, 278–279; key resources in, 279

Investment income, as charitable contribution, 260

IRAs, nonprofits as beneficiaries of, 83

and giving as percentage of income, 259; of next generation donors, 168–169; and wealthy donors' pledges, 22–23. *See also* Giving from principle; International giving; Online giving

Million-dollar visioning exercise, 57

Minkin, Tracey, 8–10

Mission matches: examples of, 68–71; exercise for, 72; ways to find, 71–72

Mission statements: action steps and, 63; examples of, 66–68; exercise and guidelines for writing, 64, 65; as tool for mission matching, 68

Mogil, Christopher, 77

More Than Money (magazine), 77–78

Ms. Foundation for Women, 153; Gulf Coast disaster role of, 102–103

Multiyear giving plan, worksheet for, 121

N

National Alliance for Choice in Giving, 148

National Center for Family Philanthropy, 171

National Charities Information Bureau, 91

National Committee on Responsive Philanthropy, 147

National Network of Consultants to Grantmakers, 171

Natural Capital Institute, 268

Needs philanthropy: as current philanthropic practice, 97; interventions and impacts of, 276*tab*; overview of, 98*tab*

Net worth (U.S.), comparative, 82

New Tithing Group, 77; *Wealth and Generosity by State* (paper) of, 254

New Ventures in Philanthropy, 263

Newman, Paul, 177

Next-generation donors, 237–252; and community-informed decision making, 168–169; early learning programs for, 239–240; and giving cards, 242; giving discussion and suggestions of, 248–252; global and multicultural perspective of, 238; as grantmakers, 244–246; guidance for, 242, 281–282; inspiring stories of, 243–244; managing transition to, 170; mentoring exercise for, 243; and messages of caring to counteract consumer messages, 242; methods of giving, 168–169; and models for partnering, 169; and online giving, 242; participation in family philanthropy, 167–168; practices for engaging, 170; and programs to develop financially literate youth (FLY), 240; provisions for, 229–234, 235; questions and answers for, 246–248; resources for, 170, 238, 239–240, 246, 248, 251; and service learning, 238; transition to, 281–282; ways to encourage, 245; youth advisory committees (YACs) model for, 244–246

Nonprofit group(s): budget, donor review of, 203–204; change strategies of, 46; effectiveness evaluation and review of, 92–95; examples of, 27; importance of healthy transitions in, 193. *See also* Independent sector; *specific group*

Nonprofit venture forums: and funding for small social change organizations, 158; as model for showcasing nonprofit groups, 158; venture fairs of, 158–160

O

Omidyar Network, 158

One Percent Club (Minnesota), giving formula of, 255

Online giving: of next generation, 242; new opportunities for, 141–146; through nonprofit and for-profit Web sites, 141–146; and philanthropic dialogue, 146–147; plan for, 45

Oxfam, 101, 102

P

Packard, David and Lucile, 164

Partnering, models of, 169

Personal giving plan: alignment of practice and principles in, 51, 133; articulation of core values in, 39, 106; broader societal or cultural change goals in, 51; clarification of giving intent in, 122–123; database for nonprofit selection in, 107; development, 32, 105–135; as element of an integrated plan, 105–106; exercises and template for creating, 109, 110–114; financial advisor's help with, 105, 107; focus on results and evaluation in, 132; functions of, 106–107; and gifts of time or social connection, 42; goal of security through community in, 108–109; guide for, 13–14; and leveraging strategies, 108, 132; multipronged approach to, 96–97; and portfolio building for optimum balance, 97–100; review of activities and impacts, 125–131; samples of, 114–115; and timing of donations, 107; as tool for greater impact, 124. *See also* Choosing where to give; Deciding how much to give

Personal giving strategy: comprehensive, steps for building, 59–60; development of, 45–62; exercise for discerning patterns in, 48; for giving plan development, 132; ideas for effective change making in, 61; impact evaluation in, 61; and integrated change making, 58; review and reflections on recent giving in, 47–50; and social change research, 61; visioning exercises for developing, 53–57

Personal values, and behavior as givers, 39

Philanthropic and legacy advisors: and donor-advised funds, 156; nonprofit recommendations of, 92

Philanthropic practice: course of, 6–8; essential ingredients of, 31; and investment across levels, 97; learning curve in, 131–133; levels of intervention in, 96–97, 98–99*tab*; making choices in, 39; types of relationships in, 194, 195*fig10.2*. *See also* Independent sector; Nonprofit groups

Philanthropist(s): definition of, 31; motivations of, 132; role, learning levels and activities in, 131–133; stereotypes of, 32, 33; as volunteer, 39; vision and values exercises for, 40–42

Philanthropy: meaning of, 31; overarching goal of human security in, 108–109

Pittleman, Karen, 168

Plan B 2.0: Rescuing a Planet Under Stress and a Civilization in Trouble (Brown), 282, 284

Pledgebank Web site, 141

Pooled funds, 138, 139; defined, 140. *See also specific type of fund*

Portfolio of philanthropic investments, 97–100; donation of appreciation from, 260

Price, Susan, 239

Private foundations: community members on boards of, 272; defined, 140

Private monitoring groups, 91

Private philanthropy: critical roles and power of, 25–27; government partnering with and support for, 25

Property donation, 82, 107–108

Public figures as donors, 22–23

Wolf, Edward N., 82

Women donors, and transformational philanthropy, 100

Women Donors Network, 281; members and activities of, 263–264

Women Moving Millions: Women Making History campaign, 258–259

Women's Fund of Greater Milwaukee, values and mission of, 69

Women's Funding Network, 259

Women's global funds, methodology of, 273

Workplace giving, 139, 147. *See also* Community-based workplace funds

Y

YES! organization, 238; guidance for transformative donors in, 281; Leveraging Privilege for Social Change program of, 170

Youth Giving Circles, curriculum of, 242

Youth on Board, 246

YouthGive, 242, 240

HOW TO USE THE CD-ROM

SYSTEM REQUIREMENTS

PC with Microsoft Windows 98SE or later

Mac with Apple OS version 10.1 or later

USING THE CD WITH WINDOWS

To view the items located on the CD, follow these steps:

1. Insert the CD into your computer's CD-ROM drive.

2. A window appears with the following options:

   Contents: Allows you to view the files included on the CD.

   Software: Allows you to install useful software from the CD.

   Links: Displays a hyperlinked page of websites.

   Author: Displays a page with information about the author(s).

   Contact Us: Displays a page with information on contacting
   the publisher or author.

   Help: Displays a page with information on using the CD.

   Exit: Closes the interface window.

   If you do not have autorun enabled, or if the autorun window does not appear, follow these steps to access the CD:

1. Click Start → Run.

2. In the dialog box that appears, type d:\start.exe, where d is the letter of your CD-ROM drive. This brings up the autorun window described in the preceding set of steps.

3. Choose the desired option from the menu. (See Step 2 in the preceding list for a description of these options.)

IN CASE OF TROUBLE

If you experience difficulty using the CD, please follow these steps:

1. Make sure your hardware and systems configurations conform to the systems requirements noted under "System Requirements" above.

2. Review the installation procedure for your type of hardware and operating system. It is possible to reinstall the software if necessary.

To speak with someone in Product Technical Support, call 800-762-2974 or 317-572-3994 Monday through Friday from 8:30 A.M. to 5:00 P.M. EST. You can also contact Product Technical Support and get support information through our website at www.wiley.com/techsupport.

Before calling or writing, please have the following information available:

- Type of computer and operating system.
- Any error messages displayed.
- Complete description of the problem.

It is best if you are sitting at your computer when making the call.